Relationships:

Why Love Relationships Fail

Love relationships fail because at no time in our training by society are we given a factual model of what a love relationship is, or how to make one succeed. There are fundamentally three levels on which intimate relationships operate, and our social training only prepares us to deal with one of them – the most superficial one – and even that one ineptly. This superficial level is called the expectations level. It is usually the only level we address consciously.

The expectations level consists of all our self-images and self-importance. When we primp ourselves in front of a mirror, what we are primping is our expectations of other people. It's the level of our daydreams and fantasies, whereon everyone is as impressed with us as we are with ourselves.

On the expectations level what interests us the most about a prospective partner is his or her physical attractiveness, manner of dress and bearing, social and educational background, future prospects, how "cool" he or she is, how he or she reflects back on us, what others will think of us for having chosen this partner.

On the expectations level a "love relationship" is actually an approval agreement, a contract, To Wit: "The party of the first part hereby agrees to pretend to honor, love, cherish and obey the party of the second part; in return for which considerations the party of the second part agrees not to hurt, betray, nor expose to public embarrassment the party of the first part (see appended schedule of specific acts which shall be deemed to constitute 'hurt', 'betrayal', and 'public embarrassment'). Any violation of this agreement by either party shall be considered valid grounds for spitefulness, vengeance, and all manner of carrying on like a big baby."

On the expectations level we submit ourselves to another person not for love, but for approval. Love and approval have nothing to do with one another. Love is a light, joyous, happy feeling; receiving approval is a tight, clinging, possessive feeling, which does, however, have an ego rush behind it. That ego rush is not joy – it's glory, self-importance, which we have been trained to seek instead of love.

The expectations level must eventually wear out because its basic premise is getting something for nothing. On this level everything we're putting out ("giving") is phony – it's just to impress other people, or to get something more in return. We're putting out phoniness in the hope of getting something real (happiness) back. And that's not how the universe is set up. There are no free lunches or free rides out there.

What fools us is that most of the messages we receive – from our parents and peers, our teachers and preachers, our leaders and the media – are that the expectations level works; and if it doesn't, that's our fault and we should be ashamed of ourselves.

For whom is it working? Look around. How many truly happy marriages are you aware of (of more than ten years' duration, since it can take that long or longer for the expectations level to wear thin). Sure, there are some, but not many; and usually the people involved in truly happy marriages are very, very special people in their own right.

Isn't this true? But there are also lots of relationships which appear to be happy on the surface, but are actually miserable underneath: both partners have learned to repress their true feelings and resign themselves to unhappiness without showing it. These people never get beyond the expectations level.

The reason why the expectations level inevitably crashes – although it can and often does mellow into true love after the crash – is because it is wholly narcissistic: it doesn't include the other person. It does not permit the other person to be a person, but only a reflection of our own fondest self-images. It doesn't allow the other person space to be real – to have feelings of his or her own.

For example, is our partner permitted to have sex with whomever he / she wishes? Is our partner even permitted to be sexually turned on by anyone but us? Is our partner permitted to tell us that we are not a satisfying lover? The list could go on and on. Only sexual expectations are mentioned here because those are practically universal, but we have all sorts of other fences we try to erect around our partners to keep them pristine and unsullied for us – expectations that they will agree with us about money, child raising, career, religion, etc.; expectations that they will forego making their own decisions in order to support us.

The expectations level must eventually crash under its own weight by sheer exhaustion. When people are involved with one another in an approval agreement, or any agenda that is not love, then everyone has to work overtime in order to convince the other or to convince oneself; and this is painful to bear.

The expectations level would be problematical and contradictory enough if it were the only level on which we relate with other people. Unfortunately, there are two deeper levels which actually govern the course of our relationships, and these deeper levels contradict the expectations level.

The level which underlies and controls the expectations level, which assures that the expectations level will eventually crash, or be maintained in great suffering, is the conditioning level. It's the level of our basic conditioning by society, which is to hate ourselves. Beneath the glitter and glory of our expectations, our self-images, is the grim truth that we are actually ashamed of ourselves. We are taught to be dissatisfied with ourselves by our parents and society.

Whereas the expectations level is set up so that people will be "nice" to each other (make the agreement: "I won't expose you as a liar and phony if you won't expose me as a liar and phony"), the conditioning level is set up to divide people, to make them fear and distrust each other. We are not trained to relate intimately with one another, but rather to wage war upon one another – to feel hurt, jealous, competitive, critical; to pick at each other and bend each other out of shape – rather than to be happy and accepting. The parent / child relationship is the basic war setup; the man / woman war is grafted on top.

While on an expectations level we tell ourselves that what we want is to live happily ever after, we are conditioned by our society to hate ourselves and to deny ourselves the very love which we consciously tell ourselves that we are seeking. We are trained by our parents to hate ourselves in precisely the same fashion in which our parents hated themselves.

The conditioning level is the level which psychotherapy addresses (unfortunately, after the damage is already done). We are so overwhelmed by our parents when we are little – so awed by their divinity – that we are afraid to express, or allow ourselves to feel openly, anger at them, or any other feeling of which they would not approve – which contradicts their expectations. Thus our parents' expectations level becomes our conditioning level.

Society calls infatuation with our own self-images "love"; and so on an expectations level we tell ourselves that we are going into relationships to get "love"; whereas on a conditioning level we are going into relationships to deny ourselves love – to pinpoint, through the mirroring of another person, precisely how we ourselves are incapable of giving and receiving love.

One might well wonder why people would want to reenact the situations out of their childhood which brought them the most pain and trauma. The reason is that those wounds never healed properly. They are still raw and suppurating, and extremely tender to the touch. Only by tearing those wounds back open again and cleaning out all the dreck, the self-hatred, can a true healing occur. And only by staging a situation similar to the one which produced those wounds originally can the wounds be reopened (actually this isn't the only way of doing it; there are far more skillful ways of doing it, such as Active Imagination. However, this is the most popular way of doing it).

Just as on the expectations level our goal is the validation of our images, on the conditioning level our goal is to recreate all the emotional turmoil our parents inflicted on us, but this time around to grab the brass ring of love which our parents denied us.

Up until recently society has had the fifth Commandment and a raft of social sanctions in place against examining the conditioning level too closely. Freud was one of the first to take a good, hard look at this level of human interaction. And at the present time there are lots of good popular books available on the subject of toxic parents, how we all marry our father or mother, and seek in marriage the precise same hurt and nonfulfillment which our principle caregivers made us feel in infancy. The problem is that we don't bother reading these books until our relationships are already in deep trouble. These books should be required reading for all high school students.

"Don't blame your parents! Just wait until you're a parent yourself!" they (our parents) tell us. Well, that's wrong; we should blame our parents, because only by consciously blaming them are we in a position to consciously forgive them. Only when we can see that it was their own self-hatred which their parents laid on them that impelled them to do what they did to us; only when we can see them as people in as much or more pain as we, who really did try to do the best for us they knew how; only then can we forgive our parents. And only then can we forgive ourselves, and let go of our own self-hatred, no longer needing to reenact it or to blame ourselves over and over because we loved our parents, and all they cared about was being right.

The third (and deepest) level of relationship is the karma level – the level of the lessons we are trying to learn from certain people, based upon our experiences with them in other lifetimes and realities. Anything which is wrong or out-of-kilter in a relationship originates on the karma level. Our gut-level, first impressions of people are often good indicators of the kind of karma we have going with them; but our conscious minds often bury such information directly as it is perceived.

For example, it could happen that the reason we are sexually turned on by a certain person is that in a previous life we raped and tortured that person; for some aeons, perhaps, that individual has been itching for a lifetime in which to right matters. That might be the karma we have set up with someone; but all our conscious mind knows, on its level of expectation, is that we are sexually turned on by that person and want the person to validate it by having sex with us. And so we put our head in that person's noose, and wonder later on why things aren't working out as we'd imagined.

The karma and conditioning levels work in tandem to control the actual circumstances and course of a relationship. For example, if on the conditioning level we decide to reenact a parent's abandonment of us and we choose a partner who will abandon us, we might select for that role someone whom in a previous lifetime we abandoned. This can be considered a penance; but we can also look at it as a kind of "you scratch my back and I'll scratch yours" – like saying, "I made you suffer in that lifetime, and now I want to know how you felt – to feel the feelings I made you feel." On the karma level, as on the conditioning level, we try to restage events which will produce a resonance with some unresolved emotional issue in the totality of our being.

The agendas we have set up with other people on the karma level are often revealed in the very first impressions we have of them and which we immediately repress. It's hard to describe this, and it's different for everyone, but often upon meeting someone with whom we have a heavy karmic agenda going, we get a FLASH, a conscious feeling or thought, of something we desire or feel threatened by about that person. And then we immediately "forget" what we just felt, because if we have bad karma going with the person, then that flash was of a side of ourselves which we don't want to consciously face or acknowledge – a side we are calling upon that person to enact openly for us, to ram down our throat for us, until we're forced to acknowledge it. Thus we "forget" this first impression, and later on pretend we don't understand why the person we loved and trusted so much could have changed so.

Of course, we can run past-life regressions to check what sort of karma we have going with someone before getting seriously involved with them – sort of like running a credit or AIDS check on a prospective spouse. In India astrology has been historically relied upon for this sort of information. But we can also avoid difficulties just by being alert to our own gut feelings and intuitive impressions of other people, rather than ignoring this most essential information in a relationship.

Thus the basic intensity or emotional theme of a relationship is set up on the karma level; the particular script, the sequence of events which will unfold in a relationship, is set up on the conditioning level; and the costuming, the superficial appearances or show put on for the benefit of the neighbors, is set up on the expectations level.

The glare of the expectations level blinds us to what is happening on the two deeper levels; and the expectations level is a lie. What is actually going on in a relationship on the conditioning and karma levels is always quite visible; but we pretend we don't see it, we pretend we don't understand it, in order to uphold our expectations as long as possible.

By "lie" is meant something that we feel, but which we suppress or conceal. For example, if our sex partner is doing something that doesn't feel good and turns us off, and we lay there and take it because we're too embarrassed to speak up and possibly hurt our partner's feelings, then that's a lie. Any time we do not communicate something we are feeling because we are embarrassed to do so, or because we don't want to hurt or provoke the other person or become a target for his or her disapproval, we are lying. Lying leads to sneaking around behind the other person's back. Lies lead to more lies.

We can tell if lying is taking place in a relationship this way: if there is an area in which we don't trust the other person; where we withhold from the other person; where we are afraid of the other person (his / her disapproval or rejection); where we feel something other than GOOD about the person; then that is a place where we are lying. We are trained to lie to other people, and then to feel betrayed when our lies are exposed.

All a lie is, is a contradiction. Lies must always exist in pairs, whereas the truth – love – just is. For example, on the level of our expectations we might set up the pair: "I want you to be honest with me" and "I don't want to hear how turned on you are by someone else." On the level of our conditioning we might set up the pair: "I truly love you, mommy!" and "I'll never question your love for me!" On the level of karma lies don't exist per se (it's repressing this level that makes a lie out of it); but one could say that the basic lie or duality of the karma level is: "You and I are two" and "You and I are one."

All the lies in a relationship are laid down right at the beginning. By "laid down" is meant: conscious. Conscious for a moment, and then – just as consciously – repressed, ignored, "forgotten". The basic lies of the karma level may be laid down in the first few seconds of a relationship. The lies of the conditioning level (the game plan of who's going to hurt whom, and how) are usually laid down at the time the relationship is formalized – when the mutual decision is made to commit, to get serious as it were. And the expectations level is a complete lie from the first pop.

Anyone with their eyes open could see what's going on. Sometimes our parents, friends, or other people who care about us try to pass us warnings. But we're "so much in love" and "love is blind" and we're so "happy" that we don't want to see it. We don't want anything to call us down from this lovely cloud we're on; this lovely lie we're telling ourselves.

And for each and every lie, the piper must be paid. There's a karmic law at work in all this, and EVERY single lie, no matter how teensy-weensy, will someday have to be brought into the open and admitted, else the relationship is doomed – doomed to be something other than a love relationship, because in a love relationship there is no room whatsoever for lies of any kind, at any time, for any reason.

All the alarm about the soaring divorce rate in our society, the call for a return to "traditional values", is a bunch of baloney. Those traditional values were a total lie, and it's amazing that the human race put up with that lie as long as it did. Traditional values means you get married on the expectations level and you never question it. You learn somehow to live with a lie, with unhappiness, and you bite your tongue because the social sanctions (what the neighbors might think) against divorce were so stringent. Instead of returning to living out lies, our society ought to stop glorifying the expectations level. As is the case also with war, when society stops glorifying infatuation people will stop seeking it.

Love relationships fail because we go into them with a lot of la-de-da thought forms about who we are and what we expect to get, and we run smack into heavy karma and conditioning agendas we had no conscious idea even existed. We are not consciously aware of what expectations we have until those expectations aren't fulfilled; and we don't understand what our parents did to us until we find our partner doing the same thing – make us feel that old, familiar feeling in the pit of our stomach.

As long as we're relating to the other person on one of these three levels, we're not relating to an actual person at all, but only to our own self-reflection, our childhood wounds, or our deep-seated fears and insecurities. On the expectations level our attention is focused on the future; on the conditioning level it's focused on the past; and on the karma level it's focused on the remote past. A true love relationship, however, involves relating to a real, live person in the now moment.

Kidraising for Fun and Profit

It isn't all that hard to be a good parent. We all want to be good parents; we all try to be good parents; so with that motivation we're bound to succeed. Being a good parent is simply a matter of: 1) following our own hearts, and 2) ignoring everything society has taught us about childraising.

Fundamentally, it's not our job as parents to teach our kids how to get along in society – to worry about their achievements or how well they're doing socially – much less to chastise them for not "measuring up". Society has its Gestapo of teachers, coaches, clergymen, scout leaders, etc. – not to mention the pressure of peers, advertisers, and the media – to whip kids into line, to teach them to be "good citizens" and "team players", to "fit in" and "belong". So kids don't need more of that crap when they get home.

What kids need from their parents is love. They don't need criticism, blame, or guilt; they don't need unfavorable comparisons with other kids; they don't need to be belittled or patronized, or to be treated rudely because their parent had a bad day at work.

When our kids come home with a lousy report card, or when they've committed some other atrocity against society, do we chastise them and make them feel bad; or do we commiserate with them and try to make them feel good? They already feel bad at having transgressed society's expectations (even if they feign defiance). Therefore, to clamp down on them, to try to impose our will on them, is not going to help them any; and if they have any gumption at all, some day they'll spit it all back in our faces.

Babies do not come into this world grumpy and truculent and spoiling for a fight. Babies come into this world too spaced-out and vulnerable to be pugnacious. Therefore, if there is anger and fighting going on in a parent-child relationship, then it is logical to assume that the parent is 100% to blame for the situation.

Parents are confused, they are cowed and daunted by the sanctions society has in place if they fail in their role as taskmasters. Parents have to understand that it's okay if their kids are failing their grade or getting into fights or doing drugs or are unmarried and pregnant. If the kids are doing antisocial things or inviting dire consequences by their behavior, then obviously they're unhappy and out of kilter with their environment. It's a parent's duty then to say, "Hey, what's bugging you?" rather then "Shape up or ship out!" And if they don't want to talk to you, then you leave them alone. You give them space, respect their feelings and their right to make their own decisions.

Parents have to stop worrying about how their kids' behavior and achievements reflect back on them. Who cares what the teachers and the neighbors think? Our kids' feelings are more important. It's not a question of taking sides with the kids, but rather entails seeing things from the kids' point of view. It's not so much a matter of standing up for the kids, as standing by them. The teacher has the whole system backing him or her up; surely the kids deserve an impartial advocate, even if they're guilty as hell.

Society drives a wedge of guilt into the parent-child relationship even before the kids are born. The common fear (particularly with a first baby) that our kid might be born crippled or handicapped or something is actually fear that we won't be able to love the baby if it doesn't fulfill society's expectations.

Society puts a lot of heavy guilt trips on parents to make them feel ashamed of their kids ("Have you heard what Sarah's boy has done now?"); and parents pass those same guilt and shame trips on to their kids ("You have failed me, son."). Parents have to be reassured that no matter how their kids turn out, it doesn't mean that they failed as parents. Even if the kids turn out to be like Heliogabalus, if the parents gave them true love, then they did their job well. Even if the kids are truly weird or nasty – even if they masturbate publicly or torch the neighbor's cats – that is not the parents' fault, responsibility, or problem. It's the kids' problem.

It is not the parents' job to mold kids' characters or guide their development; to see that they have all the advantages or to teach them how to compete and succeed. The parents' only job is to love their kids, to be able to say to them, "Well, you certainly screwed up there, but don't take it to heart. You learned a lesson, you'll go on living and breathing, etc. etc." – whatever the kids need to hear at that moment to cheer up, to recover their sense of self-worth. That's what kids need from their parents, and it's the only thing they need – ultimate acceptance, no matter what they've done. And it's the parents' job to supply this.

We're not talking about indulging kids, letting them run rampant. In a "normal" parent-child relationship, the kids are taught to fear the parents' disapproval. But there are some parents who reverse the usual roles, and fear their kids' disapproval. Usually these kids become real hellions and grow up drunk with power, with little respect for other people's space. We're not talking about switching approval / disapproval roles; we're talking about dispensing with approval / disapproval altogether. Approval is as damaging as disapproval. To say to a kid, "I love you because you fulfill my expectations and make other parents envy me." is as nasty a thing to say to a kid as, "I don't love you because you bring me no glory." To discipline our kids, all we have to do is say to them, "Hey, I don't like what you did there for these reasons …." Period. Say it once, calmly, as you would do with another adult. Don't hammer at the kids and wipe your bad vibes all over them.

We must be willing to apologize to our kids when we've overstepped ourselves and made them feel bad needlessly; and this doesn't mean a half-hearted, "Oh well, maybe I overreacted there, but still you shouldn't have … ." It means a full, complete cop: "Sorry. I guess I got on your case about nothing."

The way we can tell if we're blowing it is: if we feel annoyed or disappointed in our kids, then we're wrong. If we ever feel anything other than good about our kids, accepting of our kids, sympathetic to our kids, then we're wrong. If we can't feel good about our kids at all times, then we're blowing it. This is why raising kids is such a terrific spiritual reality check – it shows us precisely how far away we are from enlightenment.

The trick is to tell kids what they're doing wrong calmly and collectedly, without releasing a dart of anger, impatience, or annoyance. Of course, to be able to do this we have to have our own self-importance under control – to be light and detached (rather than to permit ourselves to be sucked into our kids' bad moods).

If parents were enlightened beings, perhaps then they would have a moral right to interfere in their kids' lives. If parents were exalted beings (as their kids believe them to be), maybe then their approval or disapproval would have value. But the fact is that parents don't have any more of a clue as to what's really going on than their kids do. The only guide they've got is what their own parents drummed into them: fear of disapproval.

We should act towards our kids exactly the same way that we wished our parents had done for us when we were kids. It's trite to say it, but inevitably, 100% of the time, when we are angry at our kids about something, what we are angry at is precisely what our parents used to get angry at us about.

From whom did we learn that this behavior (what our kid is doing) is unacceptable? Why does this behavior anger us? Not the ostensible reason – what we are telling ourselves and the kid – but rather the actual reason why we find such-and-such a behavior objectionable: what our kid is doing openly that our parents forced us to repress. See, we all tell ourselves that we're angry at our kids because of this or that very valid reason. We all have impeccably logical reasons why we must bend our kids out of shape; close our hearts to them by labeling their feelings "acceptable" or "unacceptable"; force them to knuckle under to us in exactly the same fashion that our parents forced us to knuckle under to them. We thereby pass our own anger at our parents for having forced us to knuckle under on to our kids, as if to say to our parents, "See, Mommy and Daddy! I forgive you for having closed your hearts to me and having put more importance on your images than on my true feelings – my need as a completely vulnerable infant for the greatest tenderness, delicacy, and respect – for I have done the same thing to my own children!" And so it goes: the torch of self-hatred is handed down from generation to generation. It only stops if we quit getting angry at our kids altogether, no matter what they do or don't do. This is not all that hard to do once we make the connection that in spite of all our wonderful logic and self-justification, all we're doing when we're angry with our kids is upholding that side of our own parents which we despised the most.

To a kid his parents are God incarnate. If a kid feels he can trust his parents, then later on he'll naturally trust in God. Another way of saying this is, upon becoming parents we take upon ourselves the mantle of Godhood willy-nilly. This is a very serious presumption and responsibility. Most of us blow it. But the point is, since we are masquerading as God, we should at least do a good job of faking it.

This means giving our kids 100% acceptance and forgiveness, no matter what they've done (just as God does for us). Check out how God deals with us: when we screw up, does God dramatically appear in a burning bush and give us hell? No, God doesn't do that; God leaves us alone to stew in our own juice and to figure things out for ourselves. To treat our kids like God treats us means not making them feel worse about themselves, but rather better, as if they were still worthwhile beings, worthy of salvation and redemption, no matter how sinful they may have been. It means not being angry with them but rather tender with them; feeling what they feel instead of trying to make them feel our feelings (agree with us).

Most parents have truly loving impulses; but society sends parents the wrong messages – it makes them feel guilty about being "weak" or "soft-hearted" or "spoiling" kids. Parents just have to know that feeling with their kids – withholding all negative judgment, criticism, and blame, is okay; that it's fine to be completely tender and sympathetic all the time; that it's not a sign of weakness to understand things from the kids' viewpoint.

When you get annoyed with your kids, think of this: if they were to die in the next moment, would you still give a damn about whatever you are angry at them about? Is that what you would want your last message to them to be – annoyance over some stupid triviality?

The next time you jump on your kids for something, think about how you would feel if they were to die in your arms in the next moment; and ask yourself if whatever you're on their case about is worth trashing the short time you will spend on this earth together.

Are You Two Compatible?

Comparing the Ascendants, Suns, and Moons in Two People's Horoscopes

People have been having problems with their relationships for as long as they have been having relationships. Even Adam and Eve, under the most ideal conditions imaginable, failed to make a decent go of it. It's not surprising, therefore, that synastry- the astrology of relationships – has always been one of the most popular branches of the stellar art. In the second century A.D. Claudius Ptolemy wrote: "Concord between two persons is produced by an harmonious figuration of the stars, indicative of the matter whereby good will is constituted, in the nativity of either person. Love and hatred are discernible, as well from the concord and discord of the luminaries, as from the ascendants of both nativities."[1]

Ptolemy's method was to compare the suns, moons, and ascendants in the two horoscopes because these are the points where the natives are in closest touch with the world outside of themselves. All of the other planets, cusps, parts, etc., are derivative from these three, both in terms of their mathematical motion, and in the psychological sense of being more conditioned or subject to karma. It is in the three vital centers that one looks for the natives' free will – the ability to recognize and discard choices that have outlived their usefulness, and go on to make new ones. This is why a comparison of the harmonies and disharmonies between the vital centers in two horoscopes is so revealing of the internal adjustments two people have to make when they join together in a relationship.

Note that this technique doesn't provide the entire story by any means – the cross-aspects between planets in the two horoscopes describe the situation in greater detail.[2] However comparison of the vital centers is a good place to begin. In what follows, marriage will be given primary attention, but the same technique can be used to evaluate any relationship between two people.

Two centers are harmonious if they are either both in masculine signs, or if they are both in feminine signs. If one is in a masculine sign and the other is in a feminine sign, then they are disharmonious. A single sign is harmonious with itself, so two centers that lie in the same sign are in harmony with each other. For example, Leo is harmonious with Gemini, since both are masculine; and Capricorn is harmonious with Cancer, since both are feminine. But Leo is disharmonious with Capricorn, since the former is masculine and the latter is feminine. The procedure is to compare separately the two sun signs, then the two moon signs, and then the two rising signs, to ascertain which of these pairs of vital centers are harmonious or disharmonious.

All of the signs of the same gender are taken to be harmonious with one another because in this context "harmony" means similarity, or likeness. When a pair of vital centers lies in harmonious signs, then those centers operate in much the same way. The two parties to the relationship can always rely upon one another in that respect, or take that facet of the relationship completely for granted. If the two sun signs are harmonious, then each person respects the other's views on life and living, and they can help one another to follow out the dictates of their individual consciences and destinies. If the two moons lie in harmonious signs, then there is a feeling of good will that underpins the relationship; both parties have a genuine liking for each other, and truly wish one another the best. If the two rising signs are harmonious, then there is a commonality of everyday interests and habits that bind the two people together; they fulfill each other's images of what they are seeking in a partner.

When a pair of vital centers lies in disharmonious signs, then there is a point of conscious difference in the relationship that can become a matter of concern or even conflict. Contrasts always impose themselves upon the awareness more forcefully than similarities do, so the attention tends to go to them. When the two sun signs are in disharmonious signs, there is a clash of wills. The two parties often find it difficult to unite their goals and aims in life. When the two moon signs are disharmonious, there is a polarity in the feelings which often shows up as a lack of emotional warmth or sympathy. When the two rising signs are disharmonious, there is a conflict in the way in which the two people express themselves, and a tendency for communications between them to break down.

Ptolemy's technique illustrates an important principle of astrological interpretation, which Dr. Marc Edmund Jones termed "Negative Indication"[3]: if all but one criteria in a well-defined set are present in a natal horoscope (e.g. planets in earth-air-water but not fire; planets in succedent and cadent houses but not angular; etc.), then the emphasis goes to the absent criteria, but with a twist of the symbolism – like a parody of what it should mean – as if in overcompensation for a felt psychological lack or need. In the present case, if only one pair of the vital centers is disharmonious, then the attention in the relationship tends to dwell upon the disharmony, like an itch that can't quite be reached and scratched, often at the expense of the enjoyment of other areas in which there is a natural accord. Instead of focusing on where there is agreement – which is what happens when only one pair of vital centers is harmonious – the focus tends to dwell upon areas of disagreement. That is to say, relationships in which only one pair of vital centers is in harmonious signs tend to be smoother, less fractious than relationships in which two pairs of vital centers are in harmonious signs.

From the foregoing it might appear that the ideal relationship occurs when the two sun signs, moon signs, and rising signs are all harmonious, but this is not necessarily the case. If that were true then Bill Clinton and Monica Lewinsky would be the ideal couple, since they have all three pairs of vital centers in identical signs (Leo suns, Taurus moons, and Libra ascendants)! Too much harmony in a relationship can produce a static or stagnant situation. Have you ever met someone and recognized in him or her some quality or trait remarkably similar to one of your own? You immediately understand that part of the person, but at the same time you are left with an unsettled feeling, or an unresolved question, like a gear that encounters another cog where it should have meshed with a space. Similarities tend to reinforce themselves on one level, rather than move to new levels. Relationships mature through a continual giving way or relinquishing of individual desires in order to maintain a greater unity. Few of us are strong enough to give up our desires by ourselves; we need other people whose desires conflict with ours to give us a reason to change and mature. Relationships, like pearls, seem to require a certain amount of irritation in order to grow. But when all three pairs of vital centers are in harmonious signs, this irritation – and with it something very vital – is largely missing. The relationship may seem somewhat nebulous or insubstantial since there aren't any solid differences to grab onto or push against. Instead of being a challenge, the relationship may become a competition, or a game of one-upmanship. For example, in the words of one of the Fitzgerald's biographers, "Both Scott and Zelda had entered a new period in their lives: both drinking heavily, and seemingly to dare each other to ever more reckless and outrageous acts. ... They both dived into the Mediterranean from a great height, and drove their car too fast along winding roads. Once, after a fight with Scott, Zelda threw herself under the wheels of their car and dared him to run over her - and he even started to move the car."[4] When all three vital centers are harmonious, each party tends to confirm him or herself all the more in their own individual resolve, rather than join with the other to move to some new level of realization. The focus of attention, therefore, has to be kept outside of the relationship itself if it is to lead anywhere. Some outside objective or goal to which both parties are dedicated should always be kept in view. These people have many common interests: the more they can concentrate on the final result rather than on who is going to have the privilege of accomplishing it, the more will the harmony between them pay off in a smooth efficiency and ability to avoid getting side-tracked.

The converse situation, when all three pairs of vital centers are in disharmonious signs, makes for rather intriguing relationships, on the principle that opposites attract. People who are quite unlike us can provide us with a fascinating complement by helping us to recognize exactly where our strengths and limitations lie. They embolden us to exhibit different facets of ourselves, to try out different roles, to experiment. We can learn a great deal from these people, not only because they present us with an alternative point of view and way of doing things, but also because in the mirror of their reactions to us we see ourselves and our aspirations standing out in bold relief. There is a sense of newness and freshness that grows out of the continual awareness of differences –you never know what to expect next! As an example, consider the first meeting of Isadora Duncan and Gordon Craig: "Here stood before me brilliant youth, beauty, genius; and, all inflamed with sudden love, I flew into his arms with all the magnetic willingness of a temperament which had for two years lain dormant, but waiting to spring forth. Here I found an answering temperament, worthy of my metal (sic). In him I had met the flesh of my flesh, the blood of my blood."[5] This type of relationship, however, is generally better for romance than for marriage, since the fact that none of the pairs of vital centers is harmonious means that the paths in life diverge sharply, and so a frustrating gap between the two people can come into being. At every turn there are differences of approach that must be reconciled; one or the other must always give way. Hence an exceptional amount of inner adjustment is incumbent on both parties in order to make the relationship work. Each must learn to recognize when the other is more in tune with the situation at hand, and forgo their own inclinations and impulses at such times. By the same token, each must learn to sort out their own ideas and feelings to determine where they must "draw the line" and let their own desires prevail. These relationships both bestow and require a peculiar fluidity and ability to adapt.

When the two sun signs are harmonious, while the two moon and rising signs are disharmonious, then there is a basic similarity of outlook on life, or a sense that the two lives are heading in the same direction. These people can come back together again after years of separation and pick right up where they left off, because the essential thing is the long view: life in its more ultimate or long-range aspects. Friendship, therefore, seems to be the most pronounced feature of the relationship. However, there are numerous areas of more superficial division: the two personalities are quite distinct, and opinions are apt to differ on how things are to be done in actual practice. Nonetheless each is willing to free the other to go their own way and do what they feel they must do to fulfill themselves. Whether they cherish or obey is moot, but they certainly honor one another. An example consider John F. and Jacqueline Kennedy: "The marriage had become, by now, little more than a matter of mutual convenience – a union of two mercurial, strong-willed, stubborn people who, like so many children of the rich, were rather used to getting their own way, and were not happy when they didn't. Any romantic love that might have once existed between them had long since evaporated. … And so a perfectly sensible business deal was struck during those first White House months. She would supply the elegance, the charm, the class that he wanted. And he, in turn would let her do pretty much whatever else she chose."[6]

When only the two sun signs are disharmonious (with harmony between the two moon and rising signs), then there is likely to be disagreement with regard to life philosophies, and ultimate aims and goals. Often the backgrounds and upbringings contrast; in any case the two parties have very different views of the world and their places in it, and they shape their lives toward different ends. There may be some possessiveness, or a tendency for each to try to force the relationship to fit their own image of how it ought to be. The resulting conflict of wills can make mutual commitment over the long haul a matter of concern, especially in the initial stages of the relationship. In the case of Elvis and Priscilla Presley, "Elvis would 'lock' his women in. It was rough for her because Elvis was a pretty jealous man, too, and with a woman as beautiful and fine as Cilla, you could see why. ... Hence the double standard that developed in Elvis's treatment of his wife. (Elvis's producer) wanted to cast Priscilla in movies. She also had numerous other opportunities. Nobody knows exactly what happened to these opportunities, but it is assumed that she disregarded them at Elvis's command."[7] In counterbalance to this separative tendency on the ideological level, there is a strong emotional bond and usually a shared set of everyday interests and tastes. Both like to do the same sorts of things, and they like to do them together. When only the sun signs are harmonious, it is everyday functioning that becomes a problem; when only the sun signs are disharmonious, it is the overview, the question of where the relationship is heading in terms of each party's individual aspirations, that is at issue. Each must learn to let the other make their own way in life, and respect the other person's choices.

    When two people have their moons in harmonious signs (while the two sun and rising signs are disharmonious), then their personalities and temperaments are in accord. Their reactions to things and feelings about life are similar, so they can be perfectly candid and reveal their deepest feelings to one another. There is a strong empathy and tenderness between them; rarely do they need to explain themselves or justify their actions to one other. Each intuitively understands the other's motivations and accepts them for what they are, rather like a mother accepts her children for what they are, unquestioningly. And like a mother who knows her children will leave her when they grow up, these people are aware that their life paths diverge, and that each will want to make their own place in the world. There is a recognition that there are limits to what they will able to accomplish working together, that they can help each other best by providing moral support, and cheering the other on in their struggle with life's vicissitudes. They know they always have someone who is receptive and kindly disposed towards them to whom they can return to unburden themselves and rest their spirits. For example, after Jane Fonda's separation from Ted Turner after eight years of marriage, she commented: "Ted is a soul mate. I care about him. He means the world to me. He taught me to be happy." They separated, she said, "because we changed. I changed. ... Are we happier by ourselves than we were together? It's not clear."[8]

    When only the two moon signs are disharmonious (with both sun and rising signs harmonious), then the feelings tend to be at odds, or at least not meeting. Individual likes and dislikes are apt to differ. Frequently the parties have separate outside friendships rather than share the same friends in common, since each needs people outside the relationship with whom they can hope and dream. Within the relationship there is often a distance or detachment where a sympathy and understanding would normally be. Each party may feel at pains to fulfill real or imagined expectations of the other, and so find it difficult to relax comfortably in the relationship and just be themselves. There may be an air of formality and impersonality, with the two parties hurting one another either inadvertently or quite consciously as they struggle to express their needs to each other. Breakups are especially acrimonious and spiteful; Prince Charles and Princess Diana are a good example, as are Woody Allen and Mia Farrow who "had a huge, explosive break-up when Farrow found porno pictures in Allen's apartment of her daughter Soon-Yi with

Allen on 1/13/1992. Their split was official in August 1992, complete with bitter accusations and legal volleys."[9] On the other hand, in these relationships there is a sense of common direction in life and a mutual moral commitment, as well as the ability to see past the momentary emotional obstacles that occasionally keep them apart. Each party has to keep their own preferences and inclinations on a leash, and learn to take satisfaction in the happiness of the other, neither judging nor rejecting that which the other person holds sacred.

When the two rising signs are harmonious (while the two sun and moon signs are disharmonious), then there is a similarity in the roles that the two people play in life. Each is willing to accept the other pretty much on his or her own terms, in hail-fellow-well-met fashion. Their fondest images of themselves are mutually reinforcing: they do things like walk in the rain and watch sunsets together. They can really sit down and talk to one another; even without talking they understand each other very well, because their relationship is based on an instantaneous communication. This is one reason why it is helpful for an astrologer to have his or her rising sign harmonious with that of a client. Nevertheless, the parties in such a relationship recognize that there are wide differences between them on deeper levels, which inclines them to maintain their distances and not place undue reliance upon one another to come through in a pinch. Even though they have the best of intentions towards each other, they are not always able to supply the kind of emotional support that the other needs. These people help each other most, in bad times as well as good, by supplying an abundance of friendly interest and help in not taking things too seriously. For example, after going public and receiving approbation for her outspoken opinions on such matters as women's rights and abortion, Betty Ford felt "it bothered me that while I was getting so much praise Jerry was getting criticism. He was a good sport. He was proud of me and even in cases where he didn't agree with my views, he was all for my spouting them. … You know, if you bring up a subject long enough with a man, why finally he gets so tired of it he agrees to anything. There might be a woman on the Supreme Court now if I'd just brought it up more often."[10]

When only the two rising signs are disharmonious (with both sun and moon signs harmonious), then there is some source of misunderstanding or non-communication that often bogs down an otherwise smooth relationship. Each party wants to talk while the other is interrupting. They are able to see through one another quite clearly, and so they may become impatient with each other's posturing on the one hand, and overly thin-skinned or sensitive to criticism on the other. They may try to outguess or keep one jump ahead of each other, or keep bringing up the same old divisive issues as if for the sport of contention. They allow the present moment to escape them in a welter of verbiage. They may try to force one another to live up to an impossible image. For example, after a trip to India to visit the birthplace of his idol Gandhi, Martin Luther King, Jr. "felt, as in India, that much of the corruption in our society stems from the desire to acquire material things – houses and land and cars. Martin would have preferred to have none of these things. He finally said to me, 'You know, a man who dedicates himself to a cause doesn't need a family.' I was not hurt by this statement. I realized that it did not mean he loved me and the children less, but that he was giving his life to the Movement and felt he therefore could not do as much for his family as he might in other circumstances. He saw a conflict between duty and love … But I knew that, being the kind of man he was, Martin needed us."[11] The inability to communicate can be very frustrating, since there is usually a profound emotional tie that binds them: a good deal of what each has to accomplish in life as an individual, the two of them can accomplish as well together. Each must learn to put aside their own train of thought and really listen to the other, permitting them their whims and peculiarities, and taking care not to tread upon their aplomb.

The foregoing descriptions of the various combinations of harmony and disharmony may appear somewhat extreme. The individual case will be more or less so, depending upon the type of relationship involved (since we tolerate different things in our intimate relations than in our casual acquaintances), and also upon the maturity of the two people. Learning how to turn obstacles into advantages is what growth is all about. In synastry, as in every department of astrology, free will is the overriding factor.

Notes

[1] Centiloquy XXXII. J. M Ashmand, *Ptolemy's Tetrabiblos*, Foulsham London 1917, page 228.

[2] For example, the principal astrological signature of sexual attraction between two people is shown when a man's sun, Mars or Jupiter conjoins or opposes a woman's moon or Venus. Of these cross-aspects between horoscopes, the sun-moon and Mars-Venus combinations are the most powerful sexual bell-ringers. Take up to 10° orbs of inexactitude, but only consider conjunctions and oppositions. Note that the reverse case (e.g. man's moon or Venus conjunct or opposed to woman's sun or Mars) is not a sexual signature – it merely indicates that the woman is the leader or initiator in the relationship.

For gay men sexual attraction is shown when one man's sun, Mars or Jupiter conjoins or opposes the other's sun, Mars, or Jupiter. Here the sun-Mars combination is the strongest. For lesbian women sexual attraction is shown when one woman's moon or Venus conjoins or opposes the other woman's moon or Venus. The moon-Venus combination is stronger than two moons or two Venus's.

The absence of any sexual signature between two peoples' horoscopes doesn't necessarily deny sexual attraction, particularly if one or the other party has natal sun, Venus, or Mars in Scorpio. However, without a sexual cross-aspect there could be a problem due to one or the other person becoming bored with the sexual relationship.

Other features of relationships (apart from sexual attraction) are shown by other cross-aspects between planets – e.g. Saturn-Jupiter contacts indicate trust; Venus-Saturn or moon-Saturn aspects indicate that the delicate sensibilities of the Venus or moon person will feel hurt by the brusqueness of the Saturn person, who in turn dislikes being clung to. And so on and so forth. The cross-aspects tell little stories. They are like little scripts of karma from previous lifetimes together, which have to be acted out again in this present lifetime.

[3] Marc Edmund Jones, *The Essentials of Astrological Analysis*, Sabian, Stanwood WA 1970. See also Bob Makransky, "Dr. Jones' Methodology", *Planetary Strength*, Wessex Astrologer 2011 and Bob Makransky, "The Natural Disposition", *Considerations* XVIII:4 2003-4

[4] Ruth Prigozy, www.zeldafitzgerald.com/fitzgeralds/index.asp, (F. Scott Fitzgerald Society website)

[5] Isadora Duncan, *My Life*, Liveright, NYC 1927, p 182.
[6] Stephen Birmingham, *Jacqueline Bouvier Kennedy Onassis*, Grosset & Dunlap, NYC 1978 p 106.
[7] Dee Presley, Dee; Billy, Rick and David Stanley, *Elvis – We Love You Tender*, Delacorte, NYC 1979 p 200-01
[8] news report on WENN 6/21/2000 posted at www.imdb.com/name/nm0000404/news
[9] Lois Rodden, *AstroDatabank* version 2.0, 1998
[10] Betty Ford, *The Times of My Life*, Ballantine NYC 1978, p 229-30
[11] Coretta Scott King, My Life with Martin Luther King, Jr., Avon NYC 1969, p187

* * * * * * * * *

Sexual Signatures in Synastry

I find it amusing when people state that they "don't believe in astrology." If people only knew how much information they were giving out when they reveal their birth time, date, and place, they would be much more circumspect. In particular, sexual signatures are an infallible guide to when there is an innate sexual attraction between two people. This doesn't always lead to out-and-out sex; but it can useful in getting one's way with people. Recently my girlfriend introduced me to her boss (for business reasons). The boss, she warned me, was bitchy, critical, and impossible to please; and my girlfriend disliked her intensely. But when I saw that the boss's horoscope and my own shared both major sexual significators, I knew that she and I would get along just fine; and so it proved (and my girlfriend's relationship with her boss improved as a result of our interaction).

Sexual turn-on is strongest when the man's sun, Mars or Jupiter conjoins or opposes the woman's moon or Venus. We will allow 6° orbs of inexactitude in measurement, but this is just a rule of thumb. Even 10° orbs "work", but the effect is lessened. This might be a good place for a statistical study.

For example, if a man's Mars is in 12° Leo; and a woman's moon or Venus is between 6° and 18° Leo (conjunction) or Aquarius (opposition); then there is a powerful sexual attraction between the two people. However, the sexual attraction is obviously stronger the closer the conjunction or opposition is to exact. In this context oppositions are not considered malefic; on the contrary, oppositions between horoscopes are better in sexual relationship. Opposites attract. However some of the effect is vitiated if the conjunction or opposition occurs over the line of the sign (e.g. from, say 29° Aries to 1° Taurus or Scorpio). Note that the reverse case (e.g. man's moon or Venus conjunct or opposed to woman's sun or Mars) is not a sexual signature – it merely indicates that the woman wears the pants in the relationship.

Of these cross-aspects between horoscopes, the sun-moon and Mars-Venus combinations in particular are the most Pavlovian sexual bell-ringers. Oftentimes I've met a woman who had her moon on or opposite my sun; or her Venus on or opposite my

Mars; and I made a mental note of the fact at that time. But nothing happened, and I certainly didn't provoke anything. However inevitably, at some future time, perhaps years down the line, without any conscious purpose on either side, there unexpectedly came a moment when we happened to look into one another's eyes and suddenly FLASH!

If you go back over all the people you've ever had such a flash with in your life and compare their horoscopes to your own, you'll see exactly what I'm getting at.

The Mars-Venus connection (when the man's Mars lies on or opposite the woman's Venus) is pure sexual attraction – fun, light, flirty, and ready to boogy. On the other hand the sun-moon cross-aspect (when the man's sun falls on or opposite the woman's moon), indicates a more profound connection; it's unquestionably sexual, but goes much deeper than the Mars-Venus combination. When you are with someone who shares this signature with you, you feel like you are home, with the person you are meant to be with, with the person who fulfills your deepest needs. There's a profound understanding between you two with no need for words; a tender sympathy and sense of belonging.

In other words, the existence of any of these sexual signatures between two people's horoscopes assures a strong sexual attraction, even if this is going on beneath the surface, unconsciously. In our sexually repressed society, most people do not consciously acknowledge their true sexual feelings; they pretend they are not feeling them. Nevertheless these feelings are shown in the horoscopes. When once you become aware of these signatures you can see it in the other person's eyes; behind their eyes, really. There are a lot more sexual agendas going on between people than they acknowledge consciously.

For example, when parents have signatures of sexual attraction with their children, it can mean that in a previous lifetime the parent and child were lovers, and the sexual attraction between them remains in this lifetime, albeit unconsciously on both sides. Of course, they will try to pretend they are not feeling this attraction; but it is often quite visible to an outside observer. Indeed, when parents find themselves fighting with a child of the opposite sex, particularly as the child reaches sexual maturity, it is often because the parent is sexually turned on and is trying to deny the attraction by substituting its negation.

The absence of any sexual signature between two people's horoscopes doesn't necessarily deny sexual attraction. People with Scorpio prominent (sun, Venus or Mars in Scorpio) tend to confuse the issue because they sexually attract and are sexually attracted by everybody. However, without a sexual signature between the two horoscopes there could be a problem due to one or the other person becoming bored with the sexual relationship.

For gay men sexual attraction is shown when one man's sun, Mars or Jupiter conjoins or opposes the other's sun, Mars, or Jupiter. Here the sun-Mars combination is the strongest.

For lesbian women sexual attraction is shown when one woman's moon or Venus conjoins or opposes the other woman's moon or Venus. The moon-Venus combination is stronger than two moons or two Venus's.

Having stated the foregoing rules for sexual attraction between horoscopes it behooves me to state the First Law of Stalking, or Keeping Your Neck Out Of Other

People's Nooses: all sexual attraction and infatuation are phony. When sexual electrons are going back and forth is when you should immediately put your guard up and be very careful of what you are doing, rather than blunder ahead into commitments that you could very easily regret. Sexual attraction can be, and often is, a cover for extremely difficult karma which will have to be dealt with if action is taken without forethought. Be warned, be smart, save yourself a lot of grief. Take a look at the other cross-aspects between the horoscopes.

* * * * * * * * *

Self-Transformation:

Telepathy and Lucid Dreaming

Philosophers of language tend to be fond of extolling the glories of human language as our "triumph" over the animal kingdom. In point of fact, language is but a vestigial remnant of humans' primordial telepathic ability, which we moderns have been taught to repress along with our other senses. However, we modern humans still rely upon our latent telepathic powers when language fails us. For example:

1) Mothers know exactly what their babies want; some mothers even let their milk down a few minutes before their babies wake up.

2) Lovers know the exact instant that the decision is made to go to bed together for the first time.

3) In foreign countries, we usually know exactly what they're saying to us, even if we don't know a word of their language.

4) We often know when we're being observed from afar (lift our eyes from reverie to the exact spot from which someone is watching us); this awareness is a remnant from our hunting days.

5) We often recognize someone we know from way far away, long before we can make out their features, posture, or gait.

6) And, of course, prophetic dreams, precognition, intuitive hunches – the types of so-called ESP that practically all of us have experienced at one time or another but cannot consciously control, but which our forebears relied upon in place of thinking and language. To them it wasn't "E"SP – it was a normal part of SP.

These sorts of telepathic communications are not a matter of body language or subliminal cues (as the rationalists would have it); rather, they are examples of true telepathy, which was a part of humankind's original equipment.

The most important concomitant of the invention of agriculture was the invention of the lie. As long as people could communicate telepathically, lies were not within the realm of possibility, since everyone knew exactly what everyone else was feeling every minute. Similarly, even we modern humans are not as easily fooled when we're dreaming as when we're awake: in dreams we can sense exactly who or what is evil or to be avoided, in spite of superficial appearances.

When mindlessness replaced mindfulness, thinking replaced feeling, and the inner dialogue replaced paying attention to the now moment, on a social level verbal communication replaced telepathy. And the gist of verbal communication is the lie: all thinking is a lie, in the sense that it is the denial of feeling, of not paying attention to the now moment. IT'S ALL A LIE. That's the gist of waking consciousness. All rationalism comes down to science; and all science comes down to mathematics; and all mathematics comes down to logic; and all logic comes down to a proposition known as The Law of the Excluded Middle, which states, in effect, that "either a statement is true, or else it is false." And that statement is false. The ability to lie – to ourselves, and other people – is what "elevates" us above the rest of the animal kingdom, and enables us to work hand-in-hand with demons.

Demon consciousness is far more elaborate, refined, and aesthetic (you might say) than human consciousness. In fact, demons are as far above humans, consciousness-wise, as humans are above animals; and their opinion of us is about like our opinion of animals. On the other hand, they are even nastier and more uptight than humans are (further separated from the Spirit). Actually, they're pretty slimy and sleazy. The point is that it's the demons who taught us how to lie, and the lie is what makes modern society, which is a pack of lies, possible. When good faith and mutual respect are gone, contracts and lists of duties and obligations are necessary.

Humans, guided by their demon mentors, intuitively perceived that a greater degree of mind would result from a greater sense of separatedness. And so, over millennia, by painful trial and error, they tried different experiments in separatedness. Agriculture was the big move, and then it got into greater degrees of division of labor and social complexity. Humankind went on a rambling, meandering walk for several thousand years. And it discovered that any separatedness which depends upon denial of true feelings will only lead to self-hatred and self-destruction.

And now, at this time, humankind has pretty much reached the limits of waking consciousness, having cut itself off from its very roots in dream consciousness. It will now enter into lucid dreaming. Dream consciousness is too erratic and mutable; waking consciousness is too ordered and routinized. Only in lucid dreaming do we have a healthy balance of mind and feeling working together (instead of one dominating the other). Lucid dreaming is the true union of reason and direct feeling – it is our true estate and destiny. It is the reason why humankind, at the time of the invention of agriculture, explored and refined waking consciousness. At that time waking consciousness was to humankind what lucid dreaming is to us today: a new frontier to explore and develop.

Merrily, Merrily, Merrily, Merrily

"Someday there will be a great awakening when we know that this is all a great dream. Yet the stupid believe they are awake, busily and brightly assuming they understand things, calling this man ruler, that one herdsman – how dense! Confucius

and you are both dreaming! And when I say you are dreaming, I am dreaming, too. Words like these will be labeled the Supreme Swindle. Yet, after ten thousand generations, a great sage may appear who will know their meaning, and it will still be as though he appeared with astonishing speed. ...

"Once Chuang Chou dreamt he was a butterfly, a butterfly flitting and fluttering around, happy with himself and doing as he pleased. He didn't know he was Chuang Chou. Suddenly he woke up and there he was, solid and unmistakable Chuang Chou. But he didn't know if he was Chuang Chou who had dreamt he was a butterfly, or a butterfly dreaming he was Chuang Chou." – Chuang Tzu

"The self dreams the double. ... Once it has learned to dream the double, the self arrives at this weird crossroad and a moment comes when one realizes that it is the double who dreams the self." – Carlos Castaneda, *Tales of Power*

"Indeed, perhaps what is now the REM state was the original form of waking consciousness in early brain evolution, when emotionality was more important than reason in the competition for resources. This ancient form of waking consciousness may have come to be actively suppressed in order for higher brain evolution to proceed efficiently. This is essentially a new theory of dreaming." – Jaak Panksepp, *Affective Neuroscience*.

The basic tenet of magic is, that it's all just a dream; that waking consciousness is but a more highly evolved and specialized facet of dream consciousness. Dream consciousness came first evolutionarily, and waking consciousness is an outgrowth of dreaming. Although we tend to believe that there is a vast difference between being awake and dreaming, the fact is that this is indeed merely a belief – a belief which enables us to focus our attention on waking – to isolate it and solidify it – to the exclusion of dreaming.

We make a big deal out of the difference between waking and dreaming, but the distinction between the two states isn't as clear as we usually imagine. When we run past life regressions; or even just listen to music or dance – any time we are so absorbed in any activity that we lose all sense of self perceiving self and are operating on pure "flow" – we are actually closer to being in a dream state than in a waking state. The less we are consciously controlling what is happening, but rather just letting it happen by itself, the closer we are to dreaming. The act of "going to sleep" is just a thought form we use to convince ourselves that we're not dreaming half the time anyway. We use the acts of "going to sleep" and "waking up" to separate out the two modes – to make a distinction where in fact little distinction exists. It's like two people who have been living together for years finally getting married – it's a symbolic thing, there's not much objective difference between the two states. It's as if we made up some sort of distinction like "write with your right hand on Tuesdays, Thursdays, and Saturdays" and "write with your left hand on Mondays, Wednesdays, and Fridays". If we got everyone to do this and make it an automatic habit, then after a few centuries the human race would have invented another distinction in consciousness (indeed, this is in fact what different cultures do). People would find that life on Tuesdays, Thursdays, and Saturdays was very different from life on Mondays, Wednesdays, and Fridays. But it's all an artificial distinction.

Ancient humans were doing what we would consider dreaming as their everyday state of mind. There wasn't as sharp a distinction then between being awake and being asleep. Then people slept in snatches, as infants do, and they alternated hunting off and on with dozing. Most of their hunting was done in a state of mind that we would call sleepwalking (a trance state). They weren't just wandering around aimlessly looking for game to hunt: they could sense what was out there and could project their consciousness forward into their prey telepathically and so anticipate the prey's movements. We moderns can still do this now and then, as for example when on the prowl for sex, or when we sense a business opportunity, especially when we feel lucky; but our hunter forebears relied on this intuitive faculty to eat every day. In other words, ancient hunters were more connected to their world, more psychically attuned, than we moderns are. They were able to pick up information from their environment which eludes us. But on the other hand ancient humans had less sense of a self at center than we do, just as we moderns have less sense of there being a solid, separated "us" there when we are dreaming compared to when we are awake.

Waking consciousness is something which evolves; which can be seen to evolve even between human generations. That's why people "back then" seem so naïve to us – they were dreaming more than we moderns do. We're more awake than our forebears. Consider too how wide-awake First World societies are compared with most Third World societies: First Worlders living in the Third World tend to find the natives to be "irresponsible" and spaced-out, when in fact all they're doing is dreaming more in their everyday waking lives than hup-hup First Worlders do.

The point is that there isn't as hard-and-fast a difference between being awake and dreaming as we are accustomed to believe. It is exactly that belief (that what we do when we are awake is more important than what we do when we are dreaming) which maintains the rigidity of wakefulness – the persuasiveness of the lie that what is happening to us when we are awake is "real" – that is to say, that there is some separated "us" to which things are happening – rather than that the whole shebang is just our projection. That "us" is symbolized by the thought forms of a body, and an outside world in which things happen to that body.

When we are dreaming, we have a body also, and a world outside of it. That body and world seem perfectly real while we are dreaming, but when we wake up we realize that it was all just a dream. The interpretation that we have a physical body when we are awake is also merely a belief, exactly like the interpretation that we have a body while we're dreaming is merely a belief. While we are dreaming our dream bodies operate with all five of the usual physical senses. Therefore, we really don't have any objective criteria for deciding, at any given moment, whether we are awake or asleep. In precisely the same fashion, our body when we are awake and the world surrounding it are just a dream. There is no objective difference whatsoever. That's what other people and our society do for us: assure us that we are indeed awake and that what we are experiencing is "real".

Ancient humans were more magical than we are (not as separated). They permitted dream material to freely intrude into their awareness, whereas we moderns have mechanisms in place to immediately repress any such incursion into our reality.

When dream stuff intrudes into waking consciousness we get moments of discontinuity. Any sudden start or shock or fright is a rift in our sense of continuity – or better said, a mad grab for our sense of continuity to mask such a rift. We have to say that discontinuity is unreal, and that people who experience discontinuity are crazy, or tired and overworked and in need of rest. We have to get everyone to validate this pretense – to pretend that they're not experiencing discontinuity, in order for society to exist. Society and waking consciousness are just two names for the same thing: in dreams, we are basically alone. In point of fact we're just as alone when we're awake, but we stupidly believe that we are sweating and puffing and bleeding as part of a team. Thus being awake can be defined as the pretense that we're not alone (that we are part of a society).

The reason why the dream state is so mutable is that there is little sense of separatedness in it. It is importance – the sense of urgency, of being driven, of being uptight – which stabilizes attention. We are able to focus our attention when we are awake because of our interminable, self-referent inner chatter every second we are awake. Waking consciousness is a clenching up within oneself – a moment-to-moment flinching from death – embodied in a socially-conditioned striving and intranquility within ourselves that keeps us awake. By contrast, the attention we have in dreams has little importance to it because we don't think so much; but as a result we can't control what we will pay attention to (what will happen next) as well in dreaming as we can when we are awake. What we experience when dreaming is far more immediate, vivid, gripping, and intense than in the ordered waking world. It all happens so fast that we can't separate ourselves from it as we can and do in waking life. We don't get weekends off and two weeks paid vacation in the world of dreams, and there's no TV to watch – no way to make it stop happening or pretend it's not happening. We must either be on the qui vive every instant; or else stand there in a stupor; but we are inevitably so caught up in the dream, so much a part of it, that although we are experiencing our feelings in symbolic form in dreams, there is little sense of separatedness there. Mind exists, but it's not developed.

Mind cannot develop until there is a clearly defined sense of separatedness, which gives mind a pause, a moment's rest or leisure, in which it can reflect on itself. It's that moment's rest or lull which gives birth to a sense of time and linear continuity.

Although waking consciousness originated together with multicellular life on earth, the invention of agriculture was its apotheosis as far as the human species is concerned. As compared with hunting, the invention of agriculture brought order, regularity, sleep 8 hours at night and work 16 hours during the day. Humankind had outgrown dream consciousness; it had found dream consciousness – the consciousness of infants and animals – too unstable, too ephemeral, and therefore too limiting for its free expression. Therefore humans literally constructed, piece by piece, thought form by thought form, over the surface of dream consciousness, the floating edifice of waking mind. Humankind began to think and reason.

Separation of quotidian life into 16 hours of wakefulness and 8 hours of dreaming – forcing our bodies to stay awake for such a long stretch of time – is a stern discipline, a way of clenching up, which helps block the intrusion of dream material (magical events) into wakefulness. Ancient humans mixed the two together in their awareness – waking life was as ineffable as dreaming, and everything was a source of wonder and mystery.

Native cultures, such as the Mayan people of Guatemala, maintain much of this thought form structure to this day. We North American-European-Asian moderns have learned to tone down our sensory impressions, to separate ourselves from our environment by taking everything around us for granted, by not paying attention to anything except our own incessant mental chatter. This makes our lives utterly boring and meaningless, but nonetheless provides us with our ability to focus our attention, to be methodical, concentrated and deliberate. Our hunter-gatherer ancestors were unable to focus that much attention. They had no need to.

Along with heightened focus comes a decreased sense of connectedness; a greater sense of separatedness. And along with the heightened separatedness necessary to focus attention in the waking world comes a heightened sense of isolation and anguish. In other words, suffering is an intrinsic component of waking consciousness. Without suffering, the constant self-pinching, we could not stay awake.

When we are awake we say "I am suffering!" That "I" is made out suffering (self-pity in the parlance of shamanism). To gainsay Descartes, "I suffer, therefore I am." Just as the waking "I" and the "suffering" arise together, so too do they dissolve together. If "I" ever stop suffering, the disconnected "I" dissolves too. The main cause of our self-hatred, the chief reason we are all so neurotic and out of kilter with our world, is simply because we've been awake too long.

The point is that waking consciousness is not something which is intrinsically different from dreaming, but rather something which evolved and developed out of it; which became more focused and intense and uptight as it evolved. Waking is merely a way of imposing a semblance of order and control (mind – things making some kind of sense instead of being wholly ineffable) on at least a portion of the dream. However this is a falsehood: NOTHING makes any sense – EVERYTHING is ineffable. In other words, waking consciousness – and the society which supports it – is a complete and total fabrication.

Waking mind is like the insouciance of a drunkard staggering across a battlefield where bullets whiz by all around him but who is somehow protected from it all by his blissful indifference. That is waking mind. It is so totally a fiction (the sense that we are separated from everything around us) that it can only be maintained by the constant validation of other people (our sense of being part of society). Only by all of us reassuring one another that we are separated individuals – by constantly picking at and annoying each other, just as we constantly pick at and annoy ourselves to stay awake – can we jointly uphold the fragile structure of waking consciousness. Our society assures its continuance by setting its individual members upon each other like ravenous dogs.

When society dissolves because of e.g. war or disaster, everything becomes like a dream, since it's out of control. Waking makes for more control than dreaming, but with a concomitant loss of awareness and joy. Over the next century, as the environment and civilization deteriorate, society will collapse and everything will spin out of control. That is to say, waking consciousness will dissolve back into the dream from which it emerged at the time of the invention of agriculture. The human race isn't going to be able to muddle through this one, as it has always done. Nor will there be any miraculous salvation: no one is going to be raptured up into the clouds to sit next to Jesus; and December 22, 2012 isn't going to be any improvement on December 20th. And certainly the corporations, governments, and materialistic scientists who got us into this mess aren't going to get us out of it. Each individual human being will then be at a crossroads: either lighten up and enter into lucid dreaming as your everyday mode of awareness; or enter into a nightmare.

In the same way that waking consciousness grew out of dreaming, lucid dreaming – that is to say, dreaming in which the dreamer knows that he or she is dreaming – is an outgrowth of waking consciousness. Lucid dreaming is humankind's next step in the evolution of consciousness – New, Improved, Lemon-Scented Consciousness. It's also our only hope for survival as a species.

Lucid dreaming allows us to take a pause for reflection on the dream plane: to make it stop happening for a moment to critically evaluate and redirect the experience, instead of being wholly caught up in it, forced to be constantly shifting and adjusting ourselves to it, as our hunter forebears had to do. Hunters had to more or less go with the flow, and they were better or worse hunters as they were able to be flexible and quick to see and grasp opportunities and avoid pitfalls as they arose. They were nimble, but not very capable of planning, organizing, or thinking things through.   If there was an easier way to do something, they probably wouldn't have been able to figure it out (not enough separatedness).

What happens in lucid dreaming is that we preserve the thought forms of waking consciousness, but without the importance. That is to say, lucid dreaming is waking consciousness without the driving urgency, the constant uptightness, the sense of a separated, suffering succotash of a self. We still have a self, symbolized by a body thought form, while we are lucidly dreaming; but that body is a great deal lighter and less separated than our waking body. It can fly, for one thing.

The point is, as all lucid dreamers soon realize, that the thought forms of waking consciousness can be activated in the dream state once they have been cut loose from their importance. Lucid dreaming is what waking consciousness could be (and will be) like when we get rid of our importance. To do lucid dreaming consistently we will have to come to a general conviction in our daily lives that nothing is all that important.

It is the purpose of the practice of magic to make everyday life more like dreaming – to release the fixation on a separated, suffering self. This is accomplished by cultivating the practice of lucid dreaming while we are asleep, and by going to trees or nature spirits every day while we are awake. The doorway out of wakefulness into lucid dreaming is what magicians term sensory thought forms, and what cognitive philosophers term qualia: that is to say, shifting attention from thinking to feeling the world around us. This entails quieting down our minds and listening to sounds, feeling the breeze on our skin, seeing the plants and the clouds. It's what mystics refer to as "suchness" or "thusness"; but really all it involves is just shutting up the constant stream of mental chatter long enough to see – hear – feel what's going on in the now moment – i.e., to do what we do when we're dreaming while we're awake.

The goal for us as individuals is to merge dreaming and waking – to be as light and unencumbered while awake as we are while dreaming; and to be as rational and clear-thinking while dreaming as we are when we are awake. The goal for us humans as a species is to make lucid dreaming our everyday awareness, in the same way that our hunter-gatherer ancestors made waking consciousness their everyday awareness at the time that agriculture was invented. I.e., to become magicians.

The purpose of Buddhism – at least insofar as I understand it – is to get a few exceptional people fully enlightened. The purpose of the practice of magic is to get the mass of people somewhat enlightened – i.e. enlightened enough to save the human race and the earth. No major upheaval in present society would necessarily be required to make this shift, unless humankind stupidly proves to be incapable of responding short of a total crisis. There are probable realities which go either way, which we as individuals can choose or decline to participate in, by believing what we choose to believe. All that's required to save humanity is for most people (not necessarily all) to lighten up just a little bit. We don't need everyone to don sackcloth and ashes and take to caves and become enlightened; nor do we need everyone to fall in line and believe as we do. All we need is for most people to become just a tad less greedy, selfish, suspicious, intolerant, closed-hearted and shameless. Just for most people to lighten up a teensy bit is all that's required for the human race to enter into lucid dreaming together.

In the state of lucid dreaming everyone instantly knows the truth, so pretense is impossible. By contrast, most of what transpires in waking consciousness is a pack of lies: people are talking about one thing, but what is really going on under the surface is something altogether different. It isn't like that in lucid dreaming – what we see is what we get. There's no room for phoniness because those importance coverings don't exist in lucid dreaming – that agreement is more important than truth.

Yes, Virginia, Truth does indeed exist. All that's necessary to find it is to cut through all the yada-yada nonsense of our decadent, degenerate society and listen to what our hearts are telling us. We magicians do this by going to trees and nature spirits for validation rather than to our fellow humans.

To enter into lucid dreaming from a position which starts from being awake is the same thing as astral projection. Talented dreamers have a facility for astral projection, and this can be the quickest way for them to go. But it would take most people too long to learn astral projection; it's easier for them to come at it through lucid dreaming. This is a better path for people who think too much, since it minimizes thinking. We have to start from being asleep, and then beckon our separatedness thought form to come to us without its covering of importance. If the covering of importance comes too, then we wake up. That's why so many of us find it difficult to maintain ourselves in a state of lucid dreaming without waking up: one must be calm in a lucid dream, otherwise one tends to beckon importance.

Lucid dreaming is not something essentially different from waking consciousness, only we get to it from a position of being asleep. When we start out from a position of being awake, we call it "everyday life". What do you suppose the horseless carriage is? Or the radio, TV, airplane, space rocket, computer? They are all wild, crazy dreams. A hundred years ago that's exactly what we would have considered them. And that's all they are – dreams. Humankind just incorporated that dream material into waking consciousness. That's the sort of thing waking consciousness is good for: to originate dream material of that sort. That kind of business requires slow, patient development over generations; and the dream plane is too unstable and mutable to do that kind of stuff on. The dream plane is too here and now. Since dream consciousness is more timeless than waking consciousness, it doesn't allow for the detachment that a sense of past (history) and future (planning) can give. We need a greater sense of separateness to be able to do things that slowly. That's why it is so difficult to do things like dial a phone number or read a sentence in a normal dream – these activities require a greater degree of separateness than normal dreaming affords, to be able to bring that kind of minute detail into focus.

That's the genius of waking consciousness: we lose scope and agility, but in return we get focus and a methodical way of getting at things. Waking consciousness is much more clearly focused and delimited than dreaming, even if we all become extremely myopic and uptight in the process.

The practice of magic is about turning our everyday waking lives into lucid dreaming, cultivating a somewhat "altered state of mind" as our everyday mindset. As we do this much of our sense of separateness dissolves and we feel more inner peace and oneness with our world. Spirits start talking to us, as they did to our hunter-gatherer ancestors. Our everyday life becomes more like dreaming – i.e., more magical. This is the road that each of us must travel as individuals; and which the human race as a whole will have to follow if it is to survive and prosper. It is the road of entering into a state of lucid dreaming from a position which starts from being awake (instead of asleep, as usual). This means understanding that waking consciousness is lucid dreaming; and the only reason we can't see that is because we must keep up the pretense that what we're doing is "real" and important. Therefore we can't see that it's all just a dream.

At this writing there don't seem to be too many lucid dreamers out there; but there are lots of people merrily, merrily, merrily, merrily dancing a jig on their descent into the coming nightmare. It's time now for everyone to wake up.

Importance

There are two basic types of thought forms: sensory thought forms and conceptual thought forms. Sensory thought forms are thought forms of mindfulness: they are what we experience when we are paying attention to what is happening here and now. These thought forms consist of sensory and extrasensory perceptions of the now moment: sights, sounds, smells, tastes, and feelings (both physical and nonphysical). Sensory thought forms have a high proportion of feeling to them, such as the sight of a beautiful woman; the smell of roses; the roar of the ocean; the feel of slime. Sensory thought forms are innately joyous, and any true joy in our lives derives from our operating on sensory thought forms (rather than conceptual thought forms).

Conceptual thought forms are thought forms of mindlessness, and operate when we are on automatic pilot (lost in thought, paying attention to something other than the now moment). For example, when we are driving our automobiles, most of the time we are not paying particular attention to the act of driving but have our minds elsewhere, and this entails operating on conceptual thought forms. But if we spot an accident up ahead, we snap-to and start paying attention to our driving; and this is operating on sensory thought forms.

We deliberately remember conceptual thought forms by making them important to us, and we do this by means of repetition. For example, if we want to remember a telephone number, we repeat it over and over to ourselves until we have made the conceptual thought form of that telephone number (its importance covering) strong enough to take its place in the inventory of remembered thought forms. Remembered thought forms hang around at the fringes of conscious attention, ready to spring into action to take over conscious attention in response to the remembered stimulus.

All thinking consists of conceptual thought forms. We cannot think and pay attention to the now moment at the same time. In order to think, we must conceive something (whatever we are thinking about) to be more important than paying attention to the now moment. Thus we can say that the difference between sensory and conceptual thought forms is that the latter have a covering, or gloss, of importance.

Importance may be defined as a screen of inattention: when we operate on sensory thought forms we pay attention to what is happening in the now moment; however, when we operate on conceptual thought forms, we pay attention to something other than what is happening right now by screening out (forgetting) what is happening right now; and this is accomplished by feeling that something else is more important (more urgent) to pay attention to than what is happening right now. In order to think, we have to stop paying attention to what is happening right now and focus our attention on something else, and it is importance which allows us to focus our attention by disregarding (screening out) what we are experiencing in the now moment.

Just as most of the thought forms of dreaming are sensory thought forms, most of the thought forms of wakefulness are conceptual thought forms. Indeed, conceptual thought forms are a specialized form (an evolutionary outgrowth) of sensory thought forms, just as waking consciousness is a specialized form (an evolutionary outgrowth) of dream consciousness. The reason why the dream state is so mutable (as compared to waking) is that there is little sense of importance to it. It is importance which stabilizes attention; the attention we have in dreams has little importance to it, thus we can't control what we will pay attention to (what will happen next) as well as we can in wakefulness.

The effect of psychedelic substances is to substantially lower importance (focus). For example, if we take a shower while tripping, we can feel (are consciously aware of) every individual drop of water as it hits our skin, as a discrete event. On the other hand we can't balance a checkbook while tripping because we can't focus that much attention – there's too much going on to be able to focus. To operate on conceptual thought forms – to be able to focus upon one thing at a time by separating it out from its background – is to create importance.

Importance, then, is a screen of inattention, a criterion for selecting just one of the innumerable possibilities of where attention will be placed at any given moment in order to bring just one piece of the overall picture into high focus. The feeling that something is important is sufficient of and by itself to bring that thing into focus and to disjoin it from its surroundings. It's magic: to feel something is important is to be able to separate it from its background and hold it in place.

Different cultures have historically inculcated importance in different ways. In our decadent, materialistic society we are taught to feel the validation of our conceptual thought forms by other people as glory; and to feel the beckoning of our own true feelings as shame. We are taught to seek the one and to hide the other: to deny our true senses and feelings, and to substitute instead a false distinction which other people will applaud. It is an endless loop because glory cannot be arrived at without shame: to seek glory is to seek a lie, and lies bring about feelings of shame because we know in our hearts that we are not what we claim to be – more important than anything else.

If you have ever stopped for a minute and objectively analyzed your constant thinking – your continual, moment-to-moment, all-day-long inner dialogue – you have probably realized that it consists mostly of thoughts about your past and thoughts about your future. When you think thoughts about your past, you feel feelings of shame and embarrassment – hatred of your looks; your actions; and your desires, particularly your sexual desires – which you try to hide from other people. On the other hand, when you think thoughts about your future, you fantasize scenes of glory in which you have absolute power and control (fantasies of sex and romance fall into this category); and other people dote on you with their approval, approbation, or regret for having done you wrong. Note that, as Freud pointed out a century ago, both the shame and glory manifestations of importance tend to attach to conceptual thought forms of sex.

Hiding shame from other people and seeking glory in their eyes is the chain which binds us to our unhappiness. In other words, conceptual thought forms are the stick and carrot which our society uses to enslave us. In order for us to be able to feel good about ourselves right now, in the present moment (i.e., to operate on sensory thought forms), obviously we first have to overcome our feelings of shame from our past and our fantasies of glory in some future that will never come (dethrone the importance of our conceptual thought forms).

There's no reason on earth why we shouldn't feel completely content all the time, perfectly at peace with ourselves and the world around us. The reason why most of us don't feel this way is because our conceptual thought forms are at war with our true feelings (our intent); we're too busy telling ourselves why we're not happy to allow a moment's pause to be happy. Our habitual thoughts drive us relentlessly, never allowing us a space in which to reflect objectively upon what we're doing, much less to consciously direct or control our reactions.

Importance is our sense of being trapped by life. Whatever is important to us – whatever areas of life we have chosen to be important to us in this lifetime – is what makes us feel trapped and helpless. For example, if we believe that money is important, then we'll always feel trapped by money – either trapped by our belief that we lack money, or trapped by our fear of losing it. No matter how much money we have or don't have, we are trapped by our obsessive concern over money. Clearly, money doesn't have anything to do with our "money problems"; money is just a conceptual thought form we use to symbolize our decision to be worried and jealous and unhappy.

The key point of magical training is to learn how to change the focus of where we place our moment-to-moment attention. This requires volition. We have to somehow make a space for ourselves away from compulsively indulging our customary conceptual thought forms of shame and glory, and instead pay attention to the world around us in the now moment (i.e. operate on sensory thought forms). Note that the goal of magical training is not to stop thinking altogether (which some critics of magical science – particularly materialistic academics – seem to want to believe); but rather to dethrone the moment-to-moment compulsion to think: to be able to turn thinking on when it is needed, and then turn it off at will and pay attention to the now moment the rest of the time. This facility is also known as "enlightenment".

This is what the coming transformation in consciousness is all about: when our unsustainable materialistic society inevitably collapses, the surviving remnant of the human race (if there is one) will have to redeploy importance from hiding shame and seeking glory (inflating self-importance) to following true feelings – working for the good of our mother earth and the human race as a whole. Or better said: only those who have accomplished such a redeployment, and who are able to follow their true feelings instead of the importance coverings on their conceptual thought forms (their shame and glory), will survive the coming collapse.

Active Imagination

Importance is not itself a thought form, but rather a thought form covering. It is a feeling of urgency created by the denial of a true feeling (telling oneself some sort of lie in order to fulfill society's expectations). Importance coverings are casings, like sausage casings, into which feelings can be stuffed; and they are controlled by the conceptual thought forms which created them. In a manner of speaking, importance coverings are our conceptual thought forms' thought forms. Like the Spirit does for us, we give our conceptual thought forms a certain amount of independence. Actually, about all we can do is to create them and destroy them; other than that, they roll their own. And not only are we subject to our conceptual thought forms, but we are also subject to our conceptual thought forms' thought forms – the energy which we gave our conceptual thought forms originally, which they have in turn bestowed upon their importance coverings.

This is to say that most of what we have been trained to consider "our" feelings such as jealousy, envy, greed, etc., are not actually "our" feelings at all, but rather are importance coverings on conceptual thought forms learned from our parents and society. These sorts of importance coverings are our conceptual thought forms' feelings; and as such they differ considerably from society to society (e.g. sexual jealousy is not as important in Eskimo or Yanomami culture as it is in ours). In fact we can define "society" to be the set of conceptual thought forms which are common to a particular milieu at a particular time. The way to distinguish between true feelings and importance coverings within ourselves is that we are born with our true feelings, whereas we learn importance coverings from the people around us.

The importance coverings on our conceptual thought forms assure that we will keep thinking the same thoughts over and over and over all the time. When those thoughts happen to be negative thoughts, then they tend to conjure up negative emotions such as jealousy, anger, lust, self-pity, etc. When we feel these negative emotions, we release emotional "darts" – we feel something like a clenching up / letting go of that emotion – from our tummies. The actual "physical" feeling of releasing a dart of negative energy varies from person to person; but if you pay close attention when you release such a dart, you'll notice that it stems from your solar plexus.

Demons, who subsist upon negative energy, work hand-in-hand with the importance coverings on our thought forms to generate food for themselves. They hover around us constantly waiting for us to think a negative thought and release a dart of negative energy; and then they snap it up. Therefore, to liberate ourselves from slavery to demons, it is not only necessary to cast out any demons which might be possessing us, but it is also sine qua non to stop thinking negative thoughts – i.e. to get rid of the importance coverings on our thought forms. This is done by banishing the thought forms – one at a time – and thereafter by rejecting those thoughts as they arise. This is equivalent to the nagual Julian's Method I:

"For the nagual Julian, self-importance was a monster that had three thousand heads. And one could face up to it and destroy it in any of three ways. The first way was to sever each head one at a time; the second way was to reach that mysterious state of being called the place of no pity, which destroyed self-importance by slowly starving it; and the third was to pay for the instantaneous annihilation of the three-thousand-headed monster with one's symbolic death." – Carlos Castaneda, *The Power of Silence*

Basically, then, the goal of magical training is losing importance: reaching the conviction that this or that "terribly important" thing – particularly the things we are afraid of or angry at – just isn't that important. It's only when we lose our importance that true spiritual growth becomes possible. Without importance we are content to let things unfold all in good time, without pushing-pushing-pushing to get our way or else cringing and whining helplessly in self-pity. Without importance we can turn our compulsion to think every minute we are awake OFF and listen to sounds, or feel the breeze caress our face.

But just as it takes money to make money, so too does it take losing (LOTS) of importance to understand the advantage of losing importance. It is importance which blinds us to the truth; and the truth is that nothing is important. It is our social training which makes us believe and act as though this and that and the other thing are important. Conventional thought form religions are full of that kind of crap: if you believe this, that, or the other; if you pat your head while rubbing your tummy on odd-numbered Tuesdays-Thursdays-and-Saturdays; then you will go to heaven when you die. But the truth is that belief, especially religious belief, is irrelevant. Belief is what blinds us to the truth: that only by losing importance can we see the truth, since the truth is not something which can be apprehended by an intellectual process. It can only be intuited by intent – by direct knowing – not by getting a little pat on the head from other people or from "God".

The only way to lose importance is to look at things from the Spirit's point of view. The Spirit says, "You are NOT IMPORTANT!" Obviously. If you were important, if you mattered in the least to the Spirit, it wouldn't make you die, would it? Death is the Spirit's way of cluing you in as to how unimportant you really are in the cosmic scheme of things.

The process of losing importance is very painful – don't let anyone tell you that it isn't. If you find the spiritual path enjoyable, you're not on it. Losing all your expectations, your images, your fantasies; having your sense of importance – your feeling that you are better than other people; or that God gives the slightest damn about you and that you are something more elevated than Purina worm chow – stomped into the mud and rubbed in your face (which is basically what the spiritual path entails) … ain't much fun. That's why so few people even attempt it; and of those that do, very, very few succeed. It's just so much, much easier to run away from yourself, especially in a superficial society like ours which provides so much mindless diversion, and so much phony "spirituality".

To deliberately follow the magician's path requires the utmost courage and determination: an importance of purpose which is strong enough to overcome the hypnotically obsessive importance of everyday life (a counterweight to it). Fundamentally, becoming a magician entails fighting against the current of the past 15,000 years of human evolution. It's taken the human race all that time to stabilize waking consciousness into the hard, unyielding substance it has become. Importance has to be durable – otherwise we go "insane" (lose the ability to keep dreaming and waking separated). For a single practitioner to turn back this evolutionary tide is well-nigh impossible; it will be easier to lose importance in the future, as society's impending collapse calls up magicians who will work together at the task (just as people today prop up each other's importance by mutual back-patting).

In Don Juan's (Carlos Castaneda's teacher's) heurism, the student deliberately seeks a merciless son of a bitch to stomp his or her sense of self-esteem and self-worth into the mud.* The point is that losing importance is the only way to clear out your social conditioning (conceptual thought forms of expectation) to allow your intent (direct knowing) to operate. Losing importance really does require being pushed beyond your limits – way, way beyond anything you thought you could endure – and stripping away everything, but everything, to which you cling. Going that extra mile – or being forced to go that extra mile – when you already thought you couldn't stand any more, is how you really lose oodles of importance. Thus, in the case of the human race as a whole, it will probably take some very unpleasant consequences of the forthcoming collapse of society to bring off the much-vaunted coming transformation of consciousness. People aren't going to give up their selfish materialism and comfortable, smug stupidity voluntarily. And those who are left standing (if there are any) will be those who have had all their importance (self-pity) completely stripped away.

You lose importance by stopping caring about the things you most care about – by becoming accustomed to (accepting) your fate instead of whining and complaining about your plight, and running around like a chicken with its head cut off to try to improve matters. You lose importance very time you "give up the ghost" – surrender something you were expecting or clinging to. Usually this is due to complete defeat (my guides have always said that spiritual growth is basically just a matter of exhaustion). The process can be speeded along by going to tree or nature spirits every day; but really, there's no substitute for having all your dreams and illusions stomped into the mud, and having everything you live for destroyed.

The ultimate goal is to be calm and relaxed in your heart; to be able to confront everyday life and other people with complete equanimity; even if there is a maelstrom swirling around you. And magicians aver, that there's no other way in which you could possibly learn how to do this except in a maelstrom. This is how the coming collapse of society will usher in a transformation of consciousness for the survivors.

The stages or steps of losing importance vary from person to person, of course. Chogyam Trungpa gives a good description of the process in his book Shambhala. In my own case, after years and years of resorting to tree and nature spirits, the first thing I noticed was that when I awoke in the morning, instead of an automatic blah-blah-blah-blah-blah starting up in my brain, instead I would be confronted with >BLANK<.

The next noticeable change in my wonted mentation, a few years later, occurred after being forced to make a highly unpalatable life decision – a tremendous defeat and the crash of a lifetime's dream, actually – after which I began to notice that my customary self-hatred and great-I-am (shame and glory) litanies had diminished; and also that my rancor fantasies had decreased markedly (most of my fantasy life traditionally revolved around fantasies of violence, vengeance, murder of my enemies, etc. Most of my internal dialogue consisted of thoughts of rancor and violence – in contrast to most people, whose inner dialogue consists mostly of thoughts of worry, depression, futility, hopelessness, uselessness). It's not that I no longer think rancorous thoughts; but rather that when such a thought pops up now, I can and do automatically reject it. It's also true, as the nagual Julian claimed, that my own process of losing importance was greatly speeded after the second time I reached the Place of No Pity. This happened in the middle, between when the >BLANK< feeling first began and the big defeat occurred.

Anyway, after this big defeat I began to feel the >BLANK< feeling all day long. The immediate upshot of this event was a general de-stressing of my life: little things that used to put me uptight previously ceased to do so; I began to be able to take things more in stride. It was kind of weird at first – like always being "on" (operating on sensory awareness), paying attention to everything every minute – instead of being lost in la-la land most of the time. It's a strange sensation, and it's accompanied by a strange indifference. This indifference isn't so much a listlessness per se, as it is a disinclination to become involved if you can possibly avoid it. And, because you are uninvolved, you can see all the ego games which everyone around you is playing with crystal clarity. And when you do have to act, then you act with a cold, hard detachment which is kind of scary.

The other noticeable thing with the >BLANK< feeling is an everyday equilibrium mindset of devil-may-care élan, and a sense that you can handle the things that happen okay. You get a moment-to-moment cushion of well-being: a feeling that (most of the time, anyway) things are fine just as they are now.

It is important for the aspirant to always keep in mind that importance is not lost little-by-little as you go along; it's lost in big chunks in relatively short periods of time, after years and years and years and years of a Dark Night of the Soul. As don Juan told Carlos Castaneda, "A warrior is waiting, and he knows what he is waiting for." The point is not to become discouraged when years and decades go by and it seems to you that you've made no spiritual progress whatsoever. This is the norm. Read your Saint John of the Cross. Just keep on keeping on – going to tree or nature spirits every day, doing whatever your spiritual practice is, and doing what you must do to keep the faith. When importance finally runs out, it runs out all at once – and when that happens, it takes your breath away.

Importance can be felt in the body as a heavy, viscous substance which exerts uncomfortable pressure, particularly in the regions of the heart and solar plexus: that "wad of dough in the tummy" feeling when we are frightened or angry. Most people deny this feeling by venting their importance through self-pity thought forms of whining and complaining; or else by projecting conceptual thought forms of anger, fear, jealousy, etc. onto other people. To lose importance it is necessary to confront the yucky, depressing, bodily feeling of importance directly rather than to deny it by disguising it behind conceptual thought forms or hurling it as darts at other people.

Losing importance – the goal of magical training – is exactly the opposite of what our materialistic society trains us to do. Our society trains us to clench ourselves up and repress our ability to feel; and then to preen and prance and vaunt our phoniness and shamelessness like the naked emperor; and to vomit our self-hatred onto others (blame other people for our own stupidity).

How can we lose importance? The same way we obtained it. Conceptual thought forms are cut off from their importance coverings the same way they were attached in the first place: through repetition. We first banish the thought forms (make a firm decision to destroy them), and then we continually reject those thoughts as they arise, as the importance coverings attempt to reconstruct their banished conceptual thought forms. Eventually, by refusing those thoughts, we sever them altogether from the importance coverings to which they were attached – we lose that importance. Note, however, that this can (and usually does) take years and years of inner work, particularly the daily resort to trees or other nature spirits. This is because the importance coverings on our conceptual thought forms are necessarily quite durable (as mentioned previously, if they weren't so durable we'd go "insane" – be unable to keep waking and dreaming separated).

In any event, within a day or so of banishing a conceptual thought form you'll feel more detachment in the area ruled by that thought form. Banishing a conceptual thought form gives you a space, a free moment, in which you can make a sober, reasoned decision about how you'll react to a given stimulus, instead of being compelled to react out of some stock set of neurotic reactions which may not be appropriate to the present situation. You get a pause in there instead of a blind, thoughtless, headlong rush to react. You can watch yourself as you react; you become consciously aware of what you're doing as you do it. This is the first step in controlling your moment-to-moment attention.

The Place of No Pity

"For the nagual Julian, self-importance was a monster that had three thousand heads. And one could face up to it and destroy it in any of three ways. The first way was to sever each head one at a time; the second was to reach that mysterious state of being called the place of no pity, which destroyed self-importance by slowly starving it; and the third was to pay for the instantaneous annihilation of the three-thousand-headed monster with one's symbolic death." – Carlos Castaneda, The Power of Silence

In other words, self-importance is generated from, or is propped up by, self-pity: by an interminable inner dialogue of me-me-me-me-me thoughts. This inner dialogue creates our lower self – our sense of who we are, and of how and where we fit into our society (whom we are better than; and who is better than us). All spiritual growth is a matter deconditioning the lower self, of becoming more selfless – i.e., of losing self-importance. This is accomplished by making something else more important than self-pity. There are various techniques (such as Active Imagination) for doing this; and these techniques are applications of the nagual Julian's first way of losing self-importance (cutting off each head one at a time).

As we will to lose our self-importance, we begin to obtain more volitional control over our moment-to-moment attention. We also find our ties to our society lessening: we stop caring so much about what anyone thinks of us. We thereby enlarge our capacity to listen to, and to follow, what our own hearts are telling us to do. We begin to operate on our own intuition and intent, our true feelings, rather than on fearful and unquestioning subservience to societal fiat.

The Place of No Pity is a peak moment in the lives of spiritual seekers when they are torn loose from their wonted psychological moorings and are completely wiped out emotionally – when they just don't give a damn no more. This temporarily erases self-importance / self-pity, and permits their higher selves to surface reaching the Place of No Pity also "unhooks" the lower self, which then begins to disintegrate slowly as it is battered by the vicissitudes of circumstances. When people who are still hooked to their lower selves face difficult circumstances, their natural tendency is to batten down the hatches and screw themselves down tighter – erect more defenses; close themselves up more; pile lies on top of more lies; or do whatever it takes to keep their lower selves intact. However, after a person's lower self is unhooked at the Place of No Pity, difficult circumstances make the person release more lower self by losing self-importance. When people are unhooked they become more indifferent – "Who gives a damn?" "Why work up a sweat?"

White magicians try to cultivate the attitude that nothing that happens or doesn't happen is all that important. This very sentiment is often expressed by people who lose part of their lower self willy-nilly after a near brush with death (the nagual Julian's third method for losing self-importance). They say things like, "Now, I'm just taking it one day at a time." What they are saying is that their eyeball-to-eyeball confrontation with their death has forced them to drop their customary moods and concerns. They lighten up, stop clinging to things, stop feeling ashamed of their past and fantasizing a glorified future. They become more selfless. Selflessness means that, while both good and bad things still happen to the person, there's not as much of a "me" there that things are happening to. There's less personal stake in what happens. Situations just unfold under their own momentum. Things are taken in stride – philosophically, not personally. This can't be faked – it requires reaching the Place of No Pity (or its equivalent).

To change the outward circumstances of our lives, we must first change our inner state. The way to do this is by making a definite, unalterable decision (i.e., make something more important than our self-pity). In order for us to learn how to be content with how things are right now (instead of making our happiness dependent upon this, that, or the other thing happening in some future which will never come), requires an irrevocable decision. This happens when we get disgusted with our own self-pity and decide to really change. The only way to arrive at such a decision is by exhaustion: when we've tried everything; and nothing works. We have to get to the place where we've just had enough of our suffering, and we are finally ready to take the responsibility for really changing things (instead of daydreaming that God will pull our chestnuts out of the fire for us with no effort on our parts). Magicians are convinced – and 12-step programs such as Alcoholics Anonymous concur – that only when a person is completely wiped-out and desperate can any real change occur: when the person reaches the Place of No Pity.

When we operate with our higher self, we are mentally clear, coldly efficient, pitilessly detached, and utterly determined. We no longer feel like our(usual, lower)selves – trapped in our petty little moods and concerns. Rather, we are exhilarated and free; we become one with the Spirit.

When our higher self surfaces it brushes aside all our doubts and fears. We no longer fear death, and we never say die. Indeed, it is our higher self which survives the death of the physical body. This is why we don't fear death (or anything) when we act with our higher self.

In a manner of speaking, our higher self is actually the same thing as our death. Our lower self is firmly pegged down by our fear of death. When society teaches us fear of death, what it is teaching us is fear of operating with our higher self – our intuition / intent instead of our fear of what other people might think of us. Our higher self is a state of unfettered limitlessness, just as our lower self is a state of crabbed dissatisfaction and torpor, symbolized by the prison of the body. And the way that we activate our higher self is by reaching the Place of No Pity. It is the doorway: after this point we lose our fear of death. We sever our ties to society, since it no longer has that fear-of-death hold upon us.

The reason why not everyone reaches the Place of No Pity when they are pushed beyond their limits is because the ground must be prepared. You have to have already cast out any demons which might be possessing you; and you must also be somewhat open to the idea of change (e.g. be willing to entertain ideas such as "you create your own reality", whether you really believe this or not). If you are possessed by demons (as most people in our society are); or if you are clinging to some salvation fantasy (such as that God will intervene miraculously to save your butt); then when disaster strikes you, it will just screw you down tighter rather than knock you off your pins.

In Carlos Castaneda's guru don Juan's tradition of heuristics, the teacher purposely contrives an outlandish situation to force the student to the Place of No Pity. In Castaneda's case, don Juan feigned complete madness. One day, out of the blue, don Juan attacked Castaneda verbally and physically in front of a gathering crowd in a public square in a small Mexican town, and accused him of assault and theft. Don Juan told the crowd: "Help me. I'm a lonely old Indian. He's a foreigner and wants to kill me. They do that to helpless old people, kill them for pleasure." He exhorted the crowd to restrain Castaneda and send for the police.

When the crowd turned on the stunned Castaneda, he reflexively kicked his attackers and fled in despair; but soon realized that there was no way of escape from a small Mexican town whose police would be watching all the buses, roads, and hotels. He hid and stood watching the scene from a distance until the crowd began to disperse and the police moved off. Then, as Castaneda explains in The Power of Silence:

"It was at that point that I felt a sudden uncontrollable urge. It was as if my body were disconnected from my brain. I walked to my car. … Without even the slightest trace of fear or concern, I opened the trunk … then opened the driver's door. … I stared at (don Juan) with a thoroughly uncharacteristic coldness. Never in my life had I had such a feeling. It was not hatred I felt, or even anger. I was not even annoyed with him. What I felt was not resignation, or patience, either. And it was certainly not kindness. Rather, it was a cold indifference, a frightening lack of pity. At that instant, I could not have cared less about what happened to don Juan or myself. …

"And then, as if all of it had only been a bad dream, he was again the man I knew. … 'What kind of act did you pull out there, don Juan?' I asked, and the coldness in my tone surprised me.

'It was the first lesson in ruthlessness.' he said."

I have reached the Place of No Pity twice. The first time was several years after leaving a very dysfunctional marriage. I would break up with my wife; and then my spirit guides would say, "Oh give her another chance, take her back, you'll be glad you did", so I would take her back. Things would be okay for a couple of days or a week, then the old bullshit would start again and I'd break up with her again. This went on for the better part of a year, until finally I called it quits. I learned much later that my spirit guides knew all along that there was no way that marriage was going to be saved; what they were really trying to do was push me to the Place of No Pity, but I wimped out before I got totally desperate. This is a good example of why you should obey your spirit guides – it would have saved me a lot of grief in the long run if I'd reached the Place of No Pity with my marriage instead of seeking the easy way out.

I finally reached the Place of No Pity almost ten years later, at the end of another partnership with a person who was trashing me emotionally (in my younger days I had a penchant for pretty, young, witchy women; which of course implies self-centered, immature, conflictive women). Since I am a complete ass about women, my guides have always used women to trick me – or better said, enticed me to trick myself. Anyway, when I broke up with this other woman, I completely surprised myself – something in me welled up and cried "ENOUGH!" I had finally reached the Place of No Pity – my normally wussy self was shattered and a cold, detached, pitiless higher self took over the reins – rather like how Castaneda describes it. However, I can't say that the aftermath of this experience made a major dent in my ongoing loss of self-importance. But the second time did.

The second time I reached the Place of No Pity was ten years after that, when I was assaulted and beaten up by a gang of thieves. When I got up from the ground and dusted myself off, it was as if a burden had been lifted from me: I felt in complete peace; I felt no fear of my attackers (who were still surrounding me and threatening me); and I felt no anger towards them whatsoever. This state of placidity and clarity lasted a couple of weeks, but it did move me up to a new level in a permanent way. I can say that, since this last time that I reached the Place of No Pity, it is much easier for me to reject thoughts of self-pity than it was before. Consequently it is much easier for me to shut off my thoughts altogether and listen to sounds (or to put my attention on what is going on around me, rather than on my inner dialogue). As I've been losing self-pity, I've also felt lighter and more detached from everything. I don't give so much of a damn anymore.

The coming collapse of society will force a great number of people to the Place of No Pity, willy-nilly. This is what the much-vaunted coming shift / transformation in consciousness is all about. This transition is not going to be pleasant: when things start falling apart as the earth turns against us; when people lose their faith as society fails to deliver the goods it's promised; when people's supports – everything they've been taking for granted – are kicked out from under them and they are driven to the wall of despair; then there will be a global movement to the Place of No Pity. People's higher selves will surface, and then they will know intuitively what they must do. It would be nice if this occurred in time to save the human race.

* * * * * * * * *

Science Debunked

Materialistic science, like most fundamentalist religions, is extremely unreasoning and bigoted. When confronted with phenomena which don't fit its presuppositions, it closes its eyes and pretends that such phenomena don't exist. There is plenty of evidence, from all times and civilizations, that magic and astrology work, that spirits exist and can communicate with people, and so on. Indeed, about the only civilization on earth up to this time which rejects these notions is ours. "We know better now" say the scientists. How do they know this? Have they examined the subject objectively? No, they haven't done this. Even to suggest such an investigation during this dark age of rationalistic materialism would require the utmost intellectual courage and devotion to the truth. The results would bring down ultimate rejection and vituperation on one's head from the academic establishment. This is what happened to Carlos Castaneda.

By the term "materialism" is meant the belief that, in the words of cognitive philosopher Daniel Dennett, *"there is only one sort of stuff, namely matter – the physical stuff of physics, chemistry, and physiology – and the mind is somehow nothing but a physical phenomenon. In short, the mind is the brain."* – (Dennett, Daniel *Consciousness Explained*, Penguin 1991 p. 33).

The science of magic, by contrast, takes the Idealistic view that the physical world, including the physical body and brain, are merely projections of the mind; in exactly the same way that the world of dreams and the body we have while we are dreaming are projections of the mind. Being awake is merely a more highly evolved form of dreaming, and it is only our belief that what is happening to us is real that makes it seem real (whether we are awake or dreaming).

Materialistic science believes that it is describing an objective, factual reality. In fact it is, like everyone else, creating its own reality. Scientists are not discovering the laws of nature; they are inventing them. The true pioneers of science – the Einsteins, Plancks, and Heisenbergs – are well aware of this fact even if the credulous hoi polloi of science are not. *"Philosophically ... the implications of quantum mechanics are psychedelic. Not only do we influence our reality, but in some degree we actually create it. ... Metaphysically, this is very close to saying that we create certain properties because we choose to measure those properties."* - (Zukav, Gary, *The Dancing Wu Li Masters*, Bantam NYC 1980, page 28).

It is important to remember that science is a body of knowledge that has been built up over many thousands of years by many thousands of thinkers working from many different points of view and philosophical perspectives. However it has happened here and there that science has fallen into the hands of unreasoning zealots with a particular ideological axe to grind; and when that has happened science, in the sense of being an objective search for intellectual truth, winds up being a polemic to defend some political agenda. That is what occurred in Communist Russia with Lysenkoism and in Nazi Germany with "Aryan science"; and that is what has happened in capitalistic academia over the past century with the cult of materialism. The materialists with their statistical version of truth, perhaps in overreaction to the fundamentalist Christian creationist view, have completely abandoned any pretense of intellectual objectivity. As a result a non-academic version of science has developed to investigate such important matters as the thousands of reports – which tend to be quite similar in content – of after-death experiences by people who were revived; of psychic healing; of past lives; of spirit communications; etc. (not to mention astrology). What we are debunking here is not the body of knowledge which is science, but rather the smug narrow-mindedness of materialism. The materialists have such absolute power in academia and the media, and have so confused the issue with disinformation and cowed their critics with ridicule, that any criticism of materialism and its dictatorial tactics is touted as an attack on science itself.

Modern physics says, in a nutshell, that the universe is not how it appears to be to our normal, everyday perception. This is precisely what magicians and Buddhists have been saying all along. It's great that some of academic science has finally caught up to what mystics have been saying for thousands of years. However, the materialistic life sciences such as biology and psychology, not to mention neuroscience, are still back in the dark ages. They haven't yet figured out what modern physics is saying. Biology and psychology are still laboring under the old "linear time, objective space" view. Wake up, people! Materialism cannot comprehend that time and space are completely subjective (learned rules of behavior). There is NO objective reality consisting of solid, discrete objects out there; all there is, is a dream, a mass hallucination, which we have been trained to interpret with the illusion of orderliness (time and space). There's no way that what is really going on can be described by materialism except by lying, by asserting that e.g. psychic phenomena, precognition, past lives, etc. don't exist. Since practically everybody has experienced these things at one time or another for themselves, most people know where the truth lies. However everyone's afraid of being ridiculed if they have the temerity to point out publicly that the emperor is stark naked. Most people – including many scientists who would never admit this openly for fear of reprisal – know damn well that it's materialistic science that's the lie, not magic or astrology.

We must constantly keep in mind that materialism is a religion like any other. It is an opinion which has no factual basis. It is merely a matter of faith amongst true believers, who happen to be in the majority and in absolute, dictatorial control of academia at the present time. When Georg Cantor invented set theory a century ago he was assailed by orthodox mathematicians not only because he tried to develop a calculus of infinite numbers, which was considered outside the bounds of proper scientific inquiry, but also because he invented a new type of proof which orthodox mathematicians rejected. Eventually a new generation of mathematicians came along which accepted Cantor's ideas, and now set theory is very much at the center of modern mathematical thought. The point is that what is accepted as proper science at a given time is a popularity contest pure and simple. There is nothing objective about it. And the materialistic definition of truth – statistical significance – is merely a definition of truth, not the definition of truth. Indeed, it is a rather lousy definition: statistics is not a measure of truth but rather of ignorance – an admission that you've somehow lost the thread of what's going on. Materialists throw out the baby and then fatuously scrutinize the bath water.

Statistics are not a measure of truth but rather a way of obfuscating truth. The best proof of this is that astrological and magical phenomena cannot be measured statistically. For example, according to materialist theory, buying numerous lottery tickets increases your chances of winning the lottery. But according to magical theory, buying more than one lottery ticket actually decreases your chances of winning, since it demonstrates lack of faith – trying to second-guess or hedge or fake out the Spirit.

Materialist critics of well-documented cases of past life memories dismiss this evidence as "anecdotal"; as if statistics was something other than a bunch of materialists telling each other anecdotes. Just choosing what to measure or ignore is a completely subjective opinion.

There is nothing to prove or disprove in magical science; there's nothing to debate. Magical science is a collection of pointers put together by more experienced practitioners to help their neophyte brethren understand what they are experiencing and where they are going, which is why magical and astrological texts written hundreds or thousands of years ago still speak to us today. Magical science makes no pretense of describing reality because 1) there is no "reality" and 2) all descriptions (thought forms, concepts, belief systems) are false.

There is only one canonical way of doing biology or physics; but there are lots of ways of doing astrology or magic; and they all work. For example, Franz Bardon's conception of spirits and how to invoke them (*The Practice of Magical Evocation*) is quite different from mine. Similarly, Carlos Castaneda's conception of demons (*The Active Side of Infinity*) is different from mine. This doesn't mean that one is right and the other is wrong. We are all sharing our personal experiences, which are necessarily diverse. Once you step outside of the bounds of everyday society with its consensual agreements, you no longer have any guidelines or guiderails to hang onto except for what your spirits tell you; and also the wisdom gleaned from your own experience. This is why it is useful for the magical tyro to read different authors, or to work with different teachers, to get different takes on the subject.

As long as you only look at this one little piece of the universe over here – things moving at slow speeds – then the old, Newtonian description works pretty well. But when you look at things moving near the speed of light, you need a new, Einsteinian, description to fit the observed facts. Similarly, when you look at this little piece of the universe over there – that which can be apprehended with the mind – then materialistic science works pretty well. But when you look at that which can only be apprehended with intuition; with feelings; by direct knowing; then materialistic science fails miserably. Materialists get around this by saying that there is no way to quantify feelings and intuition – subjective experience – and therefore these are not a proper subject for scientific inquiry; as if there is any other sort of experience besides subjective experience.

That magical science cannot be analyzed with statistics doesn't address the issue of whether magic is true. It is merely a commentary on the limitations of the materialistic approach to scientific inquiry. Magical events are too unique and ephemeral to be measured in a materialistic way because they are not mental abstracts but rather feelings. Take omens, for example, which have meaning only to the person for whom the Spirit is manifesting but not for anyone else who might be present. This doesn't mean that omens don't exist or are merely a figment of one person's imagination. Rather, it means that statistical analysis – the current criterion of scientific truth – is too crude an instrument to encompass or measure magical phenomena.

Statistical significance is no more a measure of truth than biblical authority is a measure of truth. Both statistics and the Bible merely represent different opinions as to where truth is to be found. Magicians reject both of these definitions of truth. (However consensual validation – two or more people witnessing the same event and agreeing on what they witnessed – is obtainable even with magical events when the participants have been trained – or are able from birth – to intuit such things. At Mayan ceremonies, for example, pretty much everyone present who has any sensitivity can pick up the messages which the spirits are sending. Similarly, replication of results by other researchers is as applicable to magical science as to materialistic science: that's how we learn it in the first place, and how experienced magicians train neophytes).

Laboratory statistical studies to prove or disprove "ESP" are silly. Magical science just doesn't work that way. For example, when I do rituals to invoke spirits, sometimes I feel the spirits' presence and sometimes I don't. You can't go into magic making arrogant demands; you can only humbly invite, which is why statistical studies of psychic phenomena will always come up empty.

If psychic phenomena, which are commonly experienced and have been reported by many people throughout human history cannot be measured statistically, then the obvious conclusion is that statistics are irrelevant to what is actually going on. The cult of materialism which has captured and imprisoned science has particularly corrupted those fields, such as psychology and anthropology, which would otherwise be most helpful in understanding what psychic phenomena (altered states of consciousness) really are, and by contrast what everyday life (an unaltered state of consciousness) really is. The absurdity of the materialist position is illustrated by the ongoing argument in biology over whether animals possess consciousness. This sort of shameless arrogance makes one wonder whether sociobiologists possess consciousness. It's precisely the same as the Nazi theories of superior race; and it's used to justify the same sort of cruelty and butchery (of course this depends upon how you choose to define "consciousness". Magical science is Panpsychist in that it considers that any being who can feel feelings possesses consciousness. Thus everything that lives – animals, plants, bacteria; even so-called inanimate objects such as our possessions, rocks, even mountains (especially mountains!) and caves possess consciousness. Since sociobiologists are apparently incapable of feeling, they are the only beings in the universe who do not possess consciousness).

Magical science is a science in the exact same sense of the word as materialistic science. However, the reality it describes and the techniques it uses are quite different from those of the materialists. The magician's worldview is no more true nor false than the materialistic, Christian, Islamic, etc. worldviews. You create your own reality. All worldviews are false because they are not and can never be true. What is really going on out there in the universe cannot in any way be comprehended by mind and its intellectual constructs (thought forms). It can only be apprehended with feeling, by direct knowing. The reason why you adopt the magicians' belief system, knowing that it is false, is to set up a counterpoint or contradiction with everyday society's worldview. This gives you a means of detaching from both worldviews, from intellection, altogether. Then feeling – intent – takes over.

There is no rational reason why the universe is the way it is. The idea that e.g. competition for scarce resources is the driving force behind evolution is the obvious conclusion that a capitalist would come to; just as the idea that things are the way they are because that is God's will is the only explanation that a Jew, Christian, or Muslim needs. But to a magician there is no reason for anything: things are the way they are as the result of completely random processes, and seeing any kind of order in how things are is narcissistic, post hoc, wishful thinking. There is no reason for anything. There is no reason, period. The only thing which exists in the universe is feelings, which we have termed "intent". And these cannot be apprehended by mind.

The present race in cognitive science to solve the mystery of consciousness is never going to be won by materialism. As long as you are looking south, you'll never see the pole star; and as long as you are looking outside yourself you'll never understand what consciousness is. Concepts are not an adequate tool for understanding consciousness. Only materialistic hubris would believe that. We have gone as far as we can with concepts. The philosophy of materialism – very much like the philosophy of fundamentalist Christian creationism – refuses to acknowledge this fact: that its tools are outmoded and new ones (namely intent: direct knowing as opposed to knowledge that can be communicated verbally) must be employed to proceed further. Just as slavish, mindless adherence to Aristotelian and Christian tradition retarded the progress of science for centuries, so too is the false doctrine of materialism retarding the progress of science at the present time.

Materialistic platforms such as the Skeptic magazines and the websites which "objectively" criticize astrology are star chambers. Like the Inquisition which forced Galileo to recant what he knew was the truth, materialistic scientists decry the truth of subjectivism. Materialistic scientists, like the Catholic church of old, have a vested interest in keeping their own teachings predominant. Anyone who dares to contradict these teachings is pilloried just as Galileo was. Carlos Castaneda, for example, who has brought us the most important new information of the past few millennia, was smeared, vilified, and drummed out of academia.

Although the materialists are quite correct that tests to prove the competence of astrologers are usually embarrassing failures, the fault, Dear Brutus, lies not in astrology but in the stigma which the materialists have heaped upon astrology, so that very few first-rate minds are attracted to the field. Part of the problem, too, is that the materialists demand an impossible standard of accuracy which astrology, because of its very nature, is incapable of providing. The universe is not as mechanistic as the materialists would like to believe; rather, it is a matter of free will and of possible outcomes. Astrology cannot predict that e.g. "at 12:37 pm on August 3rd you will slip on ice and break your left arm above the elbow." Psychics – and psychic astrologers – can sometimes do this; but they use intuition to do it, not astrology. To demand such accuracy from astrology qua astrology is unreasonable and silly.

Look at the diatribe against astrology a few years ago by 186 famous scientists, none of whom bothered investigating astrology before denouncing it! Thirty years ago French researcher Michel Gauquelin proved the existence of an astrological effect statistically, and his results have been replicated independently by other researchers. He did what these guys say they want: he proved the existence of an astrological effect according to the statistical canons of materialistic truth (see Dean, Geoffrey, *Recent Advances in Natal Astrology*, Astrological Association, Australia 1977, page 380 ff for details). Yet materialistic scientists still reject astrology. What does this say about scientists' pretensions to being champions of truth? Indeed, the materialistic model is a classic case of bad science: discarding any information which contradicts its preconceived assumptions.

Anthropology, economics, and psychology are the quintessential sciences because they make no pretense to studying anything beyond human nature. However all science is merely the study of human nature; or of human cognition, if you will; or of modern human cognition would be better said, since ancient humans' cognitive processes were very, very different from ours.

All that science studies is the way that humans make sense of the world. All materialistic scientists are doing is peering into a mirror and calling that the universe. Science is not the study of an objective reality, because there is no objective reality. Just because two humans can get together and agree that a ball, for example, is red and round and a foot in diameter doesn't really say anything about that ball. Rather, it is a description of how humans in our society make agreements amongst themselves.

This is a very difficult point to grasp, or to agree with, even if grasped. This is because you have been so indoctrinated with the assumption that you are a separated perceiver of an outside reality. Look at it like this: two Communists reading the same political news item in the newspaper will usually come to the same conclusions about it even if they can't confer on it beforehand. They already agree about the nature of their reality: they see everything in terms of class struggle, rich exploiting poor, and capital and labor continually at odds. Therefore anything that happens they will fit into that worldview, and they will agree on what really happened in that news story. Similarly, two capitalists reading the same news story will agree with each other on what actually happened in that news item. However, their view of the occurrence will probably be very much at odds with the interpretation of the Communists. In the same way, materialistic scientists confronted with objective phenomena try to fit them into their pre-conceived worldview, which a priori excludes astrology and magic.

I believe that most people know in their hearts that materialistic science is shamelessly lying when it denies the truth of magic. Of course, magical science cannot be proven true by materialistic canons of truth any more than Galileo could prove the validity of Copernican theory by appealing to the Bible, as the Inquisitionists of that time demanded. For one thing, materialistic science is based upon completely different presuppositions than magical science, such as linear time,* duality, the existence of an objective reality, and that statistics measure truth. Materialistic scientists and magicians are not looking at the same phenomena. Or rather, they are, but from irreconcilably contradictory points of view; or better said, from different taken-for-granted cognitive assumptions. The materialist looks outward for answers, whereas the magician looks inward. But I believe that in the next century conventional science will evolve to include what is now considered magic. Then it won't be considered magic at all. Modern science is in fact magic, but its practitioners don't call it that or understand it in those terms because they are blinded by the tenets of their fundamentalist religion, the chief one being that the world is mechanistic rather than alive. That it's something we can stomp on with impunity and it will never stomp back.

The ideal of materialistic science is a hell world, and that's where they're taking us. In societies where they have a modicum of respect for life they don't do vivisection or Auschwitz-type medical experiments, so they don't learn all the neat things you can learn by cold-bloodedly destroying other beings. Materialism is basically a form of black magic (except it is far more stupid and inept than real black magic).

It's not only the animal and human sacrifices that present-day scientists are involved in that mirror disrespect. Just the way astronomers look at the stars, with no ability to feel what they are seeing, is disrespectful. Probably most astronomers were originally drawn to astronomy by a sense of awe, but the disrespect which is part and parcel of materialism soon confuses young astronomers. And God help them if they avow before their inquisitional fellows an intuitive acceptance of the veracity of astrology or magic!

The materialists' argument – like their capitalist masters' argument – is that "it works." But so does a scorched earth policy against Mayan Indians work to isolate guerrillas. And so did the bombing of Hiroshima work: undoubtedly that saved many lives on both sides. But the underlying assumption in both cases is mistaken. It doesn't lead to happiness or joy. Shameless cruelty works really well; but it makes for a hell world. Shameless arrogance and contempt are an intrinsic component of materialism in all of its forms (standing above and subduing nature – and other people – instead of approaching them humbly and respectfully). Besides, capitalism and materialism don't "work". At this point in history it is very clear exactly how well capitalism and materialism are "working", and exactly where these stupid, destructive mindsets are leading us.

Science doesn't have to be so cruel and heartless. You don't have to rape the universe for knowledge. You can ask it nicely what you want to know. Luther Burbank produced many new varieties of plants by talking to them. According to Rudolf Steiner, that is how all the fruit crops which people now use were originally developed from wild plants. Ancient Mesoamerican magicians created maize from the native grass teosinte thousands of years ago in a manner which thoroughly baffles modern botanists, since the genetic manipulation techniques required for this transmutation have only existed for the last twenty years.

By choosing materialistic science in its current, heartless manifestation we are foregoing the experience of the world as joyous. Rationalism doesn't have to be divorced from magic, which is as much a science as physics or biology. Magical science just operates on different assumptions. Actually it is a different cognitive system altogether.

Indeed, Sir Isaac Newton – the founder of modern science – was a magician. In John Maynard Keynes' words, *"Newton was not the first of the age of reason. He was the last of the magicians, the last of the Babylonians and Sumerians."* The majority of Newton's writings have been suppressed by the materialistic Inquisition because they dealt with magic and alchemy: *"A large section <of Newton's papers>, judging by the handwriting amongst the earliest, relates to alchemy – transmutation, the philosopher's stone, the elixir of life. The scope and character of these papers have been hushed up, or at least minimized, by nearly all those who have inspected them."* - (Keynes, John Maynard, *Newton, the Man*; from Newman, James, *The World of Mathematics*, Simon & Schuster NYC 1956 pages 277, 282)

Materialistic science was well suited to agricultural and industrial human society. It led to a great deal of material progress. But there are too many people now; and they're messing the earth up. That sort of crabbed, niggling, arrogant, and shameless mindset won't work anymore. Materialistic science has perverted the quest for intellectual truth and embraced a smug, shallow sophistry in its stead. What the human race desperately needs, and is now ready for, is a new worldview, based upon broader principles of intellectual truth than any which materialistic science can ever encompass. The human race is on the brink of a scientific revolution greater than the one which rocked the 16th and 17th centuries. We have to start – or restart, since these were our guiding lights when humans were still hunter / gatherers – setting aside all our intellection, our opinions and beliefs, and opening our hearts to what the earth is trying to tell us.

One nice thing about magical science is that it really doesn't matter whether it is true or not. It's the best bet. Materialistic religion assumes that everything's all screwed up, but someday science will figure it all out. Magic, by contrast, assumes nothing. If you are going to be saved, it will be by your own efforts; by being wide awake instead of pulling woolly assumptions over your eyes to lull yourself into a stupor. You must take 100% responsibility for your own salvation.

Magicians believe that the God Materialism is leading us to hell in a handbasket. Three Mile Island and Chernobyl are good examples – loud and clear warnings to anyone who's not asleep – and yet they're still building them. It is true that materialistic science and technology have brought many people a high level of comfort and convenience, but at the cost of bankrupting their spirit and joy. Are you happy in your work, your relationships, your life? Do you know anyone who is?

Magic and astrology were the world religion once, and they shall be the world religion again, because people have had enough of the emptiness, meaninglessness, and short-sighted stupidity of materialism. *E pur si muove!*

* Where materialistic science sees time as linear, magic sees time as rhythmic. Materialistic science measures points and intervals along a well-ordered continuum, whereas magical science measures cycles upon cycles. This is what astrology is all about: the moment of birth can be viewed as a point along a linear continuum, as it is in rationalistic materialism; or, conversely, it can be viewed as a stage in the unfoldment of potentialities on various levels – i.e. as the intersection of many different interpenetrating cycles, as it is in astrology.

Time is *not* linear. Everything that has ever happened, and ever will happen, in all lifetimes and realities, is all going on at once, in an eternal NOW moment. It is more accurate to describe time as an emanation of birth – death – rebirth; and what we see as linear time is but a fragmentary way of apprehending this phenomenon which has evolved in tandem with human society. Linear time is a completely human invention, like golf or the latest Paris fashions; a set of rules which have no reference to anything outside of human experience (animals have a relatively undeveloped sense of linear time compared to humans – i.e. are more centered in the now moment, don't apprehend so much of a past and future as humans do). Linear time is predicated on linear thinking. When thinking stops – when the constant internal dialogue which most people engage in from the minute they awaken to the minute they go to sleep ceases – then so too does linear time.

Self-Healing:

The Treatment of Cancer and AIDS with Jorobté

Jorobté (pronounced "hore – obe –TAY" – Latin name *Cornutia grandifolia*) is a woody shrub native to Central America from Mexico through Panama. It is well-known and widely employed by native healers for "incurable" diseases such as Cancer and AIDS, and many miraculous cures have been ascribed to it. Its effectiveness in a given case depends upon the type and severity of the disease and how early in the course of the illness treatment was initiated. However, even in many "hopeless" cases drinking tea made from Jorobté leaves can dramatically lessen pain and prolong life.

Jorobté is more effective if it is the treatment of first resort, rather than a desperation measure adopted after conventional medical treatments have failed. However even then it can be very helpful in relieving suffering. In any case, the patient has to take full responsibility for his or her own treatment; this is a matter of eradicating self-pity and cultivating a positive, optimistic attitude.

Six-point Self-healing plan:

Drink Jorobté tea every day
Cast out any demons that may be possessing you
Use Active Imagination to learn why you made this decision
    – what lesson you are seeking to learn
Recapitulate the moment you called the AIDS virus into your body
    or made the decision to have cancer
Earth burials
Creative visualization of yourself as healthy

1) **Drink Jorobté tea every day**

Every morning boil 7 leaves (a handful) of Jorobté in a liter of water for 10 minutes. Then drink 4 cups of the tea (hot or cold) over the course of the day. This will help anyone with an incurable disease even if they don't follow the rest of the self-healing plan.

2) <u>Casting out demons</u>

It often happens that people who are chronically ill or depressed unknowingly call maleficent influences in to possess them, to help them defend themselves against their pain. We call these influences "demons". Demons give people a hard shell of anger, apathy, or self-pity with which to dull the feeling of vulnerability and helplessness. However, these demons also take control of their hosts lives and make their decisions for them; and it is definitely not in the demons' interests that people be healthy and happy. Therefore, the first thing to determine in the face of chronic illness is whether you may have (inadvertently) called a demon into yourself; and if so, to cast it out.

Go to whatever place you are accustomed to pray at; light a candle; and ask the deity to whom you usually pray that, if there happens to be a maleficent influence in your life which is preventing you from healing yourself, to please cast it out! You must make this prayer in a true spirit of decisiveness and determination – if you pray in a spirit of doubt or hesitation, the demon (if there is one) will use your vacillation to defeat your prayer. See, demons are always trying to convince you that you are doing everything possible to heal yourself, all the while undermining your efforts. A wishy-washy prayer to cast out a demon may make you believe that you've accomplished something, but the demon will weasel past it. Thus demons have to be cast out in a mood of unbending intent and decision. That's all that's required – unbending intent to heal yourself.

How will you know whether your prayer worked? Successful exorcisms are often accompanied by sensations of something that was inside you leaving – there may be some kind of whoosh of something flying out of you and away. But this isn't always true. One way you'll know is that in the next few days you'll feel lighter, more hopeful and optimistic. Your friends will notice the difference too – they'll remark on how much better you look or feel.

If there's any doubt, though, you can always repeat the exorcism. Just make sure to do it in a mood of decisiveness and determination. That's all – it's not difficult.

3) **Active Imagination**

A central part of self-healing is understanding what lesson you are seeking to learn from your illness. The events in your life don't "just happen"; they happen for a reason, and understanding that reason is the beginning of taking control of your life and turning your situation around instead of wallowing in self-pity. Asking your own subconscious for information is called "Active Imagination".

The easiest way to get this information – what lesson your illness is trying to teach you – is by asking for it in your dreams. Just before you go to sleep at night, ask with all your heart (determination) that you learn what the purpose of your illness is; what it is that you are seeking to learn from this experience. You should get the answer either in a dream, or else upon awakening. It may take more than one night's supplication until the answer comes, so be patient and just keep up the asking every night until the information comes to you.

Another way to find out what the lesson of your illness is, is by means of automatic writing (this technique also will usually provide more complex and detailed information than dreaming does). Choose a time when you are relaxed, alert, calm, and will not be interrupted. Lie down or sit, as you prefer, with a pen and notebook in hand (although automatic writing can also be done on a typewriter or word processor). Writing down both your questions and the replies as they come in the form of a dialogue, ask your body to please talk to you. For example, you might start this way:

Me: "My body, could you please come and talk to me? I am really trying to be open right now, and I want to hear what you have to say to me. I am trying to understand why I am sick; won't you please come and talk to me about it. Etc. etc."

This is just an example – you should ask your body to talk to you using your own words and sentiments. Keep writing, keep on coaxing, until you begin to feel an answer forming in your mind, and then write it down. The trick to making this work is to not stop writing. That's the purpose of the writing – to focus your attention on the act of writing, like when you're taking notes in a classroom, so that there's less room for doubt, hesitation, fear, etc. Keep on writing, even if you're just writing the same plea over and over again. Do make it heartfelt – not just done mechanically – and eventually you'll start getting an answer. It really is so simple and straightforward you won't believe it.

Note that when a person does automatic writing for the first time, the answers tend to come out sort of inchoate and constipated. Don't worry – just push it right on out and don't worry about whether it makes sense or not. Usually in automatic writing a few words or phrases spring into your mind at a time, a little faster than you can write them down, though sometimes you might get whole blocks or paragraphs at once. You might also see memory pictures pop up before your mind's eye, or get flashes of dream-like scenes as you write. Record all of this because it's all relevant. Something might not make sense at the moment, but it will eventually if you keep a written record of it.

If nothing comes to mind in response to your entreaties; or if all that comes to mind is gibberish; then you are blocking. Your conscious mind might say, "This isn't working. I'm not doing it right." or "There must be some trick to this!" in its effort to subvert the process. Don't fall for that ploy! Keep trying, keep on writing, even if all you get is gibberish. Only trust can open you enough to write automatically; otherwise you tangle yourself with doubt. If you find yourself blocking, try switching to your non-dominant hand. Keep on writing, and at some moment your conscious mind will relax its grip and you'll start writing automatically. Then, simply write down what your body tells you, asking any questions you like along the way. You might be surprised by the answers! The biggest surprise will probably be that you, yourself called your illness to come – that it didn't "just happen" to you; and for what reason you did this to yourself – what you are trying to learn from this experience. You can also ask your body for specific information as to diet, exercise, etc. to speed your healing process along.

4) Recapitulation

Now that you know that you, yourself decided to call your illness to you; and for what reason; the next step is to rescind that decision. This is done by recapitulating the memory of the moment when you decided to be ill, and pulling back that decision. The entrance technique is the same as that for running past life regressions; except when you are up in the clouds ask to return to earth in the memory of the moment when you called your disease to yourself.

You see the regression with your mind's eye, but it's more felt than seen – the emotions that are happening are usually more important than the actual events. One thing you might discover is that you are, for some reason or other, in a mood of self-pity.

Once you are back in the scene and feeling the feelings you felt at that time, the next step is to pull back the decision to be ill, and to cast out the feeling of self-pity. Whenever you get to the decision you made to be ill, take a short, sharp indrawn breath into your solar plexus, and at the same time feel that you are sucking the decision to be ill back into your navel. Then, with a hard, cutting motion of your hand in front of your navel, chop off your feelings of self-pity and leave them back in the scene. Don't worry about whether or not you are doing it right; if you're doing it in good faith, you're doing it right. Trust yourself.

You may not feel any immediate difference after recapitulating this memory; however, over the next few days you should feel lighter and more joyous in some indefinable part of your being. This is because you've made yourself younger – in a sense you've gone back to where you were before you decided to be ill. You should definitely see a turn-around in your healing process in the days and weeks after doing this recapitulation. If not, then just repeat the process. Remember that it is the determination with which you suck the decision to be ill back into your navel and cast out self-pity that counts the most.

5) Earth Burials

The earth has an infinite capacity not only to heal but also to absorb and dissipate negative energy, and every sort of spiritual and emotional heaviness as well as chronic illness. The usual method of earth burial is as follows:

It helps to fast the day before the burial. Dig a trench half a meter deep and somewhat longer than your body. You can do this at the beach if you like, but it's better to do it away from people who might disturb you. Line the trench with sawdust or leaves so you will have a soft bed and pillow to lie on, and make sure your face will be shaded from the sun. Disrobe and wrap yourself in a sheet with only your face exposed (the sheet serves as a protection against e.g. ants). You can smear insect repellant on your face, neck, and hair to keep bugs away. Then lie down in the trench, get comfortable, and have someone cover you with a layer of earth up to your neck with your head sticking out. Have someone visit you every hour or two in case you need a drink and to make sure you're okay. If you have to pee, just do it.

If you are very sick or in desperate need of lightening up, you should remain buried for 12 hours (dawn to dusk) the first time you bury yourself, and for at least 6 hours on subsequent burials (8 is better). How long and how frequently you bury yourself depend on how sick or heavy you were to begin with: you come to "know" when it's time to bury yourself again.

Although this ritual may seem to be an odd thing to do, you might just find that being buried is one of the most enjoyable experiences you've ever had. The earth herself is your hostess, and she will do her best to comfort, nourish, and entertain you. You will feel very different when you step out of the hole after a burial – lighter, healthier, happier.

6) **Creative visualization of yourself as healthy**

Creative visualization is a form of self-hypnosis; but so is all of life. You hypnotized yourself into thinking that you are sick, and you can just as easily hypnotize yourself back out of it again. It is to be expected that you will be doubtful and hesitant at first; but if you have even a modicum of belief in the possibility that what you are doing is valid, that will be enough to make it happen. Of course, the more heartfelt your belief, the faster and more impressive the result will be. Creative visualization is essentially the same thing as prayer, and has the same result, except that you don't invoke a deity. If you are accustomed to praying to a deity, then by all means continue to do so, since this can be even more efficacious than straight creative visualization (of course this depends upon who the deity is and what you're praying for).

We will summarize two creative visualization methods here:

1) Affirmations can be spoken aloud, voiced mentally, written down, or chanted. These are positive, uplifting statements: for example, "I'm so happy now that I'm healthy again!"; which are repeated over and over.

2) Treasure maps are collages of photographs or drawings which illustrate us getting what we want from life. The visual images can also be accompanied by written affirmations. The visual images are examined and the accompanying affirmations read with the aim of conjuring up the feeling of that image coming true in our lives.

In using both affirmations and treasure maps, the important point is to get to the feeling of the desire, and not just do it by rote. To make it heartfelt, you should be in a happy, delighted mood – lose yourself in reverie. Try to connect with a feeling of intense longing – a pang of sweet anguish – in your heart.

Creative visualization should be done for at least ten minutes or so upon awakening, and again at night before going to sleep. Try to do your visualization as you drop off to sleep. This is difficult at first because the attention needed to maintain an image in the forefront of the mind (importance) is the opposite of the attention needed to enter the dream state (surrender). The trick is to drop off to sleep with the feeling of your desire uppermost in your mind rather than the mental image, which is a lot harder to do.

You should also visualize your desires during the day – just like daydreaming, but in the present rather than the future tense, e.g., "I'm so happy now that I'm healthy again!" When you catch yourself indulging in normal daydreaming, switch it to creative visualization. The point is to stop thinking and to let yourself feel; to give yourself permission to feel as much joy as you would feel if your desire were to come true, without making that joy contingent upon whether the desire comes true or not. Then it really doesn't matter whether it comes true or not; and this clears the way for it to come true.

Visualization is similar to normal daydreaming, except the latter is done with thinking, and the former is done with feeling. Daydreaming is done in the third person and the future tense, whereas visualization is done in the first person and the present tense. In visualization you imagine yourself to be actually in the middle of the scene as if it were unfolding around you here and now; and you let yourself feel all the joy you would feel if that scene were actually happening. The secret of visualization is to convince yourself that what you are wishing for is already true, and to allow yourself to feel the feelings you would feel if that were in fact the case.

The difference between creative visualization and normal daydreaming is that in creative visualization there is no doubt: as in dreaming, the experience is too vivid and intense for doubt. In normal daydreaming, on the other hand, people don't really want the fantasy to come true. They're afraid of taking responsibility for that probable reality, for having that much power and control over their own destiny. Therefore, they detach themselves from their desire by projecting it into a future which will never come, instead of knowing, beyond a shadow of a doubt, that the probable reality will come true – by living that reality in the now moment, which is what is done in creative visualization. Healthy people are already using creative visualization unconsciously: they have no doubt about their health.

In normal daydreaming you are standing back and watching yourself, applauding yourself, patting yourself on the back. The "you" in the daydream is just a puppet; the real you is watching this puppet perform. But in creative visualization, the real you is smack dab in the middle of the action, taking primary enjoyment from being in the scene that unfolds around you, rather than standing back and watching at a distance. Whereas normal daydreaming is a means of escaping from the rigors of life, creative visualization entails knowing that you called your outer circumstances to you for some reason; and knowing that you can also change that reason if only you don't lose sight of (feeling for) the ultimate goal. It means reaching out to probable realities in which there is joy, no matter how improbable they may seem at the moment, rather than to ones which will only reinforce your self-pity

Creative visualization is a way of cutting across all those endless circles of doubt and feeling sorry for yourself, by taking primary joy in the act of visualization itself. It's like playing with an imaginary companion: a child who has an imaginary companion doesn't care if it's real or not – he or she just has fun with it in the now moment. And that's the attitude you must bring to creative visualization – take primary pleasure in imagining it happening right now, rather than worrying about whether or not it will actually come true in some future.

The secret of creative visualization is to convince yourself that what you are wishing for is already true, and you're just hanging around for a few minutes in the waiting room while the universe finds it and hands it to you. To visualize a desire as if it were already achieved means to imagine it happening in the here and now, as if it were taking place in front of you. You mustn't set up any contradictory agendas such as, "In the event that this creative visualization doesn't work for me then I'll do this other thing." You have to put all your eggs in one basket, in the probable reality in which your desires come true. The more energy you can bring to bear upon your desire, the faster you'll start seeing results. But be patient: Rome wasn't built in a day.

White Witchcraft:

Channeling Spirit Guides

Glendower: "I can call spirits from the vasty deep."
Hotspur: "Why, so can I, or so can any man;
But will they come when you do call for them?"
Henry IV, Part I

Like that character from Moliere who was delighted to learn that he'd been speaking prose all along and never knew it, each and every one of us is channeling all the time; and the only difference between "professional" psychics and mediums and the rest of us is that the psychics are aware of what they're doing – they make a special point of (call special attention to) a completely natural process that everybody already knows how to do. Everyone has spirit guides who talk to them constantly; however, most people don't listen to these messages, any more than they listen to what other people, such as their parents, spouse, or children, are trying to tell them. When a thought or feeling prompted by a spirit guide pops up in their consciousness, they just pass over it or reject it. In this essay we will discuss thought forms, spirit guides, and other beings which can be channeled, together with a simple technique for consciously channeling them.

In order to get an idea of what spirits are, it is first necessary to get a handle on what we are. Contrary to popular opinion, we are not solid, abiding objects that have individual self-existence. Although it certainly appears that the world is "real" and consists of solid, discrete objects, in fact our world is more like a movie screen, hooked up to other people's movie screens, on which we're all projecting what we're feeling inside outwards as symbols – solid objects in a physical world.

To ask Heidegger's question, "Why are there things rather than nothing?" is like asking, "Why can't soccer players use their hands? Why did God so construct the universe that soccer players can't use their hands?" In the same way, our perception of the universe as a world of solid, discrete objects is a wholly man-made restriction on our senses. Plants and animals don't perceive the world in this fashion, and neither, for that matter, do infants and lunatics. They still use their "hands" (their feelings rather than their minds) to play the game of perception. As a result, they don't "play soccer" very well, but they still have the free use of their hands –their intuition – which most people have learned to repress. The belief that we are discrete entities in a world of solid objects is just that – a belief – that makes the world of concepts, of thinking, possible.

Admittedly, the belief that we are discrete, abiding entities in a world of solid objects certainly seems to be true most of the time we are awake – it's a pretty convincing belief. But that's only because we have the door tightly shut on any evidence that contradicts this belief. That door is called "fear of going crazy or of being thought crazy." Keeping our sanity is equivalent to screening out lots of information about ourselves and the world around us which would be available if we could just loosen up a bit and drop the pretense that we exist as solid objects.

In fact, our existence is multidimensional. We not only exist in an infinite number of past and future lives, but we are also infinitely ramified in all the probable realities which branch off from this present lifetime. Every time we make a decision – big or little – we create a probable reality in which that decision was made, and another or other probable realities in which that decision wasn't made. For example, that person whom you wistfully smiled at from afar once but never spoke to nor saw again, is your spouse in another probable reality in which you did go over and strike up a conversation.

Thus, not only does the totality of who "we" are encompass infinite lifetimes in other worlds and realities, it also encompasses infinite probable realities within this present lifetime as well as all those others. Not only that, but within the confines of a single probable reality of a single lifetime, which is all we normally pay attention to or consider to be "ourselves", we are still multiple personalities. That is to say, we are not the same person from moment to moment, but in fact shift from one to another subpersonalities or thought forms in response to this or that changing stimulus. The only difference between an Eve, Sybil, or Truddi and the rest of us is that their slips are showing: they're acting out the multiple personality role openly, whereas the rest of us are marching around with our dress uniforms – our fear of going crazy – buttoned down tight.

Most of what we consider to be "ourselves" – that is, the thoughts, feelings and perceptions which occupy our conscious minds most of the time we are awake; our sense that there is a continuing "us" there – is just a collection of habits and predilections learned from our parents and society. Each of our habitual thoughts, moods, beliefs, etc. is a thought form – a learned behavior which is a being in its own right (some authors, such as Richard Dawkins and Daniel Dennett, have used the term memes instead of thought forms). Most of what we think we think, believe, or perceive is actually just what our parents and society think, believe, or perceive; and these thoughts, beliefs, and perceptions have an awareness, a sense of selfhood, and a will to live all their own. We create them with our decisions and we breathe the breath of life into them with our attention.

Basically, every time we think a thought we are channeling a thought form. However, this is an unskillful way of channeling because it's mindless. Thought forms grab our attention and say, "Think this! Think that! Think the other! In response to this, do that! Remember this! Desire that! Blah blah blah!" all day long every day. Thought forms are our automatic pilot – although we ourselves create them, we are subject to their control thereafter. We go along and just think whatever our thought forms want us to think. It rarely occurs to us to stop and ask, "Why? Why am I thinking this thought? Is entertaining this thought going to benefit me? From whence does this thought arise? At what point in my life did I first begin entertaining this thought? When did I make it a part of my inventory of habitual thoughts? Etc."

To ask these sorts of questions (and pay attention to the answers) is called Active Imagination, and it is a more functional form of channeling thought forms than is normal thinking. Active Imagination is a technique invented by Carl Jung, and it is described at great length in my book Thought Forms. In Active Imagination we interact with our thought forms, whereas in normal thinking we just snap to and salute whenever a thought form barks a command at us. Active Imagination is facilitated by automatic writing (which we shall learn how to do presently); i.e. automatic writing is a refinement of the technique of Active Imagination, but it's by no means the only way to do it. Thoughtful, introspective people are doing Active Imagination all the time without calling it that or giving any special attention to it; but, in fact, Active Imagination is a wholly different form of channeling thought forms than is normal thinking.

So thought forms – habitual patterns of thought picked up from our parents and society – account for most of what we consider "our" thoughts and feelings; and spirits – both good and evil – account for most of what's left. The chief difference between thought forms and spirits is that thought forms are within us, created by us, a part of us; whereas spirits are outside of us. When we channel (e.g. by automatic writing) we run across a whole menagerie of entities – both thought forms and different kinds of spirits – so it's helpful to know the differences between these various kinds of beings.

There are lots of different kinds of spirits in the world. We are spirits, for that matter. Some spirits are entirely useless to humans – we cannot even communicate with such entities. Others are nasty little things which are best avoided altogether. And still others can be quite helpful to humans, for a multitude of purposes.

The use of nature spirits, such as water spirits, to wash away our self-importance and help us tune in to our true feelings of joy and peace with the world, will be described in a later essay. The use of tree spirits is described at length in my book Thought Forms.

There are also spirits which oversee particular human activities such as agriculture, art, construction, cooking, healing, mathematics, mining, etc. etc. Every human endeavor has a cadre of spirits proper to it, which guides individual practitioners and also helps humanity as a whole expand its knowledge of the various arts, crafts, and sciences. A competent, inspired professional in any field is constantly receiving inspiration and new ideas from the spirits who oversee his or her field. However, as is the case also with thought forms, most people believe that any inspiration they receive in this fashion is "their" idea, when in fact it's being passed to them by spirits. To be a competent professional in any field is to be a clear channel for the spirits who oversee that field.

Finally, we come to personal spirit guides – what some people call angels. These are spirits who are assigned to individual human beings, who tend them as wards. Everybody has at least one personal spirit guide at any one time, but most people have several or lots of them, which may come and go in the course of a lifetime.

Although both thought forms and spirit guides can be channeled in the same ways (as can other spirits: Jesus and Mary, Krishna, nature spirits, demons, recently deceased people, etc.), thought forms and spirit guides are completely different kinds of entities. Thought forms are created by us: they stand in the same relation to us that we stand to God. Guides, on the other hand, are a bit above us in the sense of being wiser, possessing broader viewpoints and more loving hearts, but they aren't that far above us.

Many spirit guides have had human incarnations. Sometimes deceased friends, relatives, ancestors, or even aborted fetuses become one's spirit guides; and one of my own guides has told me that there are lives / realities in which I am her spirit guide. I presume that similar relationships between people and their guides obtain for everyone.

Up until recently in human history (last few thousand years) magical knowledge – the practical application of intuition – was handed down from generation to generation, as agricultural or mathematical knowledge is. However, because of the nature of the times, most of that knowledge was lost as skilled practitioners died off without leaving heirs. In the interim, the White Brotherhood, the "guild" of spirit guides, came in to fill the gap – to steer humanity in more or less the right direction during its sleep-walking (rationalist-materialist) phase.

There's a great network spread out across the world now, a linking up of groups of spirits and human channels, sending out filaments of light around the earth to love it and heal it. To learn to consciously channel your spirit guides is to join this fraternity of light. As long as there is light, no evil can overcome the earth.

Now we will describe how to channel spirit guides by automatic writing. But it must be pointed out that automatic writing is just a way of making channeling deliberate or special, of endowing it with an aura of mystery. By distinguishing the process of channeling in this way it is easier to understand and learn – to learn in the sense of separating it out of normal thinking and feeling, and to understand when "our" thoughts and feelings indeed arise within ourselves, and when they are being passed to us by a spirit. Channeling can be done via normal thinking and feeling; in trance; in dreams; and by automatic writing. Automatic writing, albeit not as clear as trance channeling (more admixture of the person channeling in the final product), has the advantage of providing a written record of a spirit's messages – something which is often useful for future reference. A lot of things spirits say to us make more sense in retrospect.

I've personally taught some hundred people to channel their spirit guides, and of that number only half a dozen or so have blocked so badly that they couldn't do it. But nobody needs a teacher to learn something as easy and basic as channeling. The only function my presence as a teacher serves is to prop up my students' faith, to put their noses down to it: I have a rather overbearing personality that expects and assumes that people will channel successfully – which doesn't offer my students much margin for doubt or failure. But this is just a didactic device – I'm convinced that anyone who wants to channel can channel, with no need for a teacher.

It's best to tackle automatic writing when you have some pressing personal question to ask, or when you are moved by a burning curiosity to communicate with your spirit guides. Idle curiosity may not have enough oomph behind it to forge a clear communications link. The reason some people block conscious channeling (or reject the idea altogether) is that they don't want to face up to the fact that they are not solid, continuing, individual beings, but rather are a flux of thought forms (images, opinions, beliefs, and expectations learned from parents and society) being urged this way and that by spirit forces.

In other words, to open to channel means to lay aside a lot of common assumptions about the nature of personal existence; and some people find this frightening. If you find yourself blocking, just set the project aside until you have a dire need to question your guides – that need will be sufficient motivation to break the block. Like everything else in life, channeling comes more easily to some people than to others (e.g. to people with good Neptune aspects to their sun or moon); but anyone can channel if they just keep plugging away at it.

Choose a time when you are relaxed, alert, calm, and will not be interrupted. Being at a power tree or power spot is a big help. If you are into astrology, you can use a lunar planetary hour; however this is merely a help, not a necessity. Lie down or sit, as you prefer, with a pen and notebook in hand (although channeling can also be done on a typewriter or word processor). Writing down both your questions and the replies as they come in the form of a dialogue, ask your guides to please talk to you. For example, you might start this way:

Me: "My spirit guides, could you please come and talk to me? I am really trying to be open right now, and I want to hear what you have to say to me. I have this problem that I need an answer to; won't you please come and talk to me about it. Etc. etc."

This is just an example – you should ask your guides to talk to you using your own words and sentiments. Keep writing, keep on coaxing them, until you begin to feel an answer forming in your mind, and then write it down. The trick to making this work is to not stop writing. That's the purpose of the writing – to focus your attention on the act of writing, like when you're taking notes in a classroom, so that there's less room for doubt, hesitation, fear, etc. Keep on writing, even if you're just writing the same plea over and over again. Do make it heartfelt – not just done mechanically – and eventually you'll start getting an answer. It really is so simple and straightforward you won't believe it – "Look, ma, I'm channeling!"

Note that when a person channels for the first time, the answers tend to come out sort of inchoate and constipated. Don't worry – just push it right on out and don't worry about whether it makes sense or not. Usually in automatic writing a few words or phrases spring into your mind at a time, a little faster than you can write them down, though sometimes you might get whole blocks or paragraphs at once. You might also see memory pictures pop up before your mind's eye, or get flashes of dream-like scenes as you write. Record all of this because it's all relevant. Something might not make sense at the moment, but it will eventually if you keep a written record of it.

If nothing comes to mind in response to your entreaties; or if all that comes to mind is gibberish; then you are blocking. Your conscious mind might say, "This isn't working. I'm not doing it right." or "There must be some trick to this!" in its effort to subvert the process. Don't fall for that ploy! Keep trying, keep on writing, even if all you get is gibberish. Only trust can open you enough to write automatically; otherwise you tangle yourself with doubt. Doubt is the enemy of all magic, and it can completely tear down automatic writing at the outset. Faith is the key to success here, as elsewhere, and a strong curiosity is a valuable asset as well. Bear in mind that your spirit guides will be thrilled to open this channel of communication with you, and they will do everything they can, from their side, to assist you. If you find yourself blocking, try switching to your non-dominant hand; or do it standing on your head (leaning against a wall). Keep on writing, and at some moment your conscious mind will relax its grip and you'll start writing automatically. Then, simply write down what your spirit guides tell you, asking any questions you like along the way.

Ask your guides what their names are, and if they have specific messages for you. Some people "see" their spirit guides in their mind's eye; though I've never seen my guides in this manner, I have met them in dreams. In automatic writing (as opposed to trance channeling) there is a lot of medium thrown in with the message. One of my spirit guides is also channeled by several other people, and while you can tell that it's the same entity coming through, she sounds different through each of us. For one thing, she speaks in English to those whose native language is English, and in Spanish to those of Spanish tongue. Beyond that, her diction, outlook, interests, etc. mirror those of the person channeling her. What is invariant from channel to channel is her feeling – the sense of her presence – and the tenor and direction of her thinking. But her relationships with her various channels are as diverse as the channels are.

It's difficult to generalize about spirit guides – each is different, as people are different. They will speak to us in a manner we are capable of understanding: they address us according to where we are coming from, in terms we are capable of receiving. If there's something we just don't want to hear, it's easy enough to block it, just as we tend to block out what we don't want to hear from other people. Sometimes my own guides have had to wait until I was in a particularly relaxed or unguarded frame of mind to sock something to me that I didn't want to hear. And at times I've remonstrated, "Why didn't you tell me this before?"; to which their usual rejoinder is, "We were telling you all along, but you refused to listen!"

Once you've got the technique of automatic writing down pat, you can use it to channel any spirits, not just your personal guides. This means nature spirits, recently deceased people, even Jesus, Mary, Krishna, Buddha, saints, etc. God can't be channeled this way, however, because God doesn't "talk". If you get a message purporting to come from God, it's some wise-guy spirit putting you on. Automatic writing can also be used as part of Active Imagination (a technique devised by Carl Jung for doing inner work – self-analysis for self-transformation. See my book Thought Forms for details).

You may wonder how you can tell if you're channeling evil spirits. All I can say is that all of the evil spirits which I've run across in my channeling made no bones about who they were or what they were up to. Evil spirits seek willing accomplices – they need a decision on your part to commit evil, they can't trick you against your will. However, they can come up with some pretty tempting offers sometimes. I would say, though, that if the messages you are channeling are full of fulsome praise at how marvelous you are, and pity at how misunderstood you are, and how much you have to suffer, then probably you're channeling demons. Real spirit guides will buck you up when you are feeling low; but they'll also kick you in the butt if you indulge in self-pity. Their actual goal is to get you to a place where you have your own true feelings working, so that you don't need them anymore.

Okay, now you're a professional, dyed-in-the-wool spirit channel, ready to hang out your shingle and charge for readings. Now what?

Generally speaking, spirit guides are useless for calling horse races, lottery numbers, or even for predicting the outcome of specific events. If prediction is what you want, it's better to use horary astrology, tarot, etc. than to ask of your guides. My experience is that spirit guides can predict the outcome of certain events when they volunteer the information; but they can't or won't predict outcomes merely at our behest. This is because spirit guides look at things very differently from us; they're on another wavelength, and the things which are of crucial importance to us are not of consequence to them. Spirits don't give a hang about what we call the "future", and they regard our obsession with it as an odd peculiarity of our species, scarcely worthy of serious notice. On the other hand, things that spirits believe should be simple for us (such as dropping lifelong habits, addictions, fears, etc. as a simple act of will) in fact present insuperable difficulties which spirits can't really appreciate. Even spirits who have had human incarnations tend to forget what it's like down here. Things just aren't as simple as they try to make them seem, because they don't have to deal with doubt, fear, inertia, temptation, taxes, etc.

Nor are spirit guides capable of pulling our chestnuts out of the fire for us, saving our skins, or changing the outward circumstances of our lives. There are spirits which can assist us with the concrete problems of our lives to some extent, but spirit guides are basically advisors, not employees.

Spirit guides can't live our lives for us; they can't feel our feelings for us, can't absorb or deflect our pain for us, can't resolve our problems for us, and can't find our happiness for us. All they can do is show us how to take responsibility for doing these things ourselves.

Spells, Charms, and Rituals

Spells are the same thing as prayers, but not necessarily directed towards a deity (although they can be). The reason why a magician's spells are usually more efficacious than most people's prayers is not because magicians have any special innate powers. Rather, it's because their intent is more realistic. Most people pray for their desires to come true; whereas magicians pray to be shown how to make their desires come true.

Another reason why most people's spells don't work is because they are too insensitive (i.e., have too much self-hatred) to understand that the little coincidence; or offhand remark someone made; or person they happened to bump into in their hurry; or other little "cubic centimeter" of chance which popped up in the hours or days after casting their spell, was in fact their spell coming true. Very rarely does the Spirit announce its gifts with trumpets blaring. What usually happens is that people cast their spells or make their prayers and the Spirit brings them an opportunity; but the people are too blinded by their preconceived images or are in too much of a hurry to see that their spell did in fact come true (brought them exactly what they were asking for; but they, themselves ignored or rejected it).

Most people believe that things just happen; or else that an omnipotent God could make things happen if you could somehow fake God out. Magicians believe that they must take full responsibility for making their desires come true. That's what intent is – taking full responsibility, leaving nothing whatsoever to chance. That's why magicians are never disappointed when their desires don't come true, because they did their best, and that's all they can do. It's like the Native Americans who fought against the encroaching whites, or the Jews in the Warsaw ghetto who fought the Germans, knowing all along they had no chance to win. It wasn't the winning that ultimately mattered – and it's not the winning that ultimately matters to a magician, but rather doing your best (although there are probable realities in which the Native Americans and Jews in Warsaw *did* win out in the end.).

Most people are addicted to some fantasy like winning the lottery, or marrying Mr. or Ms. Right, or meeting a true guru, and then all their problems will be over forevermore. These kinds of fantasies are useful in that they can provide a feeling of hope, false though it may be, to help get through the really hard times. However, addiction to such fantasies tends towards irresponsibility. It dissipates the very intent needed to find true happiness in life. Permanent change requires hard work and infinite patience. The final stroke of success may occur suddenly and even unexpectedly, but the preparation and toil take years and years. That's the difference between the magicians' way and average people's way. Average people are looking for a quick fix and a free ride, whereas magicians know there ain't no such thing.

In the popular American television program Charmed, the witches have a book of shadows which conveniently contains specific spells for every single situation, no matter how outlandish, that they encounter. However, while spells do exist and do work, it's not quite as simple as it appears in Charmed.

To make spells work it is necessary to understand what expectation is, and its relation to intent. That is to say, how you make things happen or not happen, the mechanism by which you create your own reality.

People trying to understand the spiritual path sometimes wonder that, if you lose your desires as many spiritual paths seem to advocate, what spice or zest does life have left? In fact, it's not desire per se that spiritual seekers try to eradicate, but rather expectation. Expectation means taking things personally, caring about what happens. It isn't so much spice and zest that are lost as urgency and grasping. The things that average people care about do indeed lose their zest and spice; but in return things like the sound of the wind whispering in the trees and the feel of its caress on your skin become exquisitely piquant, sensual, and exciting.

When most people lose their expectations, which usually occurs because something they had a lot of stake in crashes, they experience this as depression. To depressed people life is indeed an empty, meaningless wasteland with no purpose or reward. Having lost the expectations which underpin their sense of self-worth and self-esteem, they feel they have also lost all sense of purpose, or intent. Actually, depressed people are very, very close to enlightenment if they only knew it. Their problem is that usually they are demon-possessed, and their demons are blocking their vision with self-pity.

Magicians, on the other hand, deliberately seek to crash their expectations, since they know that this is the path to freedom. Losing your expectations is the only way to center yourself in the now moment instead of being trapped by the yearning for a future which never comes. True self-esteem is a matter of permitting yourself to be happy now, of being able to truthfully say to yourself: "What's happening right this minute is okay by me. I don't have to have this, that, or the other in order to be happy; and I don't need to prove this, that, or the other in order to be a worthwhile person." It's a matter of getting off your own case and other people's cases; and off God's case.

The way expectations are normally lost is by having them crash, and crash, and crash. There's really no short-cut, no other way (a near-death experience can do the job quickly, but that's not everyone's karma). If you bang your head futilely against the same wall over and over again, you finally arrive at a point of exhaustion, and you collapse on the ground in despair. At that point, the moment of finally giving up your own will, you look around and usually you can see a clear path in another direction that is open and free of obstructions. The point is that the feeling of being blocked, or trapped on the same treadmill of frustration, is a message that – for whatever reasons – you are going about things incorrectly. When you give up your self-will you usually are able to understand what that message is, to see quite clearly why you had been blocked previously.

It is necessary to lose all expectation before you can find true happiness. For example, most single people think that what they want is a relationship, but this is baloney. "A relationship" – in the abstract – is an expectation. It's not a relationship with a real, live person. Is a relationship with the wrong person what you want? Where you have to try to force them to fit an image you have which is not who they really are? Wouldn't you rather be alone than in a relationship where there's bickering and lying and betrayal going on? So, it must be better to wait until the right person comes along than to grab candidates off the street and try to bribe or coerce them into a relationship. And if the right person never comes along, so be it. Since you create your own reality, there must be some lesson or reason for your solitude. The point is to just try to be happy now, alone, instead of expecting some stranger to come along and make you happy. Unless you're happy now, who would want to hook up with such a sourpuss? This doesn't mean you have to stop wanting a relationship in order to make one happen – just stop obsessing over it. Do you remember things that you desperately wanted when you were a child that you don't give a hoot about anymore? It's like that. By not caring so much whether you're in a relationship or not, by not making your happiness depend on it, is how to make a relationship happen. Going to the trees and nature spirits every day is the actual technique used to accomplish this feat.

Releasing the pressure of expectation by lightening up is how to achieve your desires. This is why dilettante magicians can't get their spells to work properly, and also why most people's prayers don't work. They can't just send a powerful intent out there and then drop it. They worry and fret and examine whether this is happening or that is happening. They don't hold it all inside. What they're doing instead is frittering their intent away in self-pity. It's when you stop caring so much one way or the other, start letting things unfold naturally and start letting other people make the moves rather than acting on your own accord, that things start coming through for you (en passant: this is pretty much impossible to do as an act of will – in spite of all the New Age cant about "thinking happy thoughts" and "thinking abundance" – unless you are enlightened already. This is why you need an outside agent such as a truly enlightened guru, or nature spirits, to transform you.).

It's difficult to describe the difference between eager expectation, which is phony, and eager anticipation, which leads to your desires being realized, since they both feel rather alike. But with eager anticipation every little thing that happens – except, of course, out-and-out bad stuff – every gust of wind, the sound of leaves rustling, the sight of a pretty color, makes you happy and gives you a little rush of joy. Conversely, with eager expectation, only the things which seem to advance the fulfillment of your specific expectations bring you joy.

Happiness can not, should not, does not depend on the fulfillment of an expectation. Expectation pushes happiness away indefinitely. Happiness is something you feel, or don't feel, as the case may be, right now. This means finding something that's going on this very minute which is joyous and fulfilling. Stop reading a minute and take a deep breath. Go look out the window. If all you see is bricks, look up at the clouds. The only way you are ever going to be happy is to find something that is going on right this minute which gives you a little lift. Even a teensy lift in the midst of horrendous suffering is a good beginning. Then you have to work at expanding that feeling. There's no other way, no shortcut to happiness. This is what magicians mean by taking responsibility for making your own happiness. Rolling up your sleeves and getting down to work is what entices the Spirit to reach out to you and give you a hand. This is how to make your spells work: by controlling your attitude. There's no way to fake this. It's accomplished by painstaking inner work and daily visits to nature spirits over many years of time.

The difference between rituals and spells is that rituals are to invoke spirits, whereas spells are to accomplish something specific. Spells are for us, to accomplish our own ends. Rituals are for the spirits, to provide an opening or channel into this world through which spirits can realize their own intent. When you perform a ritual to invoke spirits in good faith, rest assured that they come. They may not come with bells and whistles, but they come, whether you are consciously aware of their presence or not. Therefore rituals and invocations shouldn't be done frivolously.

Once I was leading a Jewish passover seder. Like most traditional church rituals, such as the Roman Catholic mass, the seder is an invocation of spirits. I had neglected to leave the customary place at the table for Elijah. When we arrived at that part of the seder service where the door is opened for Elijah to come in, I felt a definite presence enter the room, and that presence was quite ticked off at having been called without having been served at the table. The moral is, if you're going to invoke spirits, be respectful and aware of what you're about.

Some kids under the influence of satanic rock music who invoke demons "just for fun" are in for a big surprise later in life, when the demons exact payment. These people may never be consciously aware of the fact that their fooling around with demons as kids is what brought them the ill-health and ill-luck they face as adults. In other words, there's no such thing as fooling around with the invocation of spirits, whether beneficent or maleficent. Beneficent spirits don't like being treated disrespectfully, and invoking them frivolously tends to make them angry. Any invocation of a spirit is the real thing and has consequences.

Sometimes people who have old books on spirit invocation ask me to invoke the spirits for them. My reply is that people should invoke spirits themselves. There's nothing I can do that people can't do for themselves. Usually these sorts of books give complete instructions on how the spirits should be invoked: propitious days, times, what seal should be drawn in the magic circle and in what colors, what words should be spoken, and so forth. This is all the information anyone needs to invoke particular spirits for particular purposes.

However I am reluctant to invoke unknown spirits, unless directed to by my own spirit guides. While there are indeed spirits who can bring you financial help, romance, take vengeance on your enemies, and so forth, these sorts of spirits – albeit not demons per se – often exact considerable payment in return for their favors. There aren't any freebies out there in the universe. So be careful what you get involved with. Definitely consult your own spirit guides before invoking outside spirits.

The story on spells and charms is this: store-bought amulets and books of spells are pretty much worthless. It isn't the trinkets or the words that matter, but rather the intent behind them. It's better that you write your own Creative Visualizations rather than borrow someone else's. Similarly robes, magical tools, incense, and similar trappings don't matter in the least. If you like such things, however, feel free to use them. These objects can be useful in imbuing the moment you cast a spell or ritually invoke a spirit with a sense of importance, and help to put you in the right mood. Just remember that the magical clothes, tools, and chants are irrelevant. The only thing that matters is intent.

I purchase my charms in a local Mayan Indian market. They're nothing special by themselves – sort of like what you would find for sale in an occult shop. What makes them special is that I place them on the altar when I do rituals to invoke my patron spirits, and then these spirits bless the charms. You can also take your charms to any local nature spirit or power place to be blessed. I regard blessing a charm as similar to formatting a diskette. The charm is now ready for use, but still has to be written to, or charged with the particular intent or use to which it will be put. A charm or amulet is a physical representation of a spell. Charms can be worn around the neck or on a bracelet, or carried in a pocket or purse. They act as a reminder or protection, depending upon the purpose with which they were charged. Charging charms and amulets is best done during a relevant planetary hour.

Curses are the same thing as prayers, but with a negative intent. Because curses are the product of our fellow humans, they are much more difficult to cast off than are demons. Our fellow humans are far more ornery and vexatious than are demons, who are relatively straightforward and aboveboard by comparison. My benefactress, who is a priestess of the nine Mayan gods, has told me that curses should be removed by a professional, not attempted alone if you don't know what you're doing. She removes curses as follows:

You can't do it without prayer. Say whatever prayer is appropriate to your faith – e.g. you could use the Our Father – into each radial pulse three times while burning copal (or any acrid incense, such as patchouli) around the person. Then say it three times over the forehead. You may have to repeat these nine prayers a few times until you feel the pulse calm down. You also need a spiritual bath with various herbs. We use nine for this: pipers, marigold, rue, life everlasting, all collected with prayers of thanksgiving and faith. Mash all the leaves in a bucket of water and set it in sun for a few hours. When the person comes, say the prayers, burn the copal and bathe their aura and physical body with the bath water.

My teacher (a Mayan daycounter) removes curses by having the subject take special baths for thirteen days. The person must abstain from sex during this period, and each evening take a normal shower. After the shower, the person pours a pot of tea made from special plants boiled together and cooled down over him or herself (the plants are wild marigold, rue, and chilka – a local plant thought to bring luck; with three shredded cigars and an eighth of aguardiente liquor mixed in). After the ceremonial bath two candles are lit and the subject prays for forgiveness and liberation from the curse.

I've had curses put on me, more than once in fact, in the course of some unfortunate run-ins with a black witch. After smoking cigarettes for many years I eventually developed a constant emphysematous cough which no doctor I went to could help me with. Finally I went to a Huichol shaman in Mexico who asked me to give him a candle to burn at night, to see if he could find the answer to my problem in a dream. The next morning he told me that he had seen that someone – he didn't know who, but I did – had put a curse on me. The curse had resided in my weakest place, my lungs. The shaman had me return to him several times, each time making passes over my body with feathers. He prayed and sucked something out of the top of my head and spit it into his fireplace. He gave me a decoction of herbs and peyote to drink, and prescribed a special cleansing diet for a week. On my last visit he had me open my right palm and placed a cross in it, and then had me clasp my left hand over it. At that instant a glass with a candle burning in it on the altar behind us shattered with a loud "CRACK!" and I knew at that moment that the curse had left me.

It is often said that Creative Visualization and prayer should be done with the certain conviction that your desire is already realized: that what you're visualizing or praying for is already true. The question arises, how can you fervently believe that your desire is true when the overwhelming physical evidence is to the contrary? For example, how can you convince yourself that you are in radiant good health when all the logical signs point to your dying of cancer?

In casting spells, or making prayers or doing Creative Visualizations, which are all basically the same thing, what you are trying to do is to coax a sense of abundance from within yourself. You look out at the exact same landscape that you are seeing now – of being impoverished, or lonely, or sick – and yet you try to find meaning, worth, and purpose in it. Trying to conjure up a sense of fulfillment and self-worth in the midst of misery is a trick of magic. It isn't easy, but it can be done. Is this lying to yourself? No more so than believing that God is going to wave His magic wand and take away all your troubles.

The way that you build faith that your desire will indeed come true is by seeing it unfold in omens and portents. These are dress rehearsals of your desire being realized; or at least signs that the impersonal forces of the universe are listening. This is the difference between knowing with certainty that your desire will come true, as opposed to vaguely hoping that someday it will drop down from heaven by magic. When you have true faith you can see it all coming together in omens and portents, and can guide it along. You can see what you have to do now to get from here to there, instead of running around half-cocked frantically trying this and that to make your desires come true. With true faith it's a matter of increasing joy and confidence as you go along, instead of riding a constant roller coaster of inflated hopes and crushing disappointments, and repeating the same stupid mistakes over and over. True faith is never blind. It's based on having seen positive results in the past.

However planetary hours are merely a help, not a necessity. Once you have found a propitious time to cast your spell, you must consider the form that it will take. Write down ahead of time exactly what you want, so that you don't forget anything when the time comes. However, it's best not to be too specific in what you're asking for, such as to win the lottery, or to have such-and-such a person fall in love with you. It's best just to ask for wealth, or love from some unnamed person. Let the Spirit handle the details – it knows what it's doing.

When casting a spell it is important to address the real issue, rather than the presenting problem. For example, recently I was casting a spell to bring money (during a Jupiter planetary hour the day before a sun – Jupiter conjunction). As I was lighting the candle I realized that it wasn't money qua money that I wanted, but rather the free time to write what I want to write, instead of having to spend most of my time doing menial work, which I have to do to get by economically. So, on the spot I changed my prepared spiel to a visualization of living in a remote place in nature where I have the freedom to write – write – write to my heart's content without interruption.

I usually cast spells at power places or power trees, but you can make an altar in a corner of a room. Prepare your altar with something that symbolizes the Spirit above it. This can be a picture of Jesus if you're a Christian, or just a cut-out picture of an eye, or whatever symbolizes the Spirit for you. Put a stick of sweet-smelling incense on the altar, and a candle whose color symbolizes what you're asking for: green for money, pink for love, white for health or spiritual illumination, and so forth. Also put on the altar objects which symbolize what you want: money if you want money; cut-out pictures of lovers in love if you want love; pictures of healthy, active people if you want health; a photo of yourself from a time in your life when you were happy if you want happiness; and so forth.

Just prior to the chosen time light the incense. Then, at the precise moment chosen for the spell, light the candle. Then call upon the Spirit to grant your wish. It's okay to read it, but you should do this with feeling – true longing for whatever it is that you want. Picture in your mind's eye your desire coming true as you call for it, and let yourself feel all the joy you would feel if your desire came true. Don't worry about whether you are doing it right. If you're doing it in good faith with true longing, then you're doing it right.

Watch the candle closely for an omen of how your wish will go. If it is difficult to light the candle, then it will be difficult to make your wish come true. If the flame wavers or dies, then the wish probably won't materialize. If the flame burns tall and brightly, then the wish will come true. However if the candle should fall over, forget it. Also watch for unusual occurrences while you are casting your spell: for example, the sudden appearance of singing birds (if you are outside) or shafts of sunlight suddenly appearing through the clouds. These sorts of things are good omens for your wish coming true.

If you don't feel comfortable with all the ritual, you can dispense with it. The ritual is just for your own sake, to lend a sense of importance and ceremony to the occasion – not to impress the Spirit. The only things of importance are to cast your spell with true longing, at a propitious time.

When you finish casting the spell, leave the area and let the incense and candle burn down. Then dismantle the altar and dispose of what's left of the candle and incense by burying them. Once a spell has been cast there's no need to repeat it unless you feel your own resolve weakening and want to strengthen it. Be assured that spells carried out in good faith always work, so don't waste them on anything frivolous, since then you're committed to it. Be sure you really want what you're asking for. And, pay especial attention to little things and dreams in the days after you cast the spell.

Past Life Regressions

Running past life regressions is a good way to start making a connection to your true life's purpose – the reason you were born and the reason you keep coming back. It's so simple to learn that you can easily master the basic method in less than an hour's time; yet it is so far-reaching in its ramifications that a few months of playing around with it for an hour or so every night can completely transform your life.

Most of us New Agers believe in the reality of past lives, even though we can't actually remember them. We embrace this doctrine because it seems logical: it explains the vicissitudes of our present existence as the patterns and choices we ourselves made in other lives. The ability to actually remember past lives seems to be the possession of a fortunate few, like Edgar Cayce, who are born with mysterious psychic powers far beyond our reach. But in fact, the ability to recall past lives can be easily learned by anybody – all that is required is an open mind. And there are incalculable insights (and surprises!) that await the adventurer willing to explore these byways of his or her own subconscious.

The entry technique here is adapted from William Swygard's excellent booklets on Awareness Techniques. There's no need to memorize the following instructions: either have someone read them to you (you indicate to the reader when you have accomplished each task by saying "okay"); or else tape record the instructions for your own use, leaving a little time for yourself to complete each task.

Choose a time when you are calm, alert, and will not be disturbed. If you are an astrologer, you can use a lunar planetary hour; however this is merely a help, not a necessity. Have a notebook and pen (or tape recorder) at hand. Remove your shoes, loosen any restrictive clothing, and lie down on your bed. Take some deep breaths, and then put your attention on your toes and relax them with a deep breath. Move up to your feet and relax them with a breath; then relax your ankles, calves, knees, thighs, arms, hands, fingers and so on up to your head.

Take a deep breath and imagine that you are extending your height by stretching your legs until you are about a yard longer than your usual height. Then return to normal size. Take another deep breath and imagine that you are extending your height by stretching your neck until you are a yard taller than your usual height. Then return. With another breath imagine that you are extending your height by stretching your legs until they touch the wall. Then return. Take another breath and imagine you are stretching your neck until your head touches the wall behind you. Then return.

Then take a deep breath and imagine yourself swelling up like a balloon to twice your volume; then release the breath and imagine returning to normal size. After you've succeeded at this, take a breath and imagine yourself inflating and filling the entire room; then return. When you can do this, take a deep breath and imagine inflating yourself until you engulf the entire house; then return. Next, take a breath and swell up until you are bigger than the house; and let yourself float upwards into the sky. Look down as you rise and imagine you are seeing the house, the neighborhood, the surrounding countryside, as if from an ascending balloon. Allow yourself to float freely up, up, until you are in the clouds far above the earth.

Then command yourself to descend lightly back to earth in another lifetime. Look down at your feet; how are you shod? Look at your clothes; what are you wearing? Look around you; what kind of place are you in? Inside, outside? If inside, what is the building like? If outside, what are the surroundings like? Are there any other people around you? Who are they? What are they doing? What time or country does it seem to be? What are you doing in the scene? Why are you there? You concern yourself with these sorts of questions until you feel you're plugged into the past life; then you just let the thing flow and take you where it will. If someone has been helping you, you can describe the scene to them as it unfolds; if you are alone you can take notes (dividing your attention between the scene and the note-taking).

When you first come down the scene will be fuzzy at first. You look at your feet, then your clothing, then your environment, to put the pieces of the picture into place. You ask questions of the regression to connect yourself to it – to make that life vivid and bring it into focus. For me (who is not especially psychic), regressions are rather murky: I can't usually make out faces clearly, nor colors unless they're very bright. You see the regression with your mind's eye, but it's more felt than seen – more like a series of emotional tableaux than a movie. You usually only hit the high points of a given life; you don't see all the day-to-day routine. It's not unlike a daydream or fantasy, except you soon realize that something other than your conscious mind is running it, and that something is your feelings. The experience will be more or less vivid depending on how much you block it. Don't judge the experience (by thinking, for example, "This isn't real – this is just my imagination!"). Just let it happen; if you want to evaluate it, wait until after it's over. This is not an exercise for your conscious mind, so tell your conscious mind to butt out and keep its judgments to itself.

When you first start to use this sort of technique you don't know how it's supposed to feel (you can't believe it could be this easy!), so you may have doubts about whether you are doing it correctly. Don't worry – if anything at all is unfolding before your mind's eye, you're doing it right. If there is no flow or direction (you're stopped in one scene), it means you are purposely blocking it. You'll know quite well if you're doing this. To unblock yourself at any point, just ask more questions: What time of day or season is it? What kind of building / vegetation is around you? And so on.

In running past life regressions it is useful to have a notebook or tape recorder in hand to jot down the past life as it occurs. Since the content of a regression is largely emotional, it tends to fade quickly from conscious memory, and it's often useful to have a record of it for future reference. It's a simple matter to divide your attention between the past life and the notebook. Once you get the hang of the entry technique, you can dispense with the going up in the sky and coming down each time.

You might want to experiment with running past lives involving people you know from this life. Try this: when you're up in the clouds ask to see a past life involving someone you love in this life. Then ask to see a past life with someone you dislike in this life. Simply give the command: "I'd like to see a past life with so-and-so" at the time you command to view a past life. The powers that be will steer you to the right place.

Also, you can ask questions during the regression, such as: "Do I know that past-life person in this lifetime?" and you'll usually get an answer, which will come as either a conscious thought or a feeling. The theory is that you have an infinite number of lives with every being on earth, not to mention other places, but some are closer to your present life than others – more connected to it in terms of lessons to be learned in this life – and these are the lives that usually pop up in regressions.

The question naturally arises as to whether these past life regressions actually are past lives, or whether the whole thing is just an exercise in imagination. These regressions are not always factually accurate portrayals of other times and places (unless you're very psychic). You can certainly interpolate anachronisms into them if you want to. Moreover a life supposedly taking place in ancient Rome often looks suspiciously like something out of a Cecil B. DeMille movie. In other words, you obviously filter these regressions through your present-day concepts.

Also it is often difficult to relate to the "you" in a regression. He or she doesn't act or react the way you would, and so it's hard to accept or understand in what sense that person is you; much less that you are personally responsible for all the mischief that person is doing.

Nonetheless there is an emotional truth in regressions that argues for their being taken seriously, no matter whether they are "real" (whatever that means) or merely figments. The real touch in a past life regression is with the feelings that the "you" in the regression is experiencing. There are emotional echoes – little pings of recognition – that you will know mean something to you personally, even if you are at a loss to put them into words. For example, you often recognize the people you know from this lifetime when you encounter them in regressions by the feeling you have for them. I first learned to feel the people around me (instead of merely react to them on a thought form level) by doing past life regressions: understanding how I felt about them in past lives helped me to get a grip on how I really feel about them in this life.

"We all to some extent meet again and again the same people and certainly in some cases form a kind of family of two or three or more persons who come together life after life until all passionate relations are exhausted, the child of one life the husband, wife, brother, sister of the next. Sometimes, however, a single relationship will repeat itself, turning its revolving wheel again and again." -- W.B. Yeats, *A Vision*

It is the emotional content of these regressions which is of primary importance, not whether they are conceptually real (although my spirit guides assure me that they are no more nor less real than the life you are living now). Nor is it important that you intellectually resolve the "meaning" of this or that life. You just try to be aware that such-and-such a person is hurting you in this lifetime because you asked him to, to atone for what you did to him in another life; or that your stirrings towards music, say, or agriculture reflect a valid part of your being – another life in which you were a musician or a farmer; or that your irrational anger, joy, fears, and hopes are often quite rational and logical after all.

The emotional recognition in a regression is due to an actual line which connects you to the "you" in the regression. Clairvoyants see these connections as fibers of living light, but most people sense them as feelings, emotional connections. The theory is that these fibers from other lives bind us to neurotic patterns of behavior in this one – we feel a need to keep reliving our mistakes until we get them right. By running past lives it becomes possible to recognize these patterns, which immediately releases a lot of the energy that's tied up in them; i.e., it loosens the fibers between that life and this one, allowing the conscious mind to decide if it wants to do something about the patterns (instead of being dominated by them unawares).

After running a life, it often helps to jot down the impressions you have of it. What was the main thrust or purpose of that life? What lessons did you learn? How did you feel about it after you died? There's no need to become morbid or obsessed about past lives – just draw your conclusions and move on. After you have run a great many past lives, you will begin to notice certain trends or feelings that keep recurring over and over. For example, during a difficult time in my marriage my guides directed my wife and I to run scores of past lives that we had together, so that we would understand how it was that we were at the place we had gotten to. It turned out that in most of our past lives together one of us had murdered the other one. Beyond that there were many other recurrent themes throughout our lives together that were repeated in this present life.

"The victim must, in the Shiftings, live the act of cruelty, not as victim but as tyrant; whereas the tyrant must by a necessity of his or her nature become the victim. …The souls of victim and tyrant are bound together and, unless there is a redemption through the intercommunication of the living and the dead, that bond may continue life after life."-- W.B. Yeats, *A Vision*

Because our viewpoint is necessarily couched in terms of linear time, it is inconceivable to us that everyone we have met in our lives – even strangers passing on the street whom we don't even nod to – get together on some level and agree to people each other's lives. It's very much like actors in a play getting together, rehearsing, having a performance, and disbanding at the end. The agreement takes place in what we consider to be dreamless sleep.

For most people the vast majority of past lives consist either of unremitting hardship and suffering, or else of selfishness and chicanery. I, personally, have had lots of lives as a scoundrel, and it's interesting how many bells these ring for me in my present life. It can humble you a little, or at least make you realize that in your own heart there is a killer, a drunkard, or a psychopath, no matter how pious and privileged you think you are; and they're not that far beneath the surface, either.

On the other hand, you'll find lives in which you were quite admirable – courageous, loving, and wise. These lives will also directly connect to your better side in this life, and confirm your sense of purpose and direction.

It's this emotional recognition which is the gist of the thing. This is your own heart speaking to you, giving you messages of truth which you usually ignore or take for granted until they're somehow pointed out to you. Past life regressions bring a lot of subconscious flotsam and jetsam up to the conscious mind, which is necessary because everything originates in the conscious mind, and can only be controlled or dispelled by the conscious mind; but first the conscious mind has to be made aware of it. Running past life regressions loosens our light fibers by tuning us into other moods ("life purposes") from other lives and realities.

An Example Past Life Regression

Because listening to other people's past life regressions is not unlike sitting through a slide show of their trip to Europe, I have deliberately chosen for this example the most bizarre, outré past life I've ever run. Notice how first I plug into the feelings of that lifetime, and only when that connection is made does the story unfold.

…. An old wooden shack. It looks like Appalachia, or maybe the pine barrens of south Jersey. I think it's the pine barrens. I hate my mother. I don't know if I really hate her, i.e. her treatment of me leaves me fuming; it's very unfair. She just happens to be a bitter, bitter woman who takes it all out on me. Father is dead? At least he's not present. It's just me and her. She uses me for her whipping boy, but although I fume, I bite my tongue and don't cross her. It's because I understand how unhappy she is, and that she doesn't feel she has any choice except to be the way she is. I tend to forgive her as we go along.

I seem to be more sensitive, understanding, and loving in this life than in most of my other lives (I think it's just an image). For example, I can talk to plants and animals. I try to spend as much of my time as possible off in the woods talking to my friends, the plants and animals. I run naked. I have animal vision and animal sense. I can tell when there are other humans around and I avoid them. With my mother I feel I am pretending to be a human being, but that actually I'm not. My humanness is a masquerade.

Actually, I'm kind of nuts, although I do have a lot of sixth sense intuition. It is true that I'm repressing a lot of feelings to maintain this façade of equanimity. I see now [from the vantage point of my present life] that a lot of my gentleness and communing with nature is an image, an escape from her, because I won't admit to myself how much I hate her. I pretend she doesn't affect me, that I'm not really human anyway. In other words, I'm not as gentle and spiritual as I think, that's just an image of myself that I have. I think I'm superior to human beings, that I'm on a level above them, but that's just a game I'm playing (although I can talk to plants and animals).

Anyway, I do hate my mother more than I'll let myself cop to. I try to pretend I'm above those sorts of emotions, and that she can heap all her poison on me and it doesn't affect me at all. I'm glad I'm there for her to do that to, I understand why she's doing it, it's not her fault, etc. etc.

Except one day I pop. Something in me just snaps, and I kill her. I hit her in the face with an iron bar. There's no thought behind it: she's carrying on like she always does and I'm taking it like I always do, and then the next minute I've killed her.

Then I sort of go into a state of shock. There's no precedent for this. My world heretofore wasn't that pleasant, but at least it was pat and figured out and everything had its place; and now my mother is dead and I've killed her. I'm totally at a loss; so what I do is go on as before. I pretend she's still alive. I prop her up in her chair and serve her food at meal times; we eat together; then at bedtime I carry her to her bed and tuck her in. In the morning I get her up and brush her hair, take her to the table for breakfast, etc. Even as the months go by and she starts rotting and falling apart I carry her back and forth from the table to her bed to her easy chair.

Of course, there's a part of me that knows this is a total fiction – that part is diabolical and is happy that the bitch is dead and I can mock her every day by pretending she's alive; it's like a sarcastic side of me. But the outward part – the image part – continues to pretend that nothing has changed. This is also calculated to make whoever discovers me think I'm nuts, so I won't be held accountable for killing her.

But it is the continuation of the masquerade I adopted when she was alive: "Oh yes, mother? Anything I can do for you, mother?" It's the continuation of my "nice guy", "spiritual guy" mask: that guy wouldn't have killed his mother, so of course I didn't kill my mother. The diabolical, sarcastic part of me is actually my anchor to sanity, and the nice guy mask is actually nuts. The two of them are in sort of a battle.

Probably, if I'd lived longer, the nice guy would have won and I've have gone completely nuts for good. But eventually a bunch of cops came in and shuffled me off, and everything after that is a blur of uniforms and cells – nothing that makes any sense. I guess I retreated into insanity to be able to handle it.

They must have executed me because I'm still young when I die. I meet my mother. She has not changed one iota. She is still, in the afterlife, playing all the same games she did on earth; and she was hanging around waiting for me to rejoin her and serve her. She doesn't blame me for killing her; she just wants me to take up the same role I played for her on earth; and I do it. There in the afterlife we create a perfect replica of the life we had together on earth: the same ramshackle house, furniture, etc., with her abusing me all day long and me sneaking off to be with the plants and animals. The only difference is that in the afterlife I no longer hate her. It's as if all my images finally came true – I'm truly indifferent to how she treats me, I know she's doing what she does because she can't help it, etc. I certainly don't love her, but neither am I repressing anger at her because I don't know what else to do.

We're still at it to this day – out there in the ozone somewhere she and I are still carrying on this pine barrens life as if nothing had happened.

In running past life regressions you have a safe and powerful technique for bringing useful information up from your subconscious, to help you get to your true purpose in incarnating, and to understand and accept who you really are. This is what W.B. Yeats termed being "in-phase" as opposed to being "out-of-phase" – i.e. being in tune with your true purpose in incarnating in this lifetime, as opposed to surrendering your free choice in life in order to conform to societal fiat (socially-approved images and expectations).

Bewitching

Magic is a craft. It's something you learn. Magicians usually do have supernormal powers. However, these powers are learned. There can be inborn talent, but it takes a lifetime of practice just to perfect one such power. This is why the terms "occultism", "secret science", "mysticism", and so forth are silly. There is nothing secret or hidden going on here. Magic is merely a matter of paying conscious attention to the things which your society has taught you to ignore.

Magic is what everyone is doing all the time, beneath the surface of everyday life. Most people just pretend they aren't doing it; or else they don't consider what they do to be magic. For example, infatuation is a species of mutual bewitching. Lovers bewitch one another and themselves. But they wouldn't consider this magic. They consider it "love" – at least until the bewitchment, the infatuation, wears off.

Similarly, people who cannot break free of an abusive relationship are usually bewitched by their partners. Doctors, and all healers, cure people by stimulating and encouraging the people's own faith in getting well. Good salespeople are adept at bewitching their customers. And so on.

Everyone is manipulating everyone else on a magical level all the time. Any time people command another's attention, or manipulate their feelings in any way, they are bewitching them. Thus all art is magic, and great artists are merely great magicians. Artists are highly intuitive people who can tune into profound feelings in their art and take other people with them.

Magicians are perhaps a bit more psychic to start with than average people. At least magicians rely upon and trust in their intuition more than average people do. To most people, psychic events such as precognition, prophetic dreams, omens, telepathic communications happen now and then unbidden, but are beyond conscious control. Such things happen to magicians with somewhat more frequency because magicians welcome, or intend, such things – or better said, magicians pay more attention to the little nuances in everyday life which most people miss in their mindless scurrying about. With some experience and practice magicians learn to control their psychic abilities.

For example, when faced with a problem, one thing many magicians do is to pray (intend) upon retiring at night for the solution to their problem to come to them. With a little practice they find that this works most of the time. They receive the answer in a dream that night, or else it comes in the next day or two. And as they see this technique work time and time again, it builds their faith, and as their faith builds the technique keeps working better and better for them.

Faith, the emotional content of belief, is the key to making magic work. It can move mountains. It is the lever by which you create your own reality. The only reason your thought form world works is because you put your faith in it. If you believed in magic with the same certainty that you believe turning a key in an ignition will start a car, then magic would work as well for you as science and technology do.

That's what faith is all about. There have been societies on this earth which were based upon magic, such as the Mayan Indians of Central America. These societies get magic to work for them as well as materialistic science does for us, because that's where they put their faith.

The reasons why magic often doesn't work as well as the books, and one's own spirit guides, for that matter, say that it should, are sundry. Sometimes it just isn't time yet. "To everything there is a season." All the prayers and spells in the world won't make Christmas happen before December 25th. Sometimes your prayers and spells are contingent upon the right astrological influence occurring.

Other times your prayers and spells don't work right away because you have heavy karma in the way that has to be cleaned out first. This karmic barrier to realizing your desires might stem from previous lifetimes, as well as this one. In my own case it took twenty years of just putting in the time and paying my dues between when I first made the decision to follow the magician's path, and when my spirit guides appeared in my life, which was my actual entry into the world of magic. From there it was another twenty years until I started seeing some real results from magic working on my own, without spirits backing me up. However, I never lost faith, and that's why I have succeeded so far.

The difference between magicians and average people is that magicians have infinite patience and a willingness to confront any danger and endure any pain necessary in order to realize their desires. Average people, on the other hand, always seem to be looking for a free ride or handout in life. Average people's decisions don't have enough power behind them to accomplish anything worthwhile because they back down and reverse their decisions the minute the going gets a little tough. What helped me a lot in my own quest, I see now in retrospect, was that my situation was truly desperate and miserable. I had nothing to go back to, so I had no choice but to press forward.

The Spirit always plays little games on your head to test you in your resolve. It always makes it as difficult as possible to stand by your decisions. Things never happen the way you fantasize them or rehearse them in your daydreams. Average people are ready to throw in the towel and weep in self-pity at every little disappointment. Magicians know that once a decision has been made, there's no going back unless the Spirit itself grants release. The basic principles of magic – of intent – are to make absolutely irrevocable decisions; and then to go to any extreme necessary to stand by those decisions.

Power is the same thing as luck. True power involves leaving nothing to chance. Average people, if they believe in magic at all, believe that magicians control chance. This isn't correct. Magicians, at least white magicians, don't dominate chance or enforce their own will on the universe. Rather, they are wholly dominated by it. They give up all personal expectations of their own, cease caring whether they win or lose, or get their own way or not (they don't give up wanting things; they just give up their sense of stake in whether the things happen or not). In this way magicians become one with chance and merge themselves with it. Then their will becomes unstoppable.

Magicians will to accept the Spirit's will as their own. They give up all their own images of what they think they desire and let the Spirit's desires for them prevail. When magicians synchronize their own desires with those of the Spirit, everything becomes possible for them. The great enemy of magic is doubt.

I happen to have the power to bewitch women to fall in love with me (okay, no snickering out there, this happens to be true). My spirits taught me how to do this to show me that magic does indeed work – that it is possible to make impossible things happen merely by willing it. They also wanted to teach me to hold my attention fixed upon a single object, moment-to-moment, all day long every day. They know me pretty well: they knew that the only thing that would motivate me to put out the effort and discipline needed to do this was the promise of sex.

I'll save the details of my experiences with bewitching women for my autobiography, except to say that the last time I tried it, it backfired on me in such a way that I'll never do it again. Besides, although you can get sex by bewitching, you can't get love that way, so why bother?

Psychic healing works the same way that bewitching does. The healer visualizes the patient as being well, and thus overrides the patient's doubt and self-pity. It's also possible to bewitch to stun: to disarm an angry or threatening person (or just to shut someone up) by disorienting and befuddling them (I don't know how to do this, but I've had it done to me). Any form of ensorcellment involves substituting the magician's will for the subject's will. This can only take place if the subject is willing, consciously or unconsciously. That is to say, no one can be bewitched, or healed, against their will.

Bewitching is really no different than Creative Visualization. Magicians know to keep their Creative Visualizations within the realm of reasonable possibility. Thus they don't try to bewitch famous movie stars to fall in love with them, or to win the lottery. These sorts of outcomes are too unlikely. In order to make magic work it is necessary to overcome doubt, and wishing for something that's way out of your league, or too improbable, starts off with too big a doubt debit.

When bewitching for love, for example, magicians start out with someone with whom they already have desire lines in place. This means someone with whom they have already shared feelings; someone they've already looked directly in the eye and flashed with. That flash doesn't necessarily have to have been one of love. The flash could have been anger, disgust, humor, or sadness as well as attraction. It doesn't matter. If, for an instant, two people look in each other's eyes and some emotion passes between them, then at that moment they stuck lines in each another. They bewitched one another. If there is any feeling at all between two people, whether positive or negative, then they can be bewitched through that feeling.

What passes in brief moments of direct eye contact is very powerful sexual magic. It is so potent, in fact, that it scares most people. They immediately get flustered, avert their eyes, and pretend that nothing happened. Even when the emotion that is being shared is humor or gaiety, there is a polite limit to how long direct eye contact can be engaged before it becomes threatening, i.e. sexual. Even if the emotion is anger or disgust, that just means that the feeling is so sexual that it has to be hidden by its negation.

Sexual feeling is the matrix of all feeling. Sexual feelings are actual lines which people shoot into one another, like arrows, whenever they flash on each other by sharing a feeling. These lines appear to people with psychic vision as fibers of living light. It's through the light fibers which join people that they pass emotional information, such as the psychic knowledge that the other person is hurt, or dead, or having sex with someone else. It's also through these light fibers that bewitching takes place (See the drawings of humans interacting on a light fiber level in Barbara Brennan's book *Light Emerging*, Bantam NYC 1993).

In short, if two people have ever shared any direct feeling, then there's already a sexual bond between them. Magicians can use this bond to bewitch, or to heal. They force energy through that desire line by intense visualization of their desire coming true. This brings pressure to bear upon the interpersonal barrier. This barrier is the pretense that there's nothing going on between the participants.

Sexual desire can exist from previous lifetimes and realities – this is usually what's behind the phenomenon of love at first sight. If there's an underlying sexual attraction (which can in fact be read from the natal horoscopes of the people involved) then there's fertile ground for bewitching even if the two people have not yet met face-to-face.

On the surface, the magicians act cordially but disinterestedly. They keep a poker face and they do nothing on their own account. Eventually that pressure brings about a moment in time when the Spirit itself opens the floodgates and the other person's defenses evaporate. If and when it's time for an overt move, it comes on its own in a moment of power.

In everyday society most of the actual sticking of desire lines into other people is done in the state of dreamless sleep, although the intent is set up in waking. If you have ever had a dream war with someone, that person was trying to stick a line into you, but you successfully fought them off. If you hadn't successfully fought them off, you wouldn't have had that dream. It would have remained unconscious, on the level of dreamless sleep.

Magicians, both black and white, sometimes rely upon spirit helpers to cue them on what to do and when. These messages come across as sudden ideas or inspirations. But magicians don't act unless prompted.

In other words the magicians' superficial behavior betrays nothing of what they are actually thinking or feeling. Contrast this with how most people try to make their desires come true. Most people get caught up in making obvious moves, polishing their self-presentation, trying to somehow flag other people's, or God's, attention: "Yoo-hoo! Here I am! Over here!"

This approach will work sometimes, but it's really inept. This is what the dating game is all about, which is why people find it so boring and predictable. There's no sport to it. Besides there's no true feeling to it, much less love. It's all phony.

When magicians bewitch, all their energy is held rigidly in check. Desire is inflamed by visualization, which is why magic is basically a matter of bewitching oneself. Magic is hypnotizing oneself into an intense, single-pointed desire. Magicians first have to bewitch themselves to be madly in love – they go first. Then they impose that feeling on the subject of their desire. Better said, they give the subject a powerful option.

No one can be forced to do anything against his or her own will by magic. It's quite possible for the person being bewitched to block the ensorcellment by detaching his or her light fibers from the magician. This is felt as closing up to them emotionally. What magicians, particularly black magicians, count on is that most people's wills are so weak and confused.

Magicians may use some object symbolic of their desire and pour all of their attention on it. They imagine the face of the person in it and talk with it and make love with it and cuddle with it at night. For example, in the movie Bell, Book and Candle, Kim Novak bewitched Jimmy Stewart with a cat. In the book The Witch's Dream by Florinda Donner, the protagonist bewitched his love with a devil's mask. The symbolic object can be charged like a charm.

Thus bewitching is like normal daydreaming or fantasizing, carried to an extreme. When bewitching for love, the magician visualizes him or herself in the presence of the beloved – holding hands, kissing and caressing, having fun together – as if the person were actually there. In bewitching you look the other person (the lover you desire, the boss you want a raise from, whomever) directly in the eye. In normal daydreaming and fantasizing, by contrast, you're usually not making eye contact at all. In bewitching the focus is on the other person and how enjoyable it is to be in their company (or to be rid of them, depending upon what you are bewitching for). In normal daydreaming the focus is on yourself, and other people serve only as mute witnesses to your own glory and vindication. This is the difference between bewitching and fanning the breeze with idle daydreaming. When you bewitch someone you're right there in front of them eyeball-to-eyeball. You let them do the talking and make the moves. In daydreaming they're fawning over you while you carry on a monologue.

This is another difference between Creative Visualization, what magicians do, and fantasizing and daydreaming, which average people do. Visualization is a matter of feeling, of longing, of reaching out for the object of desire. Daydreaming is a matter of conceptualizing, imaging, distancing yourself from the object of desire. Daydreaming is actually reaching out towards self-pity, not towards the realization of your true desires.

You should not daydream or have romantic or sexual fantasies about someone whom you are bewitching. They will feel this through the light fibers you have in them as a sleazy vibe, a sexual expectation, coming from you; and they will raise defenses against it. Creative Visualization, true bewitching, usually doesn't have a context of sexual or romantic excitation at all. It's too here-and-now, too spontaneous and unpredictable. It has a light, joyous feeling to it as compared to the obsessive and directed intensity of most daydreaming. Daydreams are about control, whereas Creative Visualization is about joy.

When bewitching to get rid of someone, magicians don't visualize bad things happening to that person. Rather, they visualize themselves happy, relieved, joyous, now that said person is gone. Psychic healing is done by visualizing the person as well. The point is that the visualization has to be done as if the action is unfolding in the here and now, unlike normal daydreams, which take place in the future. One has to feel all the feelings – joy, relief, health, whatever – that would be felt if the visualization were actually true. It's those feelings which are being felt which attract the object of desire; which make the visualization come true.

Conscious awareness is where all links ultimately have to be made. A magician, however, never makes links through direct intervention, by acting on his or her own accord. This is how most people blow things or trip themselves up. They fail by acting on their thought forms, by being impatient and pushy, by being unwilling or unable to trust in the Spirit to bring them what they want in the fullness of time.

This shows lack of faith. Only the Spirit can move the wheel of chance. Therefore the basic principle of magic is patience. Conscious awareness can only exist if there is also unconscious awareness – something which is being hidden. The trick of magic is to take in everything so that nothing is any longer hidden. Another way of saying this is, you must become aware of your own prejudices and taken-for-granted assumptions, since it is your own images and expectations which blind you to the truth – that you yourself are the one who is creating your reality.

Everybody already knows intuitively how to make magic work, but they don't do it much since if they succeeded they'd scare themselves silly. This is another difference between daydreaming and Creative Visualization. In daydreaming the person doesn't really want the desire to come true. He or she is just playing games, fanning the breeze. Therefore it usually takes an intense, overwhelming desire or desperation to activate average people's true magical powers. Miracles do sometimes happen, when people are 100% clear in their intent – when they permit their higher self to surface and take command. Magicians strive to make every moment a miracle.

Creative Visualization, is the same thing as prayer. Everyone intuitively understands the efficacy of prayer, but most people don't call upon it unless they're desperate. However, desperation isn't the best motivation for prayer since people create their own realities. They wouldn't be in that situation in the first place unless they created it for some reason, to learn some lesson. If that lesson happens to be learning the power of faith, that prayer does work, then their prayers will save their butts; but not necessarily otherwise.

The problem with magic as a spiritual path, and bewitching people in particular, is that it hangs us up in all the same stupid games of winning and losing that average people play in normal, everyday society. This is what I ultimately learned from my experiences with ensorcellment. The only difference is that magicians aim to be winners, whereas average people aim to be losers – to wallow in helplessness and self-pity.

Fundamentally magic is as much a dead-end street for an aspirant on the spiritual path as is seeking the validation and glory of society. The only value to magic, which seems baffling at first but which is learned through experience, by making lots of mistakes, is understanding the difference between when one is acting on one's own impulse, or when one is truly being prompted to act by the Spirit. This is the crux of the matter, and the reason why learning magic is worthwhile.

Black Magicians and Vampires

I live in Guatemala, a country which is populated largely by Mayan Indians. There's a lot of magic going on, both white and black. Every little village in highland Guatemala has people who know a lot a lot more magic than I do; but they're not particularly writing books on the subject, much less in English.

As a result of all this attention, magic works pretty well in Guatemala. What a society emphasizes is what it tends to manifest. For example, material abundance works pretty well in the First World (at least for the moment), but not in Guatemala.

I have an American friend here who started out as a Mormon missionary with no belief in black magic. He married a Guatemalan woman and had children with her. Eventually the marriage dissolved, and this woman, bent on revenge, hired a black witch to curse my friend.

His car broke down frequently. Thieves ransacked his house several times when he was away. Payments due him were defaulted or stolen. Eventually he realized that all this bad luck wasn't a coincidence. He went to a witch himself to undo the spells his ex-wife's witch was casting. The witch did a long ritual, and at the end of it she told my friend that there was nothing she could do since his wife's witch was far more powerful than she was. Further, she didn't know anyone who could undo the curse.

It is not true, as the materialists would have you believe, that witchcraft only works on people who believe in it. On the contrary, it works on everyone; but materialists view as "coincidence" happenings which magicians view as cause and effect. Black magic is not essentially different from the selfishness, greed, bad faith, and lying which take place in our everyday society and relationships. All of our jealousy;

bickering; people picking at each other; is inept black magic at work. All bad feelings are curses which do indeed cause the person they are directed at pain on some level.

In point of fact, our entire society is based upon black magic and lying. When is the last time you told the truth about what you're really feeling and thinking inside to anyone? You can't tell the truth in our society about anything which matters – any talk except for vapid thought form persiflage is completely forbidden. Black magic is simply what everybody is doing to everybody else all the time underneath all the phoniness and tea party hypocrisy; everybody is just pretending that they're not doing it. However, there are some people who are just natural born black magicians, just like some people are natural born musicians or natural born chefs. Natural born black magicians are very good at sucking other people's energy.

In order to stay alive you must eat – devour other living beings. When you eat you destroy and assimilate the energy of other beings in order to maintain your own personal continuity. Thus, being alive in the world is, by its very nature, black magic. What is actually being consumed is not flesh but rather feelings.

You have been trained to believe that you live in a world of things; however, this is merely an appearance. In point of fact you live in a world of feelings. For example: when someone steals from you, or rips you off in some other way, what they are really after isn't your money, but rather your anger. Women are used to men coming onto them for sexual favors; and practically everyone has experienced hustlers coming onto them for money. However the actual gain when someone tries to force you to do something you don't want to do is not the sex or money, the surface payoff, but rather the bending you out of shape. It's your anger and fear that such people are after. By making you react they can suck your energy. Even a refusal, if made in anger or fear, is a positive payoff to such people.

People who are mooches or invade your space in some other way; who are gratuitously nasty, threatening, or annoying; who make you feel dirty, or used, or frazzled; are actually vampires who are out to suck your energy. If you react to them in any way at all, rather than brush them off non-reactively, then they got what they wanted from you.

There are certain people who are natural vampires. Just being around them is energy-depleting, and becoming involved in an intimate relationship with them can be devastating. We all know of couples where one partner emotionally trashes the other one, but the victim can't seem to separate, or even understand what is going on. This is because the vampire has his or her victim bewitched. Alcoholics and drug addicts often literally vampirize their families and friends.

All power struggles and bad faith are no different from what real vampires do. These activities are overseen and directed by demons, who get their little share of the vigorish. The difference between everyday space-jumpers and real vampires who can stay alive for centuries is a matter of degrees of competence. The mechanism is exactly the same. If there is any shame, compunction, or humanity there at all, then the person isn't yet a real vampire. All black magic takes shamelessness as its point of departure. Therefore, disordered personalities (lacking shame) make better black magicians than do neurotics (who are overburdened with shame). Black magicians are the living dead – psychopaths who succeed by killing off all of their humanity (their ability to feel); and who destroy other people without any compunction whatsoever – without even any sense that they are doing anything wrong; any more than you feel compunction about killing a mosquito.

Suppose someone presses you for something which you really don't feel like giving, but you do it anyway and then feel put out or used in the process. What actually happened was that the person shot a line (a light fiber) of desire into you and sucked your energy – your good feelings, your joy – through it like a straw.

Practically everyone has experienced having had darts of black magic hurled at them, as when someone made you a gratuitous cutting, hurtful remark – or sent you an ugly, nasty look – which went straight to your heart and wounded you in your light fibers. The thought forms involved (the superficial, presenting events: the hurtful remarks or the nasty looks) are beside the point. What actually occurred in such moments is that the person threw a light fiber into your body (your solar plexus, heart, and head are the usual targets; sexual darts go in the genitals).

The basic principle involved in hurling darts of black magic is no different from that of the hurling of darts of sexual turn-on, which pass between people when they look into each other's eyes and flash on each other sexually. At such moments one person (or both of them) hurl light fibers into the other person. The basic intent in both types of dart – sexual and hurtful – is the same: namely, to bind the other person with the light fibers attached to that dart, to be able to pass energy to and from that person. However, darts of black magic are obviously not voluntarily received (as are sexual and love darts, through which energy is given in an effort to make the person feel good). The object of black magic darts is to give nothing, but just to suck the other person's energy (good feelings) through these light fibers by making the person feel bad (fearful or angry).

Black magicians get a little lift of energy through the lines they have stuck in other people; but the main beneficiaries are their handlers, the demons who possess them and are sucking their energy in turn. It's like a chain of suckers: demons suck the black magicians, who have to keep finding victims to suck to keep their own energy up; and then the victims call in their own demons as a protection, and then they have to find victims of their own to suck. Is it quite clear in this exposition that what we are talking about here is everyday society – everybody's relations with everyone around them: parents, teachers, bosses, coworkers, strangers in the supermarket? All this black magic is what's happening "beneath the surface" of everyday society, if you just open your eyes and see it.

What makes this subject so difficult to understand is that there is nothing visible going on, nothing you can point to or see openly. Vampirization, like bewitching, takes place on a feeling level. To the victim the feelings are as palpable as being physically attacked. If you've ever been burglarized, then you know the feeling of rape / violation you feel when you return home. That feeling is a light fiber left by the burglar to suck your energy – your anger and your fear at your own vulnerability and helplessness. That is what the burglar is really after – not whatever it is he stole, but rather your anger and fear that he can suck through that line.

In fact these lines are visible to psychic people – that is to say, to people who are born with or have developed this faculty. See Barbara Brennan's book *Light Emerging* (Bantam NYC 1993) for drawings of what these lines look like to a person with psychic vision. The only way to avoid being vampirized in such a situation is to not react at all.

To refuse the vampire in anger, for example, or to recoil in disgust, is as much a gain for the vampire as acceding to him is.

This is an important point: all "you" really are is your attention – where you are placing your attention right this moment. That's all you are, and that's all you have. What demons and vampires (and the people who love you as well) try to do is to capture your moment-to-moment attention by making you feel fearful or angry (or happy, in the case of the people who love you). The only way to plug those light fibers is to completely ignore the provocation: to cease all thoughts and feelings about the vampire – to just stop caring about him and his antics. Obviously, this ultimately requires the loss of a considerable amount of self-pity on your part since it is the victim's self-pity which encourages and engages a vampire's invasion of the victim's space. Vampires can only get into your space if you let them in. But, to muster the necessary ruthlessness to do cast them out, you must rid yourself of your use of the vampire as an excuse to pity yourself (by being afraid of him or angry at him). The ritual of cutting and casting out these lines (described below) is a good place to start, symbolizing as it does the definitive intent to cut that vampire from your life.

When I broke up with my girlfriend F., I did so in such an abrupt and unexpected manner that it surprised even me (it was as if something welled up in me and cried "ENOUGH!"). I learned later from her that after this breakup a wound opened on her left breast that suppurated for months. Anyway, for about six months after this breakup I was not my usual, heavy, mopey self: on the contrary, I felt an unwonted lightness of spirit – happy, optimistic, joyous. And then I came down into my usual dull self. I asked my spirit guides what that was all about, and they told me that for the preceding six months – since the breakup – I had been vampirizing F.'s energy, as she had been doing to me theretofore; that I had turned the equation around and used the lines that joined us to suck from her instead of permitting her to suck from me. And that when I came down six months later, she must have done something from her side to put a stop to it.

When my guides told me that, I suddenly understood F. (and my ex-wife) better. I had always supposed that on some level these women knew what they were doing to me – trashing me emotionally – but they just refused to acknowledge it (of course, I stupidly opened myself up to it by seeking women who would do to me what my mother did.). However, after I, myself, did the same thing to F. unwittingly – I realized that the women hadn't know consciously that they were vampirizing my energy and causing me great pain. All they knew was that they would be happy and joyous and minding their own business; and then all of a sudden I would appear and start screaming at them for no reason whatsoever. It wasn't until I found myself on the sucking side of the vampire equation for the first (and only) time in my life that I understood that most everyday vampires don't have a conscious clue as to what they are doing. But that doesn't mean they're not doing it.

The subject of magic is so very difficult to understand – indeed, it defies understanding. As a mathematician, I rather like explanations and causality; being able to see mechanisms involved; and so on. But magic doesn't work that way. I used to beseech my guides over and over, "HOW does she do it?" But now they answer me, "The same way you did it to F." And I have no idea how I did it that time – I couldn't repeat it at will; I didn't even know that I was doing it at the time. At this point in my magical training I know that there are no mechanisms involved; neither are there procedures. Magical events are caused by intending them; or better said, by awaiting them – there's no step-by-step modus operandi. It is true that some magical operations – such as spirit invocations – do have strict procedures; but this is more to please the spirits than intrinsically necessary to make the magic work. I, personally, eschew a lot of ritual, fancy clothes, formulaic incantations, etc. unless these have been mandated by the spirits involved themselves. This sort of claptrap is just a matter of taste, it has nothing to do with making magic work; whereas *intent* has everything to do with it. And, that intending can take place on a subconscious level. Indeed, the practice of magic is merely a matter of making that which most people do unconsciously, conscious. Becoming a magician is simply a matter of learning to look at everyday life the way it actually is, without all the stupidity, lies, phoniness, and hypocrisy.

The difference between black and white magic is that in black magic emotions are squelched (repressed) whereas in white magic emotions are felt, but not acted upon. White magic requires true discipline, whereas black magic is based ultimately upon fear and anger. White magic seeks to diminish self-importance, whereas black magic seeks to increase it. In black magic the practitioner jumps deeply into other people's space; whereas in white magic the idea is to keep out of other people's space. What both black and white magic have in common is ruthless ejection of other people from your own space.

As mentioned previously, people can only enter your space if you let them enter it. The way you let them enter is by thinking about them and reacting emotionally to them: caring what they do or don't do. To eject them from your space is a matter of ceasing to think about them. You free yourself from them when you stop caring about them, when you stop fawning or feeling offended by them, when you stop rehearsing mental scenarios of validation or vindication or vengeance. In other words, the trick to both white and black magic is to have conscious, volitional control over your moment-to-moment thoughts and desires. That's the only way you can ultimately disentangle yourself from other people's webs of black magic.

There are lots of spiritual paths which aim at the cessation of thoughts and desires. Usually a spiritual path aims at control of either one or the other of these, since to quiet our restless minds necessarily quiets down our relentless desires, and vice versa. The aspirant merely chooses a path which suits his or her own temperament. Where I'd characterize Buddhism as a path of stilling thought, the path of magic is a path of stilling desire. The black magicians and vampires you run into in your everyday life are terrific teachers in the craft of stilling desire – namely the desire to up and smack 'em one.

A fundamental principle of magic, both black and white, is being completely non-reactive emotionally; not permitting any dart of desire to escape. The white magician relaxes into a state of indifference, whereas the black magician clenches up into a state of heightened tension. The white magician reaches towards a state of mind in which nothing is important, whereas the black magician induces a state of mind in which one's lower self is the most important thing in the universe. The goals are different, but the technique of getting there is the same in either case: holding all desire inside instead of frittering it away in self-pity.

One trick I've found that works in black magic situations is to say to yourself, "What this person is really after is my anger, to reflect his own self-hatred back at him. If I give it to him, he wins! I can't let him get away with that!" Or else tell yourself, "I'm not going to feed this guy's demons!" And then laugh it off; or at least try to as best you can. When they actually throw a dart into your light fibers, you can't help but react. But then you try to shake it off instead of nursing a grievance.

Another helpful technique is to take an objective look at the person who is hassling you and see why they are doing it (from their own point of view), to get an understanding (if not sympathy) for the person. When you see how pitiful most of your enemies truly are, it makes you less interested in wasting your energy thinking about them or reacting to them.

The times I've reached my higher self in normal, everyday (not psychedelic-induced) consciousness was when my enemies pushed me there (to the [Place of No Pity](#)) by driving me beyond the limits of endurance. My enemies are the best friends I've had on the spiritual path; and this is not just one of those trite spiritual homilies – I really mean it. I couldn't have gotten to where I've gotten to (including a first-hand understanding of what demons really are and how to cast them out; what curses are and how to undo them; as well as how vampires operate and how to fend them off) without the thorough and relentless tutelage of my enemies.

Another thing that helps me is my knowledge from experience that most of the time when someone rips me off for something, whatever he ripped off is something I'm better off without. Or sometimes the rip-off gives me a whole new slant on something completely different. In other words, I try to take a detached view, and figure out what the lesson here is. It's a form of deliberately tricking yourself. This doesn't always work in the moment, of course, but with practice it's possible to detach yourself from the vampires instead of acceding to them. Another technique you can use when someone lays a bad vibe on you is to jump up and down and shake your arms and head to shake their bad vibes off of you. Also, resorting to nature spirits every day for an hour or so is the easiest and pleasantest way to intend your obsessive thoughts and moods instead of being slave to them.

All victims are willing victims. All victims are indulging themselves in self-pity: that's their payoff. To try to force other people to change is to do black magic to them. To expect or hope that other people will change is to make yourself a black magician's willing victim.

I, personally, have never met any real vampires face-to-face. However, I believe that they exist. This is partly because my spirit guides aver their existence, and partly because Carlos Castaneda also says they exist (See the *Death Defiers* chapter in Carlos Castaneda's *The Fire From Within*). Since everything in the Castaneda books that I've been able to confirm from my own experience has proven true, I'm willing to credit provisionally the points I haven't yet verified personally. Moreover, I can see the basic idea from my own experiences with black magic: from being sucked energetically by other people, and sucking them energetically in return. When you can see how people suck each other's energy in everyday life, the thing makes sense – it seems doable.

According to my guides and Castaneda, real vampires most certainly do exist. However the popular conception of them, such as Ann Rice's books, is way off base. Vampires are not sensitive, artistic, misunderstood beings who engage in soul-searching and wistfulness. They are total scumbags. They don't bite people in the neck. They just scare them to death and thereby absorb their power. They draw sustenance from their victims' fear. Vampires and black magicians don't kill people: they get people to kill themselves.

Black magic is basically the same thing that a torturer or sadist does. However, by getting a quick emotional charge out of his victim's fear, the torturer or sadist immediately wastes the energy he is drawing from his victim. To be a successful vampire, the black magician must not only repress all shame, as the torturer does, but also all feelings of satiation. The torturer or sadist hates his victim and thus dissipates the victim's fear energy with his hatred (actually he fears his victim, and the hatred is a cover of shamelessness to hide his fear).

A true vampire doesn't indulge in expressing any feelings whatsoever. To him, it's just a snack. Real vampires don't waste time or energy in ego-gloating. They step on people like most people step on bugs, without a thought. Their power comes from rigid control over their emotions: holding everything in. Vampires stifle all human feelings, all joy, compassion, and love. They give themselves wholly over to their own importance.

The next level down on the incompetence scale below the torturer or sadist is the everyday, garden variety son of a bitch whom we all know. The difference between the torturer or sadist and the common S.O.B. is that the S.O.B. uses his hatred to stoke his self-pity. Isn't it true that most S.O.B.'s think that they are the ones being imposed upon? This contrasts with the torturer or sadist who, like the vampire, is pitiless. Self-pity is a dangerous stand since it is a thin mask for shame.

If you're going to indulge in black magic, then you have to be completely shameless about it, as torturers and vampires are. That's the only way to win at the black magic game. You have to consciously acknowledging what you're doing; consciously choose evil and take responsibility for doing evil.

What common S.O.B.'s do is commit evil and pretend that they aren't doing it. Usually such people put on a mask of self-righteous justification, such as some thought form that they are "helping" the other person. Everyday S.O.B.'s repress shame instead of acknowledging and flaunting it. This is a losing set-up. To commit evil, to deliberately bend other people out of shape and not cop to what you're doing, only works so long as the victims accede to it. If the victims detach themselves from S.O.B.'s by deliberately ignoring them and their goads rather than reacting in fear or anger, then the S.O.B.'s are doomed. Shame will ultimately out.

So, how do you disentangle yourself from a black magician who's got you trapped and is vampirizing your energy, such as an abusive parent, spouse, teacher, boss; or, as happened to my friend, a bona fide witch? You have to stop thinking and caring about them. However, this is well-nigh impossible until you detach the light fibers they've stuck in you, through which they are sucking your energy. Having other people's lines in you is irritating and depletes your energy by making you think constantly about them. Detaching these lines of black magic through visualization is an easy way to begin the disentanglement process.

Pulling out lines is not difficult to do, but it is easiest if you are being directed by your spirit guides. Your guides will prop up your confidence as well as lead you step-by-step through the process

Complete instructions for pulling out the lines of black magicians are given in my book

As a stopgap, try this: take a firm stance, and imagine you are gripping with both hands a rope or cord stuck in your navel. This is the usual place where black magicians stick such lines in your body. If additionally you feel hypnotized by and unable to separate from the sexual relationship, then the person probably also stuck lines in your genitals. If there's a lot of hatred underlying the relationship, particularly accompanied by health or financial problems, then the person probably has lines in your head. You have to cast a little spell of banishment for each line the black magician has in your body.

Try to actually feel or imagine something like a rope in your hands which goes from the respective part of your body to the other person, through which they are sucking energy from you. You can look at a photograph of the person who is vampirizing you while you do this, or just visualize him or her standing there before you.

Then, with a movement of great repugnance, determination, and finality, jerk the line out of your body and cast it to the ground. You don't have to actually see the light fiber (though some sensitive people do) as long as you can feel it – i.e., imagine it is there.

If that person was really bringing you down, you should feel immediate relief and release after doing this exercise. Sometimes you don't even realize the extent to which they were bringing you down until you get their damn lines out of you. You should feel more youthful, since that's what black magicians vampirize: other people's youthfulness and joy. The next time you meet that person you'll be surprised by how different you feel about them, and by how much clearer your understanding of the dynamics of the relationship is. You'll have much more detachment and freedom from this person. It is by getting control over yourself, by being decisive rather than self-pitying, that you can take control of any relationship.

Demons

The information given in this book about demons, curses, and black magicians is not theoretical, armchair speculation. It's truth that I was forced to acknowledge at a certain point in my life when I found myself eyeball-to-eyeball with demons during an all-out battle with a black witch. I didn't believe in demons or curses before this experience even though I had been channeling spirit guides and nature spirits for some years prior. Therefore I certainly don't blame anyone else for not believing in these things. Unfortunately, they're true.

In our society the stigma attached to believing in demons is quite strong. Anyone who admits to believing in demons is considered crazy or stupid, or perhaps evil, and is no longer taken seriously. However, our society's view of this issue is incorrect. Becoming a magician requires facing up to this truth and dealing with it, not sweeping it under the rug. Magicians have to deal with how things really are and not worry about what other people might think or say about them. To our society, any discussion of demons is absurd. To a magician, the problem of demons is the most pressing issue facing the human race; and our addressing, or failing to address, this issue will decide our future, or lack of future, as a species (For another take on the issue of demons, see the *Mud Shadows* chapter of Carlos Castaneda's *The Active Side of Infinity*).

The trouble with all of the false stereotypes of black magic and demons in the popular media, particularly that these things don't exist, is that they prevent us from understanding what is really going on. As many fundamentalist Christians rightly believe, demons are everywhere. In fact, they run the whole shebang.

When we talk about demons, we're not talking about Transylvania: we're talking about trouble right here in River City. Demons are pretty much all over the place, and they run our society. The government, media, academia, churches (especially the churches!) – indeed, all of our precious institutions – are of the demons, by the demons, and for the demons. The movie The Matrix is actually a pretty good picture of what our society is really like, but with demons rather than machines behind the scenes pulling the strings. Like germs, demons are everywhere. Therefore, they are not something to be frightened of or worried about. In fact, the people who are the most freaked out by demons, such as Inquisitors and witch hunters, are usually the most demon-possessed themselves. Likewise, the people who are the most uptight about black magic are usually the ones who are doing the most black magic themselves. Most demon-possessed people, like most black magicians, consider themselves to be upstanding, righteous, pious citizens.

Demons are blandishing everybody – even those not specifically possessed – all the time. Most of your thoughts of how marvelous and wonderful you are; and how misunderstood you are; and how the people who don't appreciate you will be sorry some day; as well as most of your sexual and glory fantasies – not to mention angry and fearful thoughts – are just demons directing your thinking. Those kinds of thoughts aren't "your" thoughts at all. They are just thoughts which demons implant in your mind.

However many, if not most, of the people in our society – including practically all of our leaders in all areas – are out-and-out demon-possessed. That's how they got to be so successful (in what is basically a demonic society). Indeed, it's quite possible that you may be demon-possessed. I was possessed for the first 40 years of my life, until my spirit guides pointed that fact out to me and explained to me how to cast them out. It's no big deal, really, either to be possessed or to cast demons out. This will be explained later.

Here's a fictional example which illustrates how people unconsciously call demons in to possess them in moments of great self-pity, taken from John O'Hara's novel Appointment in Samarra. Notice how Julian English's wife calls in a demon of her own in response to Julian's demon:

"He did. What's the use of trying to fool myself? I know he did. I know he did and no matter what excuses I make or how much I try to tell myself that he didn't, I'll only come back to the same thing: He did. I know he did. And what for? For a dirty little thrill with a woman who – oh, I thought he'd got all that out of his system. Didn't he have enough of that before he married me? … Ah, Julian, you stupid, hateful, mean, low, contemptible little son of a bitch that I hate! You do this to me, and know that you do this to me! Know it! Did it on purpose! … You big charmer, you. You irresistible great big boy, turning on the charm like the water in the tub; turning on the charm like the water in the tub; turning on the charm turning on the charr-arm, turning on the charm like the water in the tub. I hope you die.

"I hope you die because you have killed something fine in me, suh. Ah hope you die. Yes-suh, Ah hope you die. You have killed something mighty fine in me, English, old boy, old kid, old boy. What Ah mean is, did you kill something fine in me or did you kill something fine."

This example is a good illustration of the way in which people call in demons to possess them when they feel especially vulnerable and in need of drastic protection. In most cases the appeal to demons is unconscious. Once demons are called in to possess a person, whether consciously or not, they don't leave unless they are deliberately exorcised.

What are demons like? They're like us humans, but are far more intelligent and cunning, and also sleazier. If you've ever met a psychopath face-to-face, then you know the type; but more so. Totally self-centered and sleazy. Demons are also really touchy, uptight, and self-important. They hate being ignored, and absolutely freak out at being laughed at. The demons which I have met face-to-face, in dreaming, appeared like normal people, but there was something very slimy about them. That is how I knew who they were.

Most of my encounters with demons were oblique. I could feel their presence because I would start getting angry for no reason. This is because I'm an angry person: a fearful person they would make fearful, a lustful person they would make lustful, and so on. Demons survive by generating and feeding off of your self-pity. They feed thoughts into your mind; then when you react by releasing a desire line in response, the demons snap them up. Demons are basically everywhere. For example, when you are driving and another driver cuts in right ahead of you and you beep the horn in anger, that's in fact an exchange between that guy's demons and your own.

Some psychopaths such as Adolf Hitler and Pol Pot got their dazzling, hypnotizing charm from the demons which possessed them. Other psychopaths like Joseph Stalin and Saddam Hussein were bestial thugs. What demons often give their hosts is an extraordinary cunning and a feel for the jugular. They sense precisely how far they can go and what they can get away with; and they have no scruples whatsoever about destroying anyone or anything that gets in their way.

Not all demon-possessed people become world leaders, of course, and not all are psychopathic. Many people who are depressed, repressed, angry and irritable all the time, constantly ill, addicted to drugs or sex or whatever, self-destructive generally, are possessed by demons. You can stand in a supermarket and watch the demon-possessed people go by: the harried mother pulling her kid in tow as she shops, yelling at the kid and yanking his arm out of its socket to drag him away from the things which normal curiosity leads him to explore; the old geezer with a perpetual scowl, pushing his shopping cart aggressively with an "out of my way, buddy!" expression on his face; the care-worn, overburdened, downtrodden people dragging themselves up and down the aisles.

It's not too hard to tell if people are demon-possessed when they get old. When they are still young, there's usually enough of the original person left there so that you can't see the demons as readily (except in certain revealing moments now and then). As the people get older, however, the demons eat up more and more of their souls and their joy. If, as people age, they get lighter and more joyous, then they're not demon-possessed. On the other hand if they get more uptight, nastier, depressed, or more self-pitying as they age, then they probably are demon-possessed. This is why it's so hard to deal with those old people – you're not dealing with the person anymore, just with a demon who subsists by sucking other people's energy (having burned out most of its host's energy).

Demons are not evil. They're doing what they have to do in order to eat, just like the rest of us. There is no evil per se in the universe. If you want to call the necessity of killing and devouring other beings in order to survive evil, then the one you've got to blame for this is the One who made that rule in the first place. That was not Satan. Demons have to eat just like everybody else. What demons eat is what we call feelings, especially uptight feelings. Demons survive by generating and feeding off of our self-pity. To demons, we humans are self-pity machines programmed by them to produce the most delectable demon delicacies with our constant moaning and groaning, and our thinking we're so great.

Demons are actually not that difficult to deal with – at least as compared with humans. Although they are incredibly intelligent and cunning, if you don't harbor evil intentions in your heart they won't bother you. Unlike humans, demons obey certain rules; they are consistent; they won't do anything against their own best interests. Humans, on the other hand, are grossly stupid, erratic, and self-destructive. Frankly, I much, much prefer to confront demons than to have to deal with humans.

What makes being a demon, or messing around with demons, evil is that there's no real joy or happiness in it. The way they feed themselves, and the way we feed ourselves under their influence, is uptight and ugly. It's a big rush of self-importance, and then lots of pain. Then another big rush of self-importance, and then lots of pain. It's a spiral of self-importance and pain. It's not very peaceful or pleasant. But it can't properly be characterized as evil per se. It's an extremely popular lifestyle for humans as well as demons. It's called society.

Prior to the invention of agriculture after the last ice age, about 12,000 years ago, humans were more or less like any other apes. They were more intelligent than most other animals, but not particularly smart. My guides have told me that if you could meet one of your ancestors from that period, you would consider it an animal. There's no level upon which we modern humans would consider those ancestors to be what we consider to be human.

It was an alliance that the human race forged with the race of demons during the Late Upper Paleolithic – early Neolithic era that made us modern humans the thinking, rational animals we are today. It was at that time that trapping, fishing, and hunting with dogs were invented – ensnaring game instead of hunting it directly. Then agriculture was invented – raising animals and plants instead of gathering them directly. Demons channeled new technologies to the human race through individuals who were inventors and innovators. They still do.

These indirect techniques for getting food necessitated a greater sense of planning for the future than direct hunting / gathering had required. The new social order demanded a new type of consciousness: perception and cognition tied to linear time. Planning for the future is what creates the future. Until the demons taught us about the future, all human beings had to work with was the now moment.

Linear time is the matrix of our separated, lower self. Our human ancestors, like infants, didn't have anywhere near as much sense of separatedness as we do. They were not as individuated as we are today. They lived in a more timeless frame of mind, a sense of belonging to the universe. Their mental process wasn't a matter of constant thinking, but rather of direct knowing what their ancestors, spirits, and the earth were telling them. They felt themselves to be part of an ongoing, natural process in the same way that we feel ourselves to be part of our society. Because they were not as separated as people are today, they felt less Angst than we do, because they had no future to worry about.

If the future didn't exist, would you care about it? It's precisely your caring and worrying about the future that conjures up its existence. You care about the future, it's important to you, because you fantasize that there's glory for you somewhere in your future. You fantasize that someday you will win the lottery, or find your true soul-mate, or become famous, or go to heaven when you die. These sorts of expectations are what trap you into striving towards a future which never arrives. The other side of that coin is your past, the things that you are ashamed of and are trying to forget about (and would never reveal to another person). Everyone in our society is taught to hate themselves, and then to hide that self-hatred away. This striving towards a future and slinking away from a past is what creates the illusion that there is such a thing as a future and a past. When striving ends, so too does linear time. Another way of saying this is: our sense of linear time is the product of our linear thinking. If we stop thinking so much about the future and past and return our attention to the now moment, like ancient humans and infants did, then the past and future lose much of their meaning. They are just not as important, so they are not as there; things are too now.

Our higher selves are timeless. Higher self is eternal: it is your touch with the Spirit. Higher self has to be squelched down into the straitjacket of linear time in order to create your uptight, niggling little lower self. We humans learned how to create a sense of linear time – a separated, lower self which is caught in a loop of constant self-reflection; of seeking glory in the future and hiding shame from the past – from our demon masters. Over the past millennia the demons have taught us everything that we modern humans now consider "human". That is to say, our civilization – all of our thinking – is demonic in origin. The qualities that we modern humans believe elevate us above the realm of animals are essentially demonic qualities. Demons taught us humans how to think because thinking requires concentrated effort. This effort, or being uptight – hiding shame from the past and seeking glory in the future – allows demons to suck human energy.

This is why adults are usually more uptight than little children, who aren't yet in a mode of constant thinking. Adults are completely accustomed to thinking every second all day long. We don't realize how much we have to squelch ourselves and our true feelings down in order to maintain this inner dialogue. This constant thinking, particularly when it's worried, or angry, or jealous thinking, provides fodder for the demons who surround us.

In other words, the invention of agriculture wasn't so much a matter of humans beginning to farm plants and animals for food as it was demons beginning to farm humans for food. Now, after millennia of inbreeding us, the demons have us right where they want us. Earlier generations of humans were hardy, robust, and self-reliant, which is hard fare for demons to digest. We moderns with our undisciplined, self-indulgent, materialistic, decadent lifestyles have become a toothsome delight for the demons who suck us. We are fat and complacent, with no minds or wills of our own. We eagerly and unquestioningly believe all the lies our government, church, media, and "science" tell us. This makes us easy to herd around and lead to the slaughter.

Our demon masters, who were overjoyed when humans invented agriculture and became a semblance of them, are presently ecstatic that humans have adopted an urban society wholly disconnected from nature. We are turning the green, loving earth into a hell world. At least, when most humans were doing agriculture, they were still attached to the earth's love and the rhythms of the universe. Now, urban society has cut humans off completely from the earth's love. When does anyone even look at a tree anymore except through a speeding windshield or a television screen? And the food – the Soylent green – which people today eat from supermarkets … Welcome to hell, folks! You don't have to wait until you die. Hell is right here, right now. The worst part of it is that most people have been trained to call this heaven. And the demons are eating it up. Eating us up.

There was nothing wrong with us humans having associated ourselves with demons for the past few millennia. We learned a lot from them. We learned how to think, for starters. Now it's time we humans went our own way and followed our own star, because continuing to serve our demon masters will just lead to our own destruction as a species. When humans allied themselves with demons they made some sort of very unpleasant denouement inevitable; and it is our generation and our kids' generation which will have to pay the piper, and see what can be salvaged from the rubble. A magician must remain undaunted even when single-handedly confronting all of the demons in the universe. Because you are.

I've cast demons out of people and also out of buildings they were inhabiting. I don't like doing this, though, because it scares me. When the demons are cut loose they dive into the nearest host they can grab onto. The time I cast demons out of a building where black magicians had lived previously, I followed my spirits' advice and lit a censer with copal incense. Then I circled the building repeating an appeal to the demons to leave: "You are not wanted here anymore, you'll be a lot happier in another place where you are more appreciated. In the name of the nine Mayan gods (my patron spirits) I cast you out!" I tried to muster confidence which I didn't actually feel for the "I cast you out!" part. Then at each corner of the building I set off a chain of firecrackers, since demons have highly refined sensibilities and dislike clamor. After the firecrackers went off at the first corner I could sense something coming loose. By the last corner I sensed they were completely loose.

I then left, but as I walked away I started talking nervously to my assistant about the ritual we had just performed, "Hey, that really worked, didn't it?" At that instant I sensed something diving into me, which really freaked me out. I started jumping up and down to shake whatever it was out of me, and at the same time I forced myself to think about something else, to blank my mind. Ever since then I try to avoid casting out demons. When it is absolutely unavoidable I do it in a place where I am protected, a nearby cave which is a Mayan holy place. I certainly don't advise casting demons out of other people unless you've got spirit helpers in whom you have the utmost faith, such as Jesus, Krishna, or Buddha, backing you up.

I'm of the opinion that people should cast out their own demons. They called them in, and they should take the responsibility for casting them out themselves. The exception to this would be in the cases of children or people who are too crazy to do it for themselves.

Sometimes people ask me, "I think my parent (or spouse or loved one) might be demon-possessed. Is there anything I can do to cast it out?" My usual answer is negative. Demons won't leave if the host doesn't want them to leave, or they'll immediately return if cast out. In our society most people don't even believe in the existence of demons, much less seriously entertain the possibility that they themselves could be possessed. Demon-possessed people are always right and the other fellow is always wrong. Moreover, most people, especially old people, have become comfortable with their demons. They're afraid to have to start living their own lives and making their own decisions again. It's easier just to be uptight and miserable and wallow in self-pity. Bit-by-bit they surrender all their joy to their demons, until in the end the demons are all that's left.

I once counseled a friend of mine who was in an extremely dysfunctional marriage, "I think you're demon-possessed. Even though I know you don't believe in demons, just for the hell of it why don't you go to the holy Mayan cave, light a candle, and ask the spirit of the place 'If, on the off chance, I am indeed possessed by demons, please cast them out.'" She did this and reported later that the moment she said those words her candle flickered even though there was no wind, and a pain – like an ice pick – shot through her head. What happened next in her life was that she split up with her husband. My interpretation of this is that without the demon's protection she was too vulnerable to handle the Punch and Judy show she was involved in, so she terminated the relationship. In other words, just casting out demons that may be possessing you doesn't automatically make you any happier. It just makes it possible for you to become happier. But there's no way to get even to square one until you clear the demons out of the way.

Luckily it's pretty easy to cast demons out of yourself. All that's required is the desire to do so, and the firm decision to get rid of them. If you are suffering from a chronic or incurable disease, or are battling against some form of addiction, then casting out demons is the first step in self-healing. It's the first step in self-healing for most of us, since so many of us are demon-possessed. Until you get rid of any demons that may be possessing you and reassert control over your own intent, all your spiritual endeavors are just whistling in the wind. Complete instructions on how to cast out demons are given in my book Thought Forms. To summarize:

To cast out demons, go to whatever place you are accustomed to pray at. Power spots or power trees are good places to do this, especially if you have faith in the power of the place or tree to brace your spirit. Light a candle and ask the deity to whom you usually pray that, if there happens to be a maleficent influence in your life, to please cast it out! You must make this prayer in a true spirit of decisiveness and determination. If you pray in a spirit of doubt or hesitation, the demon will use your vacillation to defeat your prayer. Mars planetary hours are good hours to take decisive, irrevocable action; to stand up for yourself; but this is merely a help, not a necessity.

Demons are always trying to convince you that you are doing everything possible to make yourself happy. All the while they undermine your efforts. A wishy-washy prayer to cast out a demon may make you believe that you've accomplished something, but the demon will weasel past it. Thus demons have to be cast out in a mood of unbending intent and decision. That's all that's required – unbending intent to cast the demon out. Jumping up and down and shaking your body vigorously is another way to cast them out. This is also a good way to get rid of bad moods or the bad vibes other people lay on you as well.

How will you know whether your exorcism worked? Successful exorcisms are often accompanied by sensations of something that was inside you leaving. There may be some kind of whoosh of something flying out of you and away. But this isn't always true. One way you'll know is that in the next few days you'll feel lighter, more hopeful and optimistic. Your friends will notice the difference too: they'll remark on how much better you look or feel.

If there's any doubt, though, you can always repeat the exorcism. Just make sure to do it in a mood of decisiveness and determination. That's all, it's not difficult. And, don't worry too much about this whole demon thing. If you are pure of heart, they won't bother you any.

Paganism:

Earth Magic

The salient feature of magical training is learning to use the world around us for validation, rather than the devices of people; to come to appreciate more the gurgling of water in a stream, the whisper of the wind in our ears, and the healing warmth of a tree, rather than the approval of people. All of our unhappiness in life stems from our trying to live up to the expectations of people, and our having forgotten what ancient humans knew: that we are first and foremost children of the earth, and that she loves us from the bottom of her heart.

The earth isn't insensible, as we've been led to believe. She is vibrantly alive. She can heal us, soothe us, and provide us with a sense of complete and unconditional acceptance. She can nurture and protect us even more than our human mothers could possibly do. We don't have to feel at odds with the world, like alien interlopers in a hostile environment. The earth is just busting to cuddle us with her love, if we would only make an effort to reach out to her.

We do this simply by 1) acknowledging that she is alive, sentient, and capable of communicating with us; and 2) acknowledging daily our debt to her and thanking her for all her gifts. Try doing the following earth ritual every day: dawn or sunset are the best times, but do it whenever you conveniently can. Go out to a place in nature (if possible), take off all your clothes (if possible), and prostrate yourself face down with arms outstretched above your head pointing in the direction of the sun. Begin to breathe out (exhale hard) all your angry, frustrated, depressed, negative feelings into the earth to be buried, and inhale the healing, soothing energy of the earth. Feel it fill your body with warmth on the inbreaths as the negative energy dissipates on the outbreaths. Then, when you are calm, kiss the earth and thank her, knowing that from the earth you have come, and to the earth you shall return.

Even if you don't feel anything out of the ordinary while doing this exercise, keep plugging away at it, and at some point you will realize that the earth is "talking" to you. Some naturally talented people pick up the thread the first time out; however, most people have to do it on faith for a while until the establish a clear telepathic / intuitive communications link with the earth. At that point the earth herself will give you instructions and tell you what to do; you'll just "know" it. For example, one thing she might have you do is to gaze at her. This is accomplished by slightly crossing your eyes but keeping them relaxed; calming down your thoughts; and staring without focusing at whatever feature in your field of vision most attracts your attention. The earth can give you all sorts of information in this way. If you do the earth ritual at dawn, try gazing at the vapors which rise from the earth in the early morning, since these are full of messages.

Everybody's experiences with the earth ritual are different, so about all that can definitively be said on the subject is, be prepared for some surprises! If you carry this ritual out in good faith and with the expectation of ultimate success, then in a few weeks or months you'll get it working as described. The only trick to making magic work is patience – long continuance of the same ritual act (repetition of the same desire).

Another ritual which can be used in conjunction with or apart from the daily earth ritual is the burial ritual. You use this one whenever you are especially burdened, ill, careworn, or depressed. The earth has an infinite capacity not only to heal but also to absorb and dissipate negative energy, and every sort of spiritual and emotional heaviness as well as chronic illness.

It helps to fast the day before this ritual. Dig a trench two feet deep and somewhat longer than your body. Line the trench with sawdust or leaves so you will have a soft bed and pillow to lie on, and make sure your face will be shaded from the sun. Disrobe and wrap yourself in a sheet with only your face exposed (the sheet serves as a protection against e.g. ants). You can smear insect repellant on your face, neck, and hair to keep bugs away. Then lie down in the trench, get comfortable, and have someone cover you with a layer of earth up to your neck with your head sticking out. Have someone visit you every hour or two in case you need a drink and to make sure you're okay. If you have to pee, just do it.

If you are very sick or in desperate need of lightening up, you should remain buried for 12 hours (dawn to dusk) the first time you bury yourself, and for at least 6 hours on subsequent burials (8 is better). Average people only need four hour burials to tune themselves (there's not much point in doing it for less than four hours at a stretch). How long and how frequently you bury yourself depend on how sick or heavy you were to begin with: you come to "know" when it's time to bury yourself again.

Although this ritual may seem to be an odd thing to do, you might just find that being buried is one of the most enjoyable experiences you've ever had. The earth herself is your hostess, and she will do her best to comfort, nourish, and entertain you.

Another way of making intimate contact with the earth is to walk around barefoot as much as possible. If you live in a place where you can't walk around barefoot, maybe it would be worthwhile to move to a place where you can – it is that important. Wearing shoes cuts off most of the healing energy and sense of rootedness which the earth would otherwise give us through our feet.

These rituals aren't immutable – you can alter them at will to suit your own taste and convenience. What is important is your seriousness of purpose, the strength of your desire to communicate with the earth, and your willingness to pursue this intent in a deliberate fashion – to make it one of the high priorities in your life. Then your success is assured: you will find a true sense of worth and belonging in the world which doesn't depend on what other people think of you.

Spiritual Cookery

I then asked (Dr. Steiner), "How can it happen that the spiritual impulse, and especially the inner schooling, for which you are constantly providing stimulus and guidance bear so little fruit? Why do the people concerned give so little evidence of spiritual experience, in spite of all their efforts? Why, worst of all, is the will for action, for the carrying out of these spiritual impulses, so weak?"

Then came the thought-provoking and surprising answer: "This is a problem of nutrition. Nutrition as it is today does not supply the strength necessary for manifesting the spirit in physical life. A bridge can no longer be built from thinking to will and action."

— Ehrenfried Pfeiffer, from the introduction to *Agriculture – Eight Lectures by Rudolf Steiner*

We all know that "you are what you eat"; and many of us are becoming aware that this maxim has a spiritual as well as a physical dimension. We know we simply feel better when we eat well – when our bodies, rather than our minds, dictate what we should eat or not eat. Many of us have experienced a complete change in attitude and outlook on life by simply changing our diets. Whole bodies of thought, such as the Jewish kosher laws and macrobiotics, have evolved to stress the spirituality of food, to emphasize its sacredness.

The "spiritual quality of food" is not a metaphor: food contains a light fiber energy which is as important to our sustenance as vitamins and proteins, but which is not susceptible to chemical analysis. And just as the vitamin and protein content of food can be diminished by processing or overcooking, so too can the light fiber content of food be diminished by disrespect.

Light fibers are actually the same things as good feelings. When we feel good, we literally glow. When a food plant or animal feels good, it glows. Even when it is killed for food, the glow remains as long as the killing was done with respect; that is, with a sense of connectedness and gratitude rather than mechanically.

A farmer puts the glow into his plants and animals by treating them with respect – by respecting their feelings. Practically all farmers farm for the love it; they sure don't do it for the money. They feel joyous as they ride their tractors up and down their fields, and that good feeling is communicated to the soil and plants. Similarly, most dairy farmers not only address their cows as individuals, but they also develop quirky personal relationships with them. Therefore, from a light fiber point of view, our vegetable and milk supplies are still relatively safe. Most egg farms, on the other hand, are run like Auschwitz, and that's what makes eggs poisonous to eat (not their cholesterol).

Not all cultures have been so cut off from their true feelings about food as ours is today. Many Native American tribes had a deep awareness that they were a part of what they ate – e.g., the buffalo. They lived with the buffalo, followed the buffalo, prayed to the buffalo. They were one with the buffalo, and thus to them eating was a sacrament. Modern Native Americans maintain that same attitude of reverence towards maize.

But in America today we mine food, extract the nutrients out of it, strip it, rape it, and throw it away. What little nourishment for the spirit is left in food by modern agricultural and processing methods is completely destroyed by the way we eat it. We use food in a most disrespectful manner – stuffing it in gluttonously whether we are hungry or not, whether it tastes good or not, whether we really want it or not; and then we waste food as if to piss on it. Like sex, we have turned eating from a joyous, spiritual act into a source of great shame.

An infant doesn't conceive of his food or his mother as something separate from himself; he doesn't feel more important than his food, and therefore doesn't feel disconnected from it. When an infant eats, he mingles with his food: he touches it, gets to know how it feels. It's pretty, it satisfies his hunger, it makes him happy. But when an infant first sees adults eat, it makes him feel shame. This is because we adults don't identify with our food – it's as if our food is not a part of us, as if what we are putting into our mouths is something foreign to ourselves. We attack our food as if it is separate from us, and it is the act of eating which allows us to use it. We bite it off in huge mouthfuls like ravenous hyenas, chew it and swallow it with gulps of contempt. We come together in great rituals like Thanksgiving and Christmas in which we engage in orgies of gluttony and wastefulness to jointly validate our shame, all the while calling it glory. And that lie makes us even more ashamed; so we lie about that one too, and call it glory. And so on. And nobody will look at what they are really feeling, because if being pigs has brought us glory, why look at what pigs we are?

The reason why saints can survive on so little food is because they're not attacking it, squeezing the life out of it, so it takes very little to sustain them. The Native Americans are able to survive on a diet of pretty much nothing but corn because they love the corn, and the corn loves them back, and they're able to live from that love even though from the point of view of nutrition they should slowly starve to death.

While it is true that the original light fiber energy in food can be vitiated by disrespect anywhere along the line – in handling, processing, cooking, or eating – it is also true that light fiber energy, being more flexible than vitamins or proteins, can be restored to food by respecting it and treating it as sacred – by ritualizing the activities connected with it.

First of all, it's important that you should raise at least some of your own food, even if all this means is a couple of pots of herbs or jars of sprouts grown on a window shelf. Try to throw in at least a pinch of home-grown herbs or sprouts into every meal you cook (not necessarily every dish, but every meal). Visualize yourself casting fibers of light into the food as you add your home-grown herbs or produce.

Next, bless your key, staple ingredients – salt, flour, sugar, honey, etc. You can ask any spirit helpers you are presently using to do this for you: Jesus or Mary, Krishna, nature spirits, etc. can all do the job for you. Just take them a pound of sugar, salt, or flour; address them in whatever form you are accustomed to; and ask them to please bless your ingredients. If you don't have a spirit helper, just take the ingredients to the summit of the largest or most imposing mountain or hill in your immediate area; take the mountain spirit a token portion of something special you have cooked yourself as an offering; and ask him or her to please bless your ingredients. Don't worry about whether you are doing it right: if you are doing it in good faith, you're doing it right.

Keep your sacred, blessed ingredients apart from the regular ones, but whenever you refill the sugar bowl, salt shaker, flour bin, etc. add a pinch of the blessed ingredient, and imagine that you are putting light fibers in with the pinch.

Observe that you must never be in a bad mood when you cook, nor must you eat food cooked by someone who is in a bad mood, or even an indifferent one. A burger from a McDonald's where the employees are a light, happy bunch has more light fiber energy than a plate of organic brown rice from a vegetarian restaurant where the cook is bored or is angry at the manager.

You can easily tell when food has bad vibes. It's not that it tastes bad per se; rather, it feels wrong or out of place in your mouth – there's no incentive to chew it and swallow it. Whenever you get a feeling like this about something you are eating, spit it out. Don't swallow it, even to be polite. Much processed, convenience food "tastes" like this – bland, insipid, effete, enervated – but people get so used to this kind of food that they can't tell the difference any more. They just assume that feeling lousy all the time is how you're supposed to feel, and they cease to notice that it is their food which is bringing them down.

Finally, talk to your food. Thank it as if it were alive and could understand you. Not long conversation, just a simple acknowledgment that you are aware of being in the presence of a sentient being who is worthy of your respect, who died for you, and from whom you wish a favor. You wouldn't ask a human being for a favor in a surly, disrespectful manner; on the contrary, you would ask humbly and respectfully, and feel gratitude for the favor when granted. And that is how you must address your food: take small bites, chew it slowly and mindfully, eat in silence paying attention to the act of eating, and never eat until full.

What We Can Learn From Plants

This young woman knew that she would die in the next few days. But when I talked to her she was cheerful in spite of this knowledge. "I am grateful that fate has hit me so hard," she told me. "In my former life I was spoiled and did not take spiritual accomplishments seriously." Pointing through the window of the hut, she said, "This tree here is the only friend I have in my loneliness." Through that window she could see just one branch of a chestnut tree, and on the branch were two blossoms. "I often talk to this tree," she said to me. I was startled and didn't quite know how to take her words. Was she delirious? Did she have occasional hallucinations? Anxiously I asked her if the tree replied. "Yes." What did it say to her? She answered, "It said to me, 'I am here – I am here – I am Life, eternal life.'"

- Viktor Frankl, *Man's Search for Meaning*

What we can learn from plants is how to be joyous. We can't learn that from other people, usually, because the setup with other people isn't to be joyous; on the contrary, it is to be fearful, close-hearted, and uptight. Therefore, to learn to be joyous, we have to go to the plants. If we can first learn to be joyous from the plants – who aren't out to cause us grief – we can then learn to be joyous with our fellow humans.

Of course, the joy we receive from plants doesn't have all the ego zing of a sexy partner, or a mother's approval, or the boss's congratulations; but it's always there. That's the nice thing. No matter how horribly our lives are going, or how much rejection other people heap upon us, the plants are always there being happy.

At a nearby airport there is a hedge in front of the entrance for departing passengers, and when the wind blows across the hedge the shrubs wave "Bye-bye! Bon Voyage! Feliz Viaje!" to all the passengers. Nobody pays any attention to them, but the plants don't care. They don't need people's acknowledgment and validation to be happy. They're just there, pouring love out into the world. That's their job, and the people passing by receive that love whether they're consciously aware of it or not.

The plants are what keep this from being a hell world. There are no plants in a hell world. The plants in this world are not just the bottom of the food chain; they're anchoring all of us uptight animals to the earth's love. They aren't just the source of all our oxygen; they're the source of all our joy. They just sit there casting joy out all over the place.

What we can learn from plants is that there is love surrounding us all the time, every minute, had we but the wit to see it, feel it. We are being offered love all the time, but we reject it because we don't understand that's what love is. We think love should be zappier, instead of quiet and peaceful and waving in the wind.

The love which plants offer us – the sound of leaves rustling, the smell of pine needles – is all there is. This is not a poetic metaphor: it's a cold, hard fact of life. If we want / need / desire something to make us happy beyond what the plants offer us, then we're just out of luck, because that's all there is. If we can't find happiness in what's going on outside our windows right this minute, then we're just out of luck.

To tune into plants is quite simple. First of all, you must have the conviction that there is indeed something you can learn from plants. You can't go in there with the attitude that you're better, smarter, or superior to a plant. We're all taught that we're superior to plants, just as we're taught that we're superior to other people. And just as we don't pay much attention to the people we think we're superior to, we can't tune into the feelings of plants if we think we're superior to them. It isn't hard to overcome this prejudice if we just bear in mind that in the only thing that really matters in life – being joyous unto one's self – plants have it all over us humans.

Go to the plants every single day, for at least fifteen minutes or half an hour. Go sit out under a tree – perhaps during lunch break. It's better to make such a space for yourself during the day, as a break from the buzz-buzz, but do it at night if you can't find time during the day. But go every day, preferably alone, without fail. Make it the most important item on your agenda – that this brief time you take for yourself with the plants is inviolable. If you make such a firm decision – that being joyous is an unalterable priority in your life – then the joy itself will follow naturally.

No specific instructions are needed on where you should go or what you should do there. If there's some specific tree or woods or meadow that calls your attention, then go there. If not, just go where you feel like going, or where you conveniently can go. Get away from people, if possible, and do what you feel like doing. There is no particular procedure, and you should have no particular expectations. Maybe the plants will start talking to you; if you ask them to nicely, they will. If not, you may never feel anything out of the ordinary except for a subtle feeling of relaxation, a general lightening up of your entire life, as time goes on.

What the plants are offering us is true love, if we take the trouble to avail ourselves of it. They will give it to us whether we feel what they are doing to us or not, whether we are consciously aware of it or not. So don't worry if you can't seem to feel with the plants in the beginning. All you have to do is to make a firm commitment to put yourself under their tutelage, and they will find a way to do the rest.

Be assured that the plants are actually acting on you. It takes a while to pick up the thread of what they're doing to you, but after a while you find they can calm you down and soothe you, no matter what kind of frenzy is going on in your world of people.

In other words, the interactions we have with plants are of a different order than the interactions we have going on with people. We interact with plants on an intuitive level, a feeling level; whereas we interact with other people on a thought form level (of images, expectations, defenses, competition, etc.). Most of us have forgotten how to relate on a feeling level, but the plants themselves will teach us how to do this if we make a serious effort to learn, in a day-by-day fashion.

You can't expect immediate results, but surely after six or eight months of going to the plants every day you should at least be beginning to understand what the plants are doing to you. When you get to the place where your hiatus with the plants is the high point of your daily routine – the part of your day which you most eagerly anticipate – then you can be said to have arrived: to understand what we can learn from plants.

Astrology:

Intuition in Astrology

Astrology is not just an intellectual enterprise (although it does depend on concepts); rather, it is a training ground for intuition, or what one might call "direct knowing". This is why a beginning astrologer with psychic ability will generally give more correct information to a client than a non-psychic astrologer who has been studying the subject for a lifetime. Although the study of astrology does require much left-brain activity (learning what different symbols and combinations of symbols mean), true comprehension and application of astrology is more a matter of opening up our intuitive channels, of letting go of our ego defenses, intellectual belief systems, and doubts, and of learning to respect and respond to our gut feelings.

This was easier to do for astrologers in centuries past than it is now, because the trend in our modern society has been toward rationalistic and materialistic solutions to problems. We are taught to rely upon so-called objective thinking, and to distrust our own feelings, which cannot be corroborated and therefore leave us standing alone. Indeed, the modern trend in astrology has been to move away from intuition.

One trend in this direction is represented by humanistic astrology, which eschews prediction and opts instead for a Gestalt approach, relying upon psychological mumbo-jumbo instead of telling people what's really happening, and probably going to happen, in their lives. Humanistic astrology has something of a sour grapes flavor to it; beyond that, it can do a disservice to clients who are not (usually) as interested in a holistic analysis of their human potential as they are in solid information about their love lives, finances, health, etc.

Another trend has been towards rationalistic astrology, which seeks to recast astrology in terms which would be acceptable to mainstream science. Astrologers of this school try to find statistical proof for the verities of astrology, which – as Michel Gauquelin after a lifetime of effort has shown – is impossible except for the tiniest little bits here and there. These astrologers attempt to remove from astrology anything that smacks of superstition or mysticism. Thus most astrologers of the rationalistic school reject the use of "unscientific" signs and houses, even though there is no more statistical proof of the validity of midpoints than there is for signs and houses. In their toadying to the scientific establishment (which rejects them anyway, as it rejected Gauquelin) rationalistic astrologers risk being led into intellectual dishonesty.

Such trends notwithstanding, astrology is still one of the last strongholds of spiritual truth in our society. Most of what we do nowadays is done on the basis of logic, conditioning, immutable schedules, what other people expect from us or would approve of, rather than on the basis of what feels right. In other words, we do what we think we ought to do instead of doing what our hearts tell us to do. And while this is a viable strategy for success in rationalist-materialist society, you can't do astrology this way.

To be an intuitive astrologer, it helps to have the sign Aquarius emphasized in your natal horoscope. But even if you're not a "natural", it is still possible to emulate those Aquarian qualities which facilitate relating to other people on an intuitive level: democracy, seeing other people as your equals, being willing to relate to people from all walks of life and stations of society without shame, superiority, or false humility. If you are not capable of seeing others as your equals, then you are defending yourself against them; and whatever you are doing to defend yourself against them will prevent you from psychically attuning yourself to them.

To get your intuition flowing you must be willing to fly with your hunches. If it's important to you that you always be right, then you'll never make it as an intuitive astrologer. The channel through which insight flows is blocked by the door of worrying about whether you're right or wrong. Only the courage to be wrong can open you enough to feel what's going on, what the real needs of the client are, and what his or her chart is trying to tell you. Once you're no longer afraid of looking foolish, you just say the first thing that pops into your mind.

Everyone who visits an astrologer does so because some question is weighing on them. Even when they claim to be consulting you out of mere curiosity, in truth there is some problem bugging them, or else they wouldn't have come to you. It's your job as an astrologer to elicit and address their problem. This is not done by questioning them, but by examining their horoscopes and by staying open to their feelings; and this can be done even when the clients are not physically present.

In everyday life we tend to block the feelings which other people send our way. We're usually more concerned with maintaining our own self-image, with impressing people, with winning their sympathy, than we are with listening to them and understanding where they are coming from. When interpreting charts it is necessary to put aside your own attitudes and prejudices and see the clients and their problems from their own point of view, without and judgments or criticism. You have to go into an interpretation without a point of view of your own.

One good way of doing this is to begin every horoscope interpretation with an invocation. You do this silently: take a moment to ask for divine guidance in helping your clients to find the answers they are seeking. If you are a Christian you can call upon Jesus for this help; if not, you can call upon the spirit guardians of astrological wisdom to guide you to the correct judgments. The point is that by beginning your interpretation session with a prayer you wipe the ego slate clean by the symbolic act of surrendering your own will (desire to look good) and letting the powers of the universe take over.

The best training ground for intuitive astrologers is horary astrology. In horary you use little pieces of the chart (the planets and houses which govern the particular question being asked) and ignore everything else, which helps to focus your attention. One thing that tends to overwhelm neophyte astrologers is the sheer mountain of information in a birth chart, since they have not yet learned what to focus on and what to ignore. Beyond that, a horary horoscope is completely centered in the now moment, is less encumbered by personal history (yours or the clients') and is usually prompted by a strong desire for an answer; which makes it easier to tune into than a natal chart, where there are all sorts of themes and crosscurrents of emotion going on which have to be sorted out.

The flux of the universe is constant – and movement is extremely fast. What was a correct prediction a moment ago may not be valid now. A horary chart erected tomorrow may give a completely different message than one erected to answer the same question today. This is why it's best, when you are using horary astrology for your own guidance, not to go to the oracle on your own, but rather to wait until some outside event happens (which bears on the question) and to erect the horary chart for the moment of that event. Such charts are always readable, even if they contain strictures – such as a void-of-course moon – which normally defeat interpretation (in such cases the answer is usually "no" or "not yet".)

Another reason why horary astrology is a better training ground for intuition than natal astrology is because it's more symbolic, less rational. A typical horary textbook consists of a quick set of rules designed to suggest answers, and then long lists of symbols for each horoscope factor. For example, a list (Simmonite's) of places ruled by Saturn might read: "deserts, woods, obscure valleys, … dens, … church yards, ruinous buildings, … sinks, wells, muddy, dirty, stinking places." When you've memorized – or better yet, gotten a feel for – what each symbol means (in this case, Saturn-type places), you find that in the moment of interpretation one particular item pops into your mind. You don't have to rack your brains to figure out the correct interpretation from the smorgasbord of possibilities; if you know what the symbol means (how it feels), then you'll always be led to the correct interpretation of that symbol in this instance.

Thus, horary astrology is more of a "symbol bank" than natal astrology: there's less of an intellectual system to it, and what system there is, is more abstract (such as the ring-around-the-rosy technique for locating questions in houses; e.g., the father's brother's income being shown by the second from the third from the fourth = the seventh house).

Horary astrology is more like dreaming, where natal astrology is more like being awake. Things are more symbolical in horary, hence closer to true feeling (what's really going on). Just as we can learn more about our true state of feeling – what's really making us happy or unhappy – by studying our dreams, rather than by constantly examining and re-examining our waking lives, so too can we get sharper, clearer answers from horary astrology than from natal. Indeed, natal astrology becomes increasingly effective as we are able to integrate horary techniques into it.

The other day I was interpreting the chart of a young man who is leaving the service, and trying to decide what he should do next. He had Mercury in Pisces opposing (and mutual reception) Jupiter in Virgo across the 9th – 3rd house axis. I got a strong impression that he should study and go for a professional degree in some humanistic field. He asked if he should study in his native Puerto Rico or go abroad, to the States; I got the impression that he should go abroad – further abroad than the U.S. The word "France" popped into my mind, which made him chuckle when I told him because he doesn't speak French, doesn't have money to travel, and the whole idea seemed off the wall to him. Nonetheless I suggested that he look into it, to see what opportunities to study in France are available.

And that's that. That was my job as an astrologer. It doesn't matter if he never goes to France; it doesn't even matter if he's crossing the street tomorrow and gets run over by a truck. Whether my prediction is right or not has nothing to do with how well I did my job as an astrologer. There is a Zen story about the most celebrated archer in all of Japan, who has never once succeeded in hitting the bulls-eye. In astrology, as in Zen archery, the concern has to be for the process, not for the result. Because of a mysterious law of nature, that's the only way to get good results.

Now the prediction about going to France obviously has nothing to do with the horoscope feature which prompted that prediction. Neither Mercury, nor Pisces, nor Jupiter, nor Virgo, nor their combination, specifically carry the meaning "France". How "France" came out of that, I don't know. In someone else's chart that identical planetary configuration might have an altogether different meaning. And at another point in my client's life, when some other problem is bothering him, that same configuration might have a different interpretation also. Horoscope factors only mean something with respect to a particular client at a particular moment in time. Although we learn astrology inductively – we learn what, for example, Mars square Saturn means by studying the lives and characters of the natives we know who have Mars square Saturn – we cannot interpret charts inductively.

This is why most statistical studies of astrology are doomed to failure. Astrology is a wavelength we can tune into, not a dead specimen we can dissect and expect to learn anything from. We can learn to feel what Mars square Saturn means by studying its effects in a hundred cases; but we cannot arrive at a correct interpretation in the hundred-and-first case by extrapolating from a preconceived list of concepts or likely possibilities. There are just too many possibilities.

Nor can we gain anything by adding more and more points to the horoscope (hypothetical planets, midpoints, asteroids, etc.); all that does is muddy the waters. As Dr. Marc Edmund Jones pointed out, astrology should not be more complex than life itself. Rather, astrology should be a means of simplifying, of cutting across complexities and arriving at clear-cut answers. And this can only be done by bypassing the level of conscious, thinking mind.

We need to study what Mars square Saturn has meant in order to tune in to a certain feeling – the feeling of Mars square Saturn. Then when we run into a chart containing Mars square Saturn, we pick up this feeling and let it lead us to the correct interpretation. We do need a grounding in the basics – an intuitive feel for what the different horoscope factors symbolize – and this implies study. There are intuitive astrologers who can come up with the correct interpretation just by touching a chart (without even looking at it); but most of us are not blessed with such extraordinary ESP. Nonetheless, we can each develop our intuition by studying what all the different horoscope elements mean (how they each feel). The study of astrology itself serves to open our intuitive channels.

To be an intuitive astrologer requires humility. This doesn't mean false humility: not taking complete responsibility for what you're doing. It means not going into an interpretation with preconceived ideas, points to defend, a know-it-all attitude. Being an astrologer, even a beginning one, means that people are going to believe what you say. This is a big responsibility. There is a natural tendency to cop out of this responsibility by being either overly serious (playing the mountebank) or not serious enough (playing the dilettante). To be humble means to respect the client, to respect yourself as an astrologer, and to respect the craft of astrology. You have to go into each interpretation as if it were the first one you have ever done, and yet with the confidence that you will be guided to the correct interpretation. Then it all just happens by itself.

The Sunshine House System

Most of us astrologers have at one time or another wondered why astrology doesn't work as well as it's supposed to. Although adamant in defense of astrology when confronted by skeptics, we nonetheless agonize in our innermost souls as to whether the ancient astrologers were lying, or whether astrology just doesn't function as well in this decadent age; or whether -– horror of horrors! – we may just be fooling ourselves.

No, no, it can't be that. After all, that prediction we made about cousin Tillie's boyfriend was right on the button! So why then, if astrology does work so well sometimes, do we find it so hard to make it work consistently? Where does the fault lie, dear Brutus – with astrology, or with ourselves?

Actually, the problem is not with astrology per se, but with how we modern, western astrologers have been practicing it (or better said: conceptualizing it) for the past several centuries. Ever since astrology and astronomy parted company 300 years ago, both branches of the Uranian science have gone astray. They've lost contact with their true roots – the astrology spirits who, from time immemorial, have guided astrologers and helped them to make accurate judgments.

The Hindu astrologers never lost contact with the astrology spirits, and hence they haven't gone through the crisis of confidence experienced in the west. The Hindu astrologers respect the astrology spirits (heed their counsel); they respect their craft; they respect themselves; and therefore they are respected in turn by their community. We occidental astrologers – in our endeavor to turn astrology into a "reasonable" and "rational" (hence "respectable") science (which it isn't) – have turned our backs on the astrology spirits, have prostituted our craft and ourselves, and thus justly deserve the opprobrium which mainstream society heaps upon us. If we were delivering up accurate predictions, you can be sure they'd be singing a different tune.

To the astrology spirits, all statistical research is hooey. It may be interesting and even illuminating, but even if it did score little points before the Rationalist-Materialistic Inquisition (which it doesn't), it has nothing whatsoever to do with astrology. Astrology is not a matter of mind nor of logic.

The aphorisms of the ancient astrologers were not meant to be taken as rules in the modern sense, but rather as examples of how to interpret charts by the spirit (by intuition). We western astrologers have our rules – e.g. that moon in the 2nd house means such-and-such, or that Mars square Saturn means thus-and-so, etc. – and then we try to deduce meanings by using logical deduction (reasoning).

Rather, the thing should be done by feeling, not by thinking. The ancient astrologers and the Hindus did it that way. We don't need astrology spirits to interpret horoscopes; we can do that with our own feelings once we've learned how to get our intuition flowing. What the spirits want to do at this time is to teach (or reteach) us western astrologers HOW: give us concrete tools to work with.

Of course, there are some astrologers out there right now who are already doing this as a matter of course; and practically every astrologer has done it now and again: made an astoundingly accurate prediction without knowing quite how he or she did it. What the spirits want to do is to show us how to do it all the time – consistently give our clients specific, exact information rather than vague generalities such as those which are cranked out by computers.

To start with, the astrology spirits recommend changing the manner in which we calculate horoscopes. This is not because there's anything wrong with traditional house systems per se; after all, the ancient astrologers got good results from them. Rather, by misusing these horoscopes – by treating astrology and its guardians with disrespect – we western astrologers have put bad vibes over these horoscopes, and so have rendered them inoperative.

The spirits recommend abandoning all current house systems and using instead a system of 24 half-houses which are precisely analogous to the planetary hours. The exact details of how interpretation works in this system have yet to be worked out, although an algorithm for computing half-house placements of natal planets is available; i.e. these new horoscopes can be computed easily enough, and the spirits gave rules on how to interpret them, but research is lacking.

In the meantime – as a stopgap – the spirits recommend using a system of 12 houses in which the houses have the usual meanings (1st = personality, 2nd = money, etc.), but which are calculated as follows:

To obtain the houses above the horizon (7 – 12) the sun's diurnal arc (the length of time from sunrise to sunset) is divided into six parts; to obtain the houses beneath the horizon (1 – 6) the sun's nocturnal arc (the length of time from sunset to sunrise) is divided into six parts. Then these 12 division points are projected onto the ecliptic with house circles (house circles are great circles on the celestial sphere which pass through the north and south points on the horizon. The Campanus and Regiomontanus systems also project with house circles, but the former divides the prime vertical into 12 parts, and the latter divides the celestial equator into 12 parts).

Because this new house system results from a division of the sun's diurnal circle, we call it the Sunshine House System (actually Ken Gillman named it). Although we are trying to get away from logic, a moment's reflection will show that the sun's diurnal circle is indeed the most logical circle to divide to produce mundane houses. If the houses are to be considered analogous to the signs; and if the signs result from a division of the sun's yearly path (the ecliptic); then it follows that the houses should result from a division of the sun's daily path – its diurnal or declination circle; i.e., the small circle parallel to the celestial equator which passes through the natal sun.

Since the analogy requires that the angles be house cusps (or in any event, the spirits require it), projection of these 12 division points must needs be with house circles, since only a projection with house circles retains both the Ascendant and Midheaven as house cusps.

The Sunshine House System has two unusual features:

Three parameters (Sidereal Time, Latitude, and Declination of natal sun) are required to compute house cusps, rather than only two (ST and Latitude) required by all other house systems. This feature precludes a table of houses for the Sunshine House System, but in this age of computers this is not really a problem.

Opposite house cusps (except for the four angles: Asc, IC, Desc, and MC) do not lie opposite in the zodiac. In fact, it is common to find intercepted pairs of signs which do not lie opposite in the zodiac. This is an odd feature, but certainly not an objectionable one.

When I began recalculating the horoscopes in my files using the Sunshine House System, the first experiment I tried was secondary progressions to intermediate house cusps. I had always regarded secondary progressions to intermediate house cusps to be the acid test of proof for a house system (transits, because of retrogradation, are too uncertain to use as a test for timing). I had never seen secondary progressions to intermediate house cusps work in any of the half-dozen other house systems in which I'd tried them.

Needless to say, they didn't work in the Sunshine House System either. Disappointed, I was about to file the whole idea away for the duration when I happened to take a vacation and found myself in the (for me) unusual position of doing a lot of face-to-face natal consultations for complete strangers. I calculated all these new charts with the Sunshine House System, and I discovered the following:

Using the Sunshine House System and the traditional house symbolism (e.g. 7th = marriage, 8th = death, 9th = journeys / religion, etc.) I found that I obtained much clearer psychic impressions than I'd ever experienced in the 20 years I'd then been studying astrology. My astrology mysteriously reached an altogether new level. I'd be looking at some feature in a chart, and then suddenly I'd just know, beyond a shadow of a doubt, precisely what happened to that guy at age 6; or what he'll be doing in 20 years; or what's bothering him right now.

When I use the Sunshine House System, it sometimes happens that an actual picture pops up before my mind's eye; but more often it's just a feeling of something known – like reaching out for a memory of something which you know, but can't quite put your finger on – which horoscope symbols help you pin down or express in words.

The impressions definitely come from the native, not the horoscope. Nonetheless the horoscope is intrinsic to the process. All feelings take off from symbols in the horoscope; and also the horoscope serves as a focus or way of conceptualizing feelings which are in the air. It can't be done without the horoscope (at least I can't do it without the horoscope).

Although you can use intuition with everyone, the clearest impressions come from natives who are themselves psychic, or who are at least open-hearted and straightforward people. The guy who sits there with his arms crossed and with an "I dare you!" look on his face can effectively block any attempts to psychically probe him. You have to break down such a native's screen of thought forms (penetrate his defenses) before you can give him his money's worth. I can usually get an antagonistic or dubious client to loosen up by starting (in a friendly and easy manner) with his or her current progressions and transits. I get clients used to the sound of my voice; I let them know that I'm not threatening nor judging them; and then, when they're relaxed, I can start pulling impressions out of them. The point is that if you're going to be an intuitive astrologer, you have to be open to the native (rather than defending some sort of ego trip of your own). This means respecting the native, and also respecting yourself; it means giving the person emotional space, and at the same time, not permitting him or her to encroach upon yours.

There is really no other way of being able to give specific information to a client except through intuition. That's the only way to cut through all the innumerable possibilities of what the symbols could mean logically, to arrive at what they do mean in a particular case. The rationalist astrologers who believe that astrology should be based upon reason rather than intuition are only promulgating an astrology of distrust: distrust in the spirit, distrust in their own abundant inner knowledge, and distrust in the craft of astrology. We are not advocating "blind faith" in astrology here; we're talking about concrete results that we can each validate for ourselves in our own practice.

The Sunshine House System is a link, given to us by the astrology spirits, to help us activate and utilize our latent intuition. If you use a house-based astrology in your practice, I highly recommend your giving the Sunshine House System a whirl. I think you will be surprised and gratified to find how such a simple adjustment as changing the house system you use can produce such an amazing difference in the specificity and accuracy of your predictions.

*Notes channeled from the spirit guardians of astrological knowledge on the application of the Sunshine House System:

As a point of departure it is suggested that you look to the rulers of the horoscope houses (the connections which the rulers make by aspect and reception with the rest of the horoscope) as an augury of how the affairs symbolized by the houses will go. For this purpose the spirits suggest using not the modern rulerships of the signs by the planets (e.g. sun ruling Leo, moon ruling Cancer, Mercury ruling Gemini and Virgo, Venus ruling Taurus and Libra, etc.), but rather the ancient, original rulerships, which are as follows:

Sun rules Capricorn	Jupiter rules Aries
Moon rules Cancer	Saturn rules Scorpio
Mercury rules Libra	Uranus rules Sagittarius
Venus rules Pisces	Neptune rules Aquarius
Mars rules Virgo	Pluto rules Gemini

Evidently, the rulers Uranus, Neptune, and Pluto were not part of the original scheme, but are a later addition by the spirits. In this scheme Taurus and Leo have no rulers.

For example, if Libra is on the second cusp, then Mercury is the significator of money matters; if Scorpio is on the seventh cusp, then Saturn is the significator of partnership; etc. The aspects these planets make to other planets in the natal chart – together with the houses which these planets rule in turn – show where the native can expect help or hindrance with regard to the matters signified (such as money or partnership).

The houses which have Taurus or Leo on their cusps point to problem areas in life, where decisive action is needed but the native tends to drift rudderless, with no plan, objectivity, or sense of direction. If in a horary chart Taurus or Leo rule either the querent or quesited, then the question is not answerable (there's nothing the native can do about the situation except abide).

In progressions, directions, and transits, look to the house ruled by the moving body (rather than that ruled by the aspected natal planet) to see what areas of life will be affected.

If you open your mind and look at the Sunshine House Horoscope, the thing will just hit you in the face. You'll understand so much more about your horoscope than you ever did before – the things that have always puzzled you about your chart will suddenly make sense in a highly personal and intuitive way.

Monday's Child

It is said that the planetary hours are all that remains of pure astrology, and that they contain everything.

This is a fair statement because planetary hours astrology is basically an astrology of luck, whereas conventional astrology of the zodiac and houses is an astrology of karma. Conventional astrology depicts people as socially conditioned beings: it shows how they relate to others, what lessons they are seeking to learn in this lifetime, and how they adjust (or fail to adjust) to the expectations of their parents, spouses, children, co-workers, boss, neighbors, etc.

By contrast, planetary hours astrology depicts people as spiritual beings, and shows their relationship to the abstract: their personal (as opposed to social) power and effectiveness, and their ability to make their own decisions and choose their own destinies.

Planetary hours astrology shows you at your best, at your "you-est." It shows how you tune out static, stress, and external pressure and make contact with your own sense of self at center. It shows how you unhook yourself from society's wheel of rewards and punishments and operate on your own, at your own pace. It shows your most natural and joyous state of being, wherein you need nothing outside yourself to feel whole fulfilled, and at peace.

This is why planetary hours astrology is an astrology of luck: it points out the moods and mindsets you are in when you are operating at your peak of performance. The following interpretations are not necessarily descriptions of how you act every day, but rather of how you act when your luck is flowing. They describe that side of your personality which you should seek to enlarge until you are able to act with complete effectiveness in your everyday life.

When we look at the day of the week you were born, as opposed to your rising sign in conventional astrology, we are looking at a wholly positive side of your personality and relationship with your environment. Your weekday symbolizes the expression of your highest self, rather than some sort of mask you wear or set of mannerisms designed to elicit some stock response from other people. Your weekday symbolizes a more genuine interaction with other people than does your rising sign. Your weekday shows you in your most relaxed and natural state of being – the side of you which others find most inviting.

Observe that the astrological day begins at dawn (not midnight).   Therefore, if you were born between midnight and dawn (i.e. if your natal Sun falls in the first three houses of a conventional horoscope), then you should read the interpretation for the day of the week before your birthday. For example, if you were born on a Tuesday between midnight and dawn, then you should read the interpretation for Monday. If you don't know what day of the week you were born, the free downloadable Planetary Hours tables calculates the weekday your were born as well as your planetary hour (see further along).

SUNDAY: You are outgoing, self-possessed, poised, and dignified. You have unlimited self-assurance and elàn, and unhesitatingly take your rightful place (preferably in the center) of any social group of which you are a part. Because you basically respect yourself as a person, you are able to respect other people as well, and this naturally wins you their respect in turn. You are a natural-born leader, not because you flaunt yourself, but precisely because you are willing to honor other people's viewpoints as being valid from their own side. Although you can have a prissy, prima-donna streak, your lofty noblesse oblige is executed with sufficient good humor so as not to ruffle other people's sensibilities. Indeed, they respect your calm reason and objective judgment. You are practical and down-to-earth, and your unvarnished forthrightness induces other people to look up to you and cede you the lead.

MONDAY: You are soft, childlike, spontaneous, and possess the eager cheerfulness of a puppy. You are playful and mischievous, and take a positive, constructive view towards life and its problems. You try to avoid conflict, not because you're a shrinking violet, but because you have a genuine love of peace and harmony. You have a strong sense of your own personal space, and a respect for that of others; you are both gentle and firm (on the negative side, unyielding). Because you basically feel good about yourself and truly like yourself, you make it easy for other people to like you as well. You are able to keep cool and collected no matter what is going on around you, because you are very attuned to your own inner voice, and you follow your own intuition with little regard for what other people might think of you. Thus you have a somewhat Bohemian or off-beat streak, a determination to just do your own thing in your own time.

TUESDAY: You are irrepressible, adventurous, and peppery. You have a shrewd, analytical mind which sees clearly through the ulterior motives of other people, and which instantly grasps the possibilities of profit in any situation. Although not combative per se (you don't go looking for trouble), you don't shrink from conflict either. You are fearless in confronting other people directly – eyeball to eyeball, cheek to jowl, and in fact you seem to come alive at any hint of confusion or doubt in an opponent. You are opportunistic without being especially ambitious. You love challenge for its own sake, but have little patience for thinking in terms of long-term goals or empire building. Indeed, you are scornful of what most people consider "security", and prefer living by your own wits to planning for your future. You regard the trappings of comfort –

dependence on possessions, other people, and worldly responsibilities – as encumbering baggage to be avoided whenever possible. You prefer keeping loose, agile, and free of commitments so you are always able to land on your feet no matter how hard life buffets you about.

WEDNESDAY: You are unabashed and plain-spoken, and do not hesitate to speak your mind and speak to the point. Your tart, no-nonsense approach to people and your ironic sense of humor cut through pretense and empty gesticulating and go right to the heart of matters. You do nothing for show or effect. Because you feel no need to prove anything to yourself, you feel no need to put on airs, but are able to relax and just be yourself in any company; and your simplicity enables other people to be out-front with you in turn. You tend to rely upon bull-headedness rather than subtlety or guile to get your way; and while your frankness can at times be bruising, your earnestness and sincerity win the admiration of others.

THURSDAY: You are soft-spoken, polite, and considerate. You possess a detached intellectual curiosity and an open, nonjudgmental attitude towards others. You are forward-looking and hopeful, and are willing to tackle even arduous jobs with a spirit of dedication and enterprise. You are able to carry out any task smoothly and cheerfully because you don't let your personal feelings get in your way. You prefer not to make waves, not because you are shy or feel threatened by people, but rather because you don't need any ego-bolstering from them. You are able to find satisfaction in the punctilious discharge of your responsibilities, and hence you can afford to be generous with others – to live and let live. You are optimistic and always prefer to look at the bright side of things rather than become bogged down in disagreements or bickering.

FRIDAY: You possess a starry-eyed idealism, freshness, and naivete. Your innocuousness and artlessness disarm other people and put them at ease. You're not afraid to let it all hang out, to express your true feelings openly and make yourself vulnerable to other people, because you feel you have nothing to be ashamed of or to hide. You are thoroughly candid without being brusque; on the contrary, you are soft, open, and approachable. Albeit gregarious, you don't let yourself become too dependent on the approval and validation of other people to buttress your own sense of self-worth. At root you know that your own motives are good, so that you are capable of reaching out to others in a spirit of good will and good faith. Because you basically trust your own motives, you are able to trust in the ultimate good nature of other people as well.

SATURDAY: You are serious-minded and reserved, and possess a dignified mien and bearing. Your patience and forbearance are the product of a true faith in yourself and the power of the universe to sustain you. You are high-minded and courageous, and are always willing to stand alone on your own two feet. You are hard-working and thorough, without demanding any special recognition for your efforts. You are basically self-starting and self-motivating, and therefore you have little need for or interest in the carrot or stick for encouragement. Although you can be independent to the point of contrariness, and maddeningly aloof and blasè, your self-reliance is a model for and stabilizing influence upon other people.

From both the mathematical and symbolical points of view, the weekday you were born is analogous to your rising sign in conventional astrology, and your planetary hour ruler is analogous to your sun sign. Although it is possible to place all the planets – not just the sun – in the scheme of 24 planetary hours, the calculations for doing this are complex. What standard tables of planetary hours show is the sun's position in the 24 hours.

What your conventional sun sign shows is a somewhat ostentatious and manipulative side of your personality – the way in which you bid for power and control. By contrast, your planetary hour ruler shows your most decisive and confident mode of action – how you behave when you are free of all doubt, hesitation, or ulterior motive. It shows how you are able to inspire yourself, and by extension, how you are most able to inspire others.

SUN HOUR: You are bright, exuberant, positive, and have a winning personality. You take great pride in your personal fitness, and you cultivate at least one interest or area in life in which you are thoroughly expert and competent. You are lordly and gracious without being snobbish or stuffy. Indeed, your personal flair and idiosyncracies are your most delightful assets; you charge off like Don Quixote with complete assurance and faith. You have a conspiratorial twinkle in your eye and a sense about you like a little kid up to no good. Your dashing self-confidence and good-natured panache captivate other people and assuage any difficult situation.

MOON HOUR: You are moody, changeable, wistful, and other-worldly. Your gentleness and sense of pathos tend to arouse the protective instincts in others. You like things simple and straightforward, and always need to find a basis of harmony and accord. You are by no means a patsy or pushover, but rather don't feel any overriding need to defend your point of view. You don't so much shun harshness as you willingly bear trials and tribulations without complaint. You maintain a cheerful, philosophical, and consoling attitude which eschews blame or remorse.

MERCURY HOUR: You are objective, inquisitive, and have a light touch with others. Albeit sociable, you are emotionally remote. You play the role of detached spectator or impartial arbiter, not because you're afraid to stand up for your beliefs, but because your reach is for understanding rather than proving that you're right. In fact, you have a highly original point of view and a wry sense of humor, together with a fine appreciation of the ironies of existence. Without especially trying to, you make a favorable impression on people because you are fair, high-minded, and more interested in communicating clearly than in imposing your own ideas.

VENUS HOUR: You are sociable, playful, and devil-may-care. You have an easy manner and a soft, non-assertive approach to other people. You are not so much pliant or indolent as you are blithe and indifferent. You are always able to find some level on which you can enjoy yourself, come what may. You take a creative approach to life, and are able to lavish your complete attention on any relationship or hobby which excites your interest. Although you can have a complacent, self-satisfied streak, your buoyant good humor enlivens any group you are in.

MARS HOUR: You are gutsy, spunky, and never say die. You have a critical, analytical mind and a willingness to roll up your sleeves and get down to work at whatever business is at hand. You are proud of your ability to reason things out, and to take complete responsibility for yourself and the situation in which you find yourself. You are willing (and indeed prefer) to go it alone rather than compromise your own personal vision and designs. Although you can be impatient, argumentative, and authoritarian, your pioneering spirit and utter faith in your own powers makes you a steadying influence on others.

JUPITER HOUR: You are expansive, outgoing, and optimistic. You throw yourself into your work and relationships with unstinting vigor and joie de vivre. You feel the most alive when you are sharing common goals, interests, and experiences. Although you drive yourself with a high-wire energy, you are patient and accepting in your dealings with others. You are a good teacher and organizer because you are willing to give others the benefit of the doubt. You are conscientious and fair, and are a model to others of unselfishness, keen insight, and whole-hearted enthusiasm.

SATURN HOUR: You are grave, determined, and indomitable. You have a heavy, brooding, grumpy air and a low, daunting growl, which effectively prevents others from trying to cross you. You are hard, tough, and cannot be deflected from the path beneath your feet. You depend upon no one but yourself, and are ready to go to any extreme or take on any burden single-handedly rather than surrender an inch of your independence. You are not so much uncooperative as disinterested; not so much unsympathetic as pitiless. Although you can be cool to the point of rudeness, you nonetheless inspire others with your activity and staunch singlemindedness.

I have long been an admirer of the heuristic method employed in Ronald Davison's *Astrology* – perhaps the best beginner's book on natal astrology ever written. The basis of this system is a set of keywords, and a concise but elegant set of key phrases and ideas. Davison succeeded magnificently in reducing natal astrology's complexities to a bare-bones armature, over which the neophyte astrologer could drape his or her own ideas and intuitive insights. I have often wondered whether the same sort of systemization might not be applied to the theory of transits.

The basic system for interpretation of transits given here is meant to be suggestive, not definitive. You could call it a rough sketch. Only transiting conjunctions and oppositions are taken into account here; not because other aspects cannot be effective – they often are (particularly transiting squares). But by only taking transiting conjunctions and oppositions into account we are obeying Dr. Marc Edmund Jones' injunction to keep things as simple as possible. This system of interpretation is based upon the fundamental idea that when a transiting planet conjoins or opposes a significant point (planet, angle, etc.) in your natal chart, then:

1) the nature of the expected event is described by the symbolism of the transiting planet;
2) the nature of your emotional response – or the area of your life affected – is described by the symbolism of the natal point contacted.

Following this assumption, the following table of Keywords results:

KEYWORDS FOR THE TRANSITING AND NATAL PLANETS:

Transiting Planet (nature of external event)		Natal Point (nature of your response)
DECISIVE	SUN	DETERMINATION
HEARTFELT	MOON	ASSURANCE
ENCOURAGING	MERCURY	UNDERSTANDING
SOCIABLE	VENUS	INTIMACY
FORCEFUL	MARS	ADVANCEMENT
CHEERING	JUPITER	FULFILLMENT
CHALLENGING	SATURN	DISCIPLINE
SURPRISING	URANUS	LIBERATION
UNUSUAL	NEPTUNE	ATTUNEMENT
REVEALING	PLUTO	CLARITY
	NORTH NODE	GUIDANCE
	SOUTH NODE	GRATIFICATION
	PART OF FORTUNE	NOVELTY
	ASCENDANT	REORIENTATION
	MIDHEAVEN	HOPE
	DESCENDANT	COOPERATION
	LOWER MERIDIAN	RESOLUTION

See Appendix I below for more detailed interpretations for the transiting and natal planets.

Before giving some examples of how to apply these keywords to actual cases (using Theodore Roosevelt's life and horoscope as the model), let us consider some basic issues in transit theory. What follows below is meant to be a mere suggestion – a set of pointers – based upon one practitioner's own experience. This is not to imply that there aren't other approaches which can be equally or more effective in a given horoscope or for a given practitioner. Astrology – like healing – is a science; but it is even more so an art. There's no right way or wrong way of doing it: all approaches made in good faith, in a true spirit of searching for truth, are valid.

Overall Expectation: The technique of transits – like that of zodiacal primary directions – tends to produce concrete physical events in one's outward life (whereas secondary progressions tend to produce emotional or psychological states – karmic lessons – rather than actual events per se. Although they can and do). Transits – unlike zodiacal primary directions – fail frequently. Also, major events in the life can and do occur without any relevant transit, progression, or direction which can be held to account for that event. That's life. Astrology is not a tocsin which unerringly sounds the alarm at the precise moment it's supposed to. This doesn't mean that we have to use every astrological point imaginable – e.g. the transit of the moon's node to the quincunx of the Chiron – Lillith midpoint – to "prove" anything. Nor does it mean – as the rationalistic materialist critics of astrology would have it – that astrology is a false doctrine. On the contrary, astrology models life perfectly, because life is imperfect.

Note: the given interpretations do not take into account whether the transiting planet and the natal planet contacted are intrinsically harmonious or disharmonious in nature, which modifies the interpretations. For example, a transit to natal Mars by a planet intrinsically disharmonious with it would tend to impede or block ADVANCEMENT rather than facilitate it. See the Table of Harmonious and Disharmonious Planetary Combinations in Appendix II.

The Natal Chart: It is often said that transits cannot bring events which are not promised in the natal chart; but I haven't found this guideline especially useful in interpretation. House positions and rulerships do not seem to be as important in determining how a transit will operate as do the essential meanings of the transiting planets and natal points involved. Do, however, pay attention to any aspect in the natal chart between the planet which is transiting and the planet or point being transited, since e.g. a natal sextile or trine will tend to bring fortunate events even if the transiting aspect is an opposition or square (though usually these necessitate expending effort or overcoming conflict in order to benefit the native); and a natal square or opposition will tend to bring conflicts or disappointments of inflated hopes even to nominally benefic transits.

Transiting Planets: In a general way, the transiting conjunctions and oppositions of Uranus and Saturn, respectively, are the most effective. Transiting Jupiter and Mars can be quite effective, especially when transiting their own positions in the natal chart. The effects of Neptune and Pluto tend to be more vague; but not necessarily (the point is, don't count too much on them). The other, swifter, planets tend to be less effective, except in combination. That is to say, when transiting swift planets conjoin or oppose each other within a degree or two of a significant position in the natal chart, then this mutual transit is likely to produce a noticeable event. For example, the Superior Conjunction of Mercury or Venus (the transiting Superior Conjunction of these planets with the sun) in conjunction or opposition to a significant point in the natal horoscope, usually produces, within orb of a day or two, a noticeable event.

Orbs: As in the theory of primary zodiacal directions, the tendency is for the event to trail (rather than lead) the exact date of the aspect in time.

Outer planets which transit the same natal position three times (direct, retrograde, direct) or five times (direct, retrograde, direct, retrograde, direct) may produce an event anywhere within the time frame between the first and last direct transits; but the overall tendency is for the event to occur at – or shortly after – the first direct transit (and in the case of the slower planets, the following year or two is spent in clean-up or reorganizing in response to the effect of the first direct transit). But this is not always the case. For example, an informal study of the Demi-Uranus Return (Uranus' transit to opposition its natal place) – which occurs in early 40-something natives – shows that the expected SURPRISING event which brings LIBERATION can occur anywhere between the first and last direct transits.

Transiting Uranus tends to produce events sharply-defined both in nature and in timing. Transiting Saturn produces events which – albeit sometimes associated with a particular moment in time – even then spread their effects out over a period from a few months before, to a year or two after, the exact date of the first direct transit. Transiting Neptune is vaguer (of course); transiting Pluto can produce definitive, transformative events (like 180 degree changes – deaths and rebirths), whose repercussions go on over a year or two of time. Jupiter's return to its natal place – and sometimes its transit of the Ascendant – produce joyous, serendipitous events within a month of the exact transit date. The swifter planets in combination refer to events that should be timable within a day or two of the exact time of the transit – usually following it rather than preceding it.

Your emotional response – or the area of your life affected – here we follow traditional astrological symbolism, e.g. that the sun symbolizes honor, reputation in the world, career, life work, life purpose; the father, the husband, boss or authorities. The moon symbolizes feelings, mood, past life influences, the mother, the wife, employees; and lacunae in one's quotidian life (travel, sickness, psychic experiences – any break with wonted routines). Mercury symbolizes mind – the particular set of self-justifications and images with which you present yourself to the world for approval (or rejection); as well as routine issues and relationships: siblings, neighbors, coworkers, children. Venus is love in the sense of infatuation, embellishment, art, creativity, sociability, the girlfriend or female lover, art for art's sake. Mars is aggressive energy – courage, valor, athletics, self-sacrifice for a cause; male friends and lovers, dynamism. Jupiter is enthusiasm, benevolent impulse with no thought of reward; money, religious / philosophical interests; aunts and uncles, as well as detached advisors and friends who wish the best. Saturn is discipline, limitation, karma. We all have dues to pay – which are accessible in our past life regressions – and Saturn symbolizes where (by house position) and how (by sign position) we have to slow down and wake up to the lessons which our life is teaching us. It symbolizes frustration, obstruction, older people, difficult people. Uranus introduces an element of disruption and surprise into our lives, without which we could never understand the meaning of freedom. Neptune is psychic, intuitive, otherworldly knowledge (or its opposite – morbid, indwelling, spaced-out irresponsibility). Pluto is cunning and obsession; as well as complete transformation – ability to begin anew after total wipeout.

Examples of Interpretation of Transits:

In these examples the cookbook interpretations – cobbled together from the keywords in the Table and the Detailed Interpretations from Appendix I, are given first; and these are followed by a description of what actually happened in Theodore Roosevelt's life at that time. Examples for the slower planets (which often spread their effects out for a year or more) will be listed first; followed by examples for the swifter planets (which are usually effective only for a day or two). Exact dates of transits by the slower planets to TR's chart are given in Appendix III.

Jupiter: Transiting Jupiter's return to its natal place every twelve years usually brings a month of serendipitous events – new spiritual or business connections, new ideas, new relationships – which become of great importance in the future. In TR's case Jupiter's return in 1870-71 was also accompanied by its transit of his Ascendant, which augurs a CHEERING event: an opportunity to lighten up, join together with others, and take a detached, generous, and conciliatory overview; and this event brought him FULFILLMENT and REORIENTATION – he found that things fell right into place with no effort on his part. He got to do something he'd wanted to do for a long time, and he began a new phase or epoch in his life.

What happened in summer-fall 1870 was that twelve-year old TR was very sickly, plagued since birth by chronic asthma. His father challenged him to make his body; and the boy began working out daily at a local gymnasium as well as in a gymnasium at home which his father had stocked with athletic equipment. His sister later wrote: "For many years one of my most vivid recollections is seeing him between horizontal bars, widening his chest by regular, monotonous motion – drudgery indeed." (this belies the "no effort on his part" interpretation from Appendix I – but nothing is perfect). He exercised throughout winter-spring 1870-71, and by the summer of 1871 he had cured himself and strengthened his body immensely. "Glorifying in his newfound strength, he plunges into the depths of icy rapids and clambers to the heights of seven mountains. ... Along with this physical exuberance, he develops a more studious interest in nature."

Saturn: Transiting Saturn's aspects are not necessarily bad; but even the good ones require considerable discipline or sacrifice. Also, what Saturn giveth, Saturn taketh away. In TR's life, transiting Saturn opposed Venus and conjoined Jupiter just before crossing his Ascendant from summer 1884 through summer 1885, which one might expect would bring a CHALLENGING event – having to overcome obstacles directly; not shrinking from difficulties but holding his own ground and securing his position in life. This event emphasized INTIMACY and FULFILLMENT and brought REORIENTATION: He attended to family, social, or relationship matters which impacted on his gregarious, romantic, enthusiastic side; and found that things fell right into place with no effort on his part. He got to do something he'd wanted to do for a long time; and he began a new phase or epoch in his life.

The preceding fall he made his first trip out west and loved it. That winter his mother and wife died suddenly (the same day) which completely shattered him emotionally, and to get his mind off it he returned to Dakota in June 1884; made some important new friends; found a perfect site for a ranch house, and bought it. He returned east in October and spent the winter writing *Hunting Trips of a Ranchman*. In April 1885 he returned to Dakota and finished building his ranch house, bought a herd of cattle, and spent the month of June on a roundup through the Badlands. According to his biographer this experience changed him drastically: "Some extraordinary physical and spiritual transformation occurred during this arduous period. It was as if his adolescent battle for health, and his more recent but equally intense battle against despair, were crowned with sudden victory. The anemic, high-pitched youth who had left New York only five weeks before was now able to return to it 'rugged, bronzed, and in the prime of health.'" Long afterward he said that "If it had not been for my years in North Dakota, I never would have become President of the United States."

Another example: Transiting Saturn conjoined TR's natal moon and opposed his Mars between summer 1886 and late spring 1887, which augured a CHALLENGING event to his ASSURANCE and ADVANCEMENT. Obstacles had to be confronted directly; he couldn't shrink from difficulties but had to hold his ground and secure his position in life. His deep-seated instincts came to the surface and he had to pay attention to what his own inner voice was telling him. His forward motion was blocked; his plans and projects shattered; and he was depressed by failure and despair for the future.

TR remarried in December 1886, but the event to which this transit probably refers is the destruction of his western ranching business and dream due to the terrible winter of 1886-87, which killed all of his cattle. He made a trip out west in April 1887 to survey his losses, and returned east thoroughly depressed. "The losses are crippling. For the first time I have been utterly unable to enjoy a visit to my ranch. I shall be glad to get home." Returning broke, with no political prospects, he determined that he would have to write for a living, and so began working on his magnum opus *Winning the West*.

Uranus: Transiting Uranus crossed TR's natal Venus – Jupiter opposition from late 1901 through late 1902. This SURPRISING, unexpected, serendipitous event shook TR out of his ordinary routines and doldrums and brought him INTIMACY and FULFILLMENT: he attended to family, social, and relationship matters which impacted on his gregarious, romantic, enthusiastic side. He found that things fell right into place with no effort on his part, and he got to do something he'd wanted to do for a long time.

This period corresponds to TR's first year in the White House, which he entered the preceding September 1901 upon President McKinley's assassination. It was like releasing a fish into water: that first year he began the first major national anti-trust case (against Northern Securities); he introduced his plan for a Panama Canal; he settled a major, violent strike in the anthracite coal fields; and he squared off with Germany over a crisis in Venezuela. It was a year of triumph and success on all fronts (except for a serious accident suffered on 9/03/1902 when his carriage was hit by a trolley car, which killed his bodyguard; almost killed him; and was the beginning of a life-long leg pain which required many operations over the next few weeks). But by the end of 1902, TR was assured of renomination in 1904: "The power of one man thus to cover his party with the mantle of his own strength is unprecedented in the history of American politics."

Neptune and Pluto: Transiting Neptune crossed TR's natal moon – Mars opposition; and transiting Pluto crossed his Ascendant; from late summer 1908 through mid-1910. Transiting Neptune produces UNUSUAL events – odd, out-of-the-ordinary occurrences; strange vibrations and undercurrents; which provoke powerful attractions or repulsions on his part. The event impacted upon his ASSURANCE (his deep-seated instincts came to the surface; he had to pay attention to what his own inner voice was telling him) and also impacted his ADVANCEMENT – impelling him forward to make new plans or projects, motivated by a sense of progress, accomplishment, and hope for the future. At the same time the interpretation for transiting Pluto conjunct Ascendant is a REVEALING (disorienting, transformative) event which forced him to take command, rise to the occasion, get on top of things. This event produced a major REORIENTATION: he began a new phase or epoch in his life.

This period embraced TR's last few months in office and the victory of his hand-picked successor (Taft) whom TR believed would follow his policies. Just before he left office, TR's Great White Fleet returned from its round-the-world cruise, which one of his biographers called "the apotheosis of Roosevelt." From March 1909 – March 1910 he went on a safari in Africa which was the fulfillment of a long-held dream; and he wrote a series of articles on his adventures. He returned to the U.S. on 6/16/1910 to a triumphal welcome (a parade up Broadway hosted by the mayor of New York). His friends considered that he had become a changed man: "He was just the same in manner, in appearance, in expression, yet there was something different. We, all of us who had been closely associated with him in the past, felt it. I spoke of it. Senator Lodge spoke of it. Secretary Meyer … spoke of it; and so did Nick [Longworth]. Loeb and I, for we rode together in the procession, talked almost entirely of him and each of us felt that there was a change in him. Mr. Meyer thought he had grown older, but it wasn't that. Loeb, Senator Lodge, and I figured it out to be simply an enlarged personality. To me he had ceased to be an American, but had become a world citizen. His horizon seemed to be greater, his mental scope more encompassing."

The swifter transiting planets produce transient events – perhaps within a day or two of the precise date they are due. They fail often. Transiting changes of station (from direct to retrograde or retrograde to direct) usually work quite well; mutual transits (the conjunction or opposition of two transiting planets falling on or opposite a significant point in the natal horoscope) are usually more effective than single-body transits.

Mars: Transiting Mars conjoined its natal place on 3/2/1879, bringing a FORCEFUL event: intense involvements with other people (though not necessarily conflictive) in which he had to take a position, stand up for himself, be willing to fully commit himself; the upshot of which brought him ADVANCEMENT: impelling him forward, motivating him with a sense of progress, accomplishment, and hope for the future. What happened was that the previous day TR embarked on a fabulous two-week hunting trip to Maine, where he made some fast friends for life: "The emerging politician got great satisfaction out of his ability to converse, on equal terms, with backwoodsmen as well as Boston Brahmins. So, too, did the hunter exult in chasing a caribou for thirty-six hours through the snowy forest, with neither tent nor blankets to protect him. The naturalist collected specimens, while the sometime invalid worked up 'enough health to last me till next summer.'"

Sun-Venus: Transiting Venus' superior conjunction with the sun on 2/18/1890 conjoined TR's natal Midheaven, auguring a DECISIVE, SOCIABLE event: one which calls for an exercise of will in which he had to follow his heart and stay his course; do what he felt was right; involving encounters, gatherings, or events which played upon his affections (note that sun and Venus form an intrinsically disharmonious combination so their conjunction is usually brings disagreement, conflict, tension in relationships).

Falling on his Midheaven, this transit impacted on TR's HOPE – it gave him something to set his sights on or to shoot for.

Three weeks earlier Congress had appointed a committee of TR's enemies to investigate him; and on 2/19/1890 hearings began: "As always when confronted by a challenge, Roosevelt instantly took the offensive. He intended so to dominate the hearings that he would be entirely vindicated." (which is what happened).

Mercury: Transiting Mercury turned retrograde on 5/28/1883 on TR's natal Jupiter, which produced an ENCOURAGING event which changed his attitude, viewpoint, or self-image. He saw himself in a new light, in a new role vis a vis other people, and need tact, aplomb, and confidence in his own abilities. This event brought him FULFILLMENT – he found that things just fell right into place with no effort on his part. He got to do something he'd wanted to do for a long time.

That evening TR was guest of honor at a meeting of the Free Trade Club, where he met Henry George. But more importantly, "a chance meeting occurred which directly influenced the future course of his life." TR met Commander H.H. Gorringe, who invited him on a buffalo hunting trip out west, which was a dream TR had nurtured for a long time. This invitation was the beginning of TR's interest in the west; and the seed of his cattle-ranching venture in Dakota, begun the following year.

Appendix I: Detailed Interpretations

I: Detailed Interpretations for Transiting Planets
(nature of event)

Sun: DECISIVE – Calls for an exercise of will in which you have to follow your heart and stay your course; do what you feel is right.

Moon: HEARTFELT – Something out of the ordinary which affects you on a deep level. May bring messages or guidance from the spirit world.

Mercury: ENCOURAGING – An event which changes your attitude, viewpoint, or self-image. You see yourself in a new light, in a new role vis a vis other people, and need tact, aplomb, and confidence in your own abilities.

Venus: SOCIABLE – Encounters, gatherings, or events which play upon your affections. They may symbolize a poignant moment in a personal relationship, or creative, artistic expression.

Mars: FORCEFUL – Intense involvements with other people (though not necessarily conflictive). You have to take a position, stand up for yourself, be willing to fully commit yourself.

Jupiter: CHEERING – An opportunity to lighten up, join together with others, and take a detached, generous, and conciliatory overview.

Saturn: CHALLENGING – Obstacles which have to be confronted directly. You cannot shrink from difficulties but must hold your ground and secure your position in life.

Uranus: SURPRISING – Unexpected (serendipitous or calamitous) events which shake you out of your ordinary routines and doldrums.

Neptune: UNUSUAL – Odd, out-of-the-ordinary occurrences; strange vibrations and undercurrents. May provoke powerful attractions or repulsions on your part.

Pluto: REVEALING – Events of a disorienting, transformative nature. You have to take command, rise to the occasion, get on top of things.

II. Detailed Interpretations for Natal Planets
(nature of your response)

Sun: DETERMINATION – You have to stand up for yourself, let your own views be known, make your own will prevail. You must disencumber yourself and take a step forward.

Moon: ASSURANCE – Your deep-seated instincts come to the surface. You must pay attention to what your own inner voice is telling you.

Mercury: UNDERSTANDING – You must meet or communicate with others of like mind (opposition inclines to conflicts). You may begin new projects or relationships.

Venus: INTIMACY – You attend to family, social, or relationship matters which impact on your gregarious, romantic, enthusiastic side.

Mars: ADVANCEMENT – You are impelled forward, make new plans or projects, and are moved by a sense of progress, accomplishment, and hope for the future.

Jupiter: FULFILLMENT – You find that things just fall right into place with no effort on your part. You may get to do something you've wanted to do for a long time.

Saturn: DISCIPLINE – You must work hard, dedicate yourself, exercise self-control. You have to adjust yourself to limits imposed from outside.

Uranus: LIBERATION – An expansion of your personal space and horizons. New doors open for you, and you have to release old assumptions.

Neptune: ATTUNEMENT – You need to overcome doubt, confusion and uncertainty and trust in your ability to just go with the flow.

Pluto: CLARITY – You must be calm and steady, and use sober, objective analysis. You have to put the situation into proper perspective.

North Node: GUIDANCE – You need to reconsider your position, to be fluid and receptive to change.

South Node: GRATIFICATION – Your ego gets a boost; you collect some debt from the past.

Part of Fortune: NOVELTY – You find you are able to take things in stride, to relax and enjoy yourself in a unique situation.

Ascendant: REORIENTATION – You begin a new phase or epoch in your life.
Midheaven: HOPE – You are given something to set your sights on or to shoot for.

Descendant: COOPERATION – You change the tone or direction of a close relationship.

Lower Meridian: RESOLUTION – You are required to stand your ground and consolidate your position.

Appendix II – Table of Harmonious and Disharmonious Planetary Combinations

	SU	MO	ME	VE	MA	JU	SA	UR	NE
MO	+								
ME	–	+							
VE	–	+	–						
MA	+	–	+	+					
JU	+	+	–	+	+				
SA	–	–	+	–	–	+			
UR	+	–	+	–	+	+	+		
NE	–	+	–	+	–	+	–	+	
PL	+	–	+	–	+	–	–	–	–

Appendix III – Exact Dates of Theodore Roosevelt Example Transits

JU conj JU = 8/15/1870 – 12/15/1870 R – 4/06/1871
JU conj ASC = 9/22/1870 – 11/05/1870 R – 5/02/1871
SA opp VE = 7/10/1884 – 1/14/1885 R – 3/21/1885
SA conj JU = 8/05/1884 – 12/08/1884 R – 4/24/1885
SA conj ASC = 6/02/1885
SA conj MO = 8/12/1886 – 2/06/1887 R – 4/25/1887
SA opp MA = 8/22/1886 – 1/21/1887 R – 5/10/1887
UR conj VE = 12/28/1901 – 7/07/1902 R – 10/15/1902
UR opp JU = 3/05/1902 – 4/18/1902 R – 12/07/1902
NE conj MO = 9/23/1908 – 11/16/1908 R – 7/11/1909 – 2/19/1910 R – 5/04/1910
NE opp MA = 8/13/1909 – 1/04/1910 R – 6/14/1910
PL conj ASC = 8/26/1908 – 10/26/1908 R – 7/01/1909 – 12/28/1909 R – 5/18/1910

(Excerpted from *The Mountain Astrologer* magazine, issue # 145, 6-7/2009)

* * * * * * * * *

Neptune Sextile Pluto

The planets Neptune and Pluto entered orb of a sextile (* = 60 degrees apart) aspect in the mid-1940's; and they will remain there until the 2030's. Normally aspects between Neptune and Pluto are within orb for only a dozen or so years at a time. However, Pluto is presently at a fast place in its orbit so that it is moving at about the same speed as Neptune, at the same time that the two planets are roughly 60 degrees apart, so they are both in the sextile pattern for about a century. Thus, there will come a moment in time when there is no one on earth who doesn't have Neptune and Pluto sextile in their natal horoscope. What does this mean?

The manner in which each individual Neptune sextile Pluto native adapts him or herself to their generation's ideal of taking personal responsibility for making one's own choices is shown by the value of the Neptune sextile Pluto aspect in their birth horoscope. The value is simply the orb of inexactitude: if Neptune and Pluto are within one degree of exact sextile, then the value is one; if greater than one and less than or equal to two degrees from exactitude, the value is two, and so on. This technique was devised by Dr. Marc Edmund Jones in his Lecture - Lesson on *Pythagorean Astrology*, Sabian Publishing, 1929, from which the keywords for the aspects were also taken.

DR. JONES' KEYWORDS FOR THE VALUES (Aspect Orbs)

1 = EMPHASIS (Doing)   4 = HABIT (Limitation)
2 = CHANGE (Thinking)   5 = EXPRESSION (Skill)
3 = GROWTH (Relating)   6 = EXPANSION (Self-enlargement)

1. EMPHASIS (Doing) All aspects within one degree of exactitude reveal their meaning in its purest, knee-jerk-responsive form – "as near impersonal as it is possible for them to be and yet be individual experiences." Thus natives with Neptune sextile Pluto within one degree of exactness are the most compulsively pragmatic and individualistic – not in the sense of being rebellious or flaunting their independence of spirit, but rather they are self-contained lone wolves. They are idealists off on their own tangents, hence they are not especially successful in mundane affairs unless the rest of the chart is dynamic. They have considerable self-discipline, are self motivated and self-starting, and are conscientious and dedicated. On the negative side they lack perspective: they are too focused on the path beneath their feet and easily become mired in their thinking. Their individualism manifests as a naive doggedness and scrupulosity which inspires others with its unassuming honesty and integrity. Examples: Dan Aykroyd, Mikhail Baryishnikov, John Belushi, Alice Cooper, Farrah Fawcett, Bill Gates, Michael Jackson, Magic Johnson, Jay Leno, Madonna, Maria Shriver, Stevie Wonder.

2. CHANGE (Thinking). All aspects between one and two degrees of exactness indicate flexibility, the ability to adapt oneself to changing conditions – "universals are only to be perceived in terms of constant flux." This means that natives with Neptune sextile Pluto greater than one but less than two degrees from exactitude are the most experimentally pragmatic and individualistic: eager to learn new things and to examine situations and other people's ideas and motivations from different points of view. Like the one's, the two's are hardworking and competent (all Neptune sextile Pluto natives are – Dr. Jones' keyword for the sextile is PRODUCTION), but the reach here is more towards understanding than psychological independence. They are thoughtful, introspective, and arrive at solutions to problems by thinking them through rather than bulldozing ahead. On the negative side, lacking the single-mindedness of the one's, they can come across as being indecisive, bland, and wishy-washy: too lacking in firmness to be masterful (unless the rest of the chart cooperates). Their individualism manifests as a naive intellectual curiosity which inspires others with its unpretentious open-mindedness.

Examples: David Bowie, Albert Gore, Kevin Costner, Whitney Houston, Tonya Harding, Nancy Kerrigan, Elton John, Dan Quayle, Steven Spielberg, Howard Stern, Robin Williams, Oprah Winfrey.

3. GROWTH (Relating). All aspects between two and three degrees of exactitude symbolize friendliness – "the expanding element of simple co-operation in being. It is the basis of pure social relationship, the emanation of ... self to the point of fellowship with other selves." Accordingly, natives with Neptune sextile Pluto between two and three degrees of exactitude are the most socially pragmatic and individualistic: outgoing, gregarious, eager to please; yet still original – fun-loving and mischievous, with a true sense of irony. They are cheerfully optimistic, and enjoy other people instead of analyzing them (two's) or ignoring them (one's). They live and let live, and try to turn aside from conflict and unpleasantness. On the negative side they are inclined to sidestep or slough off problems, to let things slide until they build to a crisis (rather than tackling them directly or thinking them through). Their individualism manifests in a detached, light, unconcerned manner which inspires others with its graciousness and buoyant hopefulness. Examples: Princess Anne, Prince Charles, Princess Diana, Prince, Tom Cruise, Mia Farrow, Arsenio Hall, Diane Keaton Liza Minelli, Bill Murray, John Travolta, Jann Wenner.

4. HABIT (Limitation). All aspects between three and four degrees of exactitude symbolize a tenacity and sagacity which must "observe and classify and understand." Natives with Neptune sextile Pluto between three and four degrees of exactness are the most eccentrically pragmatic and individualistic – highly self-attuned and self-assured, with great depth and delicacy of feeling. They march to the beat of a distant drum and have a spirit of errant adventure. They are calm and knowing, with good intuition and the ability to stop to listen to what their hearts are telling them. Where the two's reach out for intellectual comprehension, the outreach of the four's is less cerebral, more a passionate (and compassionate) lust for life. For the four's understanding is not so much a matter of formulating ideals as it is living one's ideals to the fullest, of drinking life to the dregs. On the negative side they are stubborn, self-willed, convinced of their invincibility and rectitude, and inclined to go to the extremes of human experience (and endurance). Their individualism manifests in their ability to stand up for themselves with utter disregard for the social consequence, and they inspire others with their nobility of spirit and their can-do Quixotism. Examples: Cher Bono, Eric Clapton, Hillary Clinton, John Denver, Goldie Hawn, Steve Martin, Bette Midler, Diana Ross, Bruce Springsteen, Rod Stewart, Alice Walker.

5. EXPRESSION (Skill). All aspects between four and five degrees of exactitude are ingenious and straightforward – "the clue to a man's heart lies in his artlessness – simplicity, smooth functioning in little things." Natives with Neptune sextile Pluto between four and five degrees of exactness are the most candidly pragmatic and individualistic: they are not particularly humble or self-effacing, but rather waste little energy in affectation or posturing – they are plain vanilla with no frills, and just get down to the real business at hand. The striving here is towards reasonableness, fairness, and clear communication with others. They possess a good-natured bonhomie, which on the

negative side inclines them towards talking rather than doing; they can be noncommittal or hedging when what is needed is fairness and taking a stand. Their individualism manifests in their unvarnished outspokenness – saying what they think without fear. They inspire others with their optimism, frankness, and impartiality. Examples: Danny DiVito, Michael Eisner, George Harrison, Janis Joplin, Stephen King, George Lucas, Jim Morrison, Eddie Murphy, Donald Trump, O.J. Simpson, Sylvester Stallone, George W. Bush.

6. EXPANSION (Self-enlargement). All aspects between five and six degrees of exactitude show a no-nonsense practicality: "bending of outer factors to inner convenience; smoothness in the accomplishment of things." Natives with Neptune sextile Pluto between five and six degrees of exactness are the most dispassionately pragmatic and individualistic: they are cool, down-to-earth, purposeful and realistic – ready to roll up their sleeves and get to work. They are deft at processing, whether this be people or problems, and they are willing to take on more than their fair share of responsibility, which on the negative side can lead them to deliberately multiply their burdens and then feel put upon; or to push into areas where their counsel is neither needed nor appreciated. Their individualism is manifested in their ability to meet and even exceed their own (rather than society's) expectations; and they inspire others with their thoroughness and selfless dedication. Examples: Connie Chung, Bill Clinton, Michael Douglas, Jose Feliciano, Aretha Franklin, Stephen Hawking, Jimi Hendrix, Calvin Klein, Martin Scoroese, Barbara Streisand, Marlo Thomas.

For everyone born in this Neptune sextile Pluto generation there comes a point in time when transiting Pluto arrives at the point that Neptune occupied in the natal horoscope (for those born in the twentieth century, this occurs at some time during one's twenties); and because of Pluto's retrograde (back-and-forth) motion the effect lasts for almost a year. The specific events triggered by transiting Pluto conjunct Neptune can occur anytime during that period; but the general tendency is for them to occur at the beginning or at the end (rather than in the middle). A lot of what might be expected to happen depends on what else is going on at the same time in other transit and progressions. Generally speaking, however, transiting Pluto conjunct Neptune presents a major challenge: important new responsibilities or commitments. At first you may doubt your ability to handle them; there's a question of whether you're really up to it. Since it's transiting Pluto, it tends to extremes: thus transiting Pluto conjunct Neptune is either extremely joyous and fulfilling (the usual case, since the planets are natally sextile); or else it's an extreme bummer (if concurrent transit and progressions are unfavorable); but it's rarely in-between. Thus Pluto means extreme something: you have to push something to the limits. What is required is acting (and reacting) according to your gut-level intuition (Neptune) to go with how you feel rather than what society has told you (the natal Neptune sextile Pluto influence). This is a year of maturation, of putting aside your rose-tinted illusions (Neptune) and coming to grips with life directly (Pluto).

* * * * * * * * *

The Mercury Cycle: Shame and Glory

If you analyze your constant thinking (your customary inner dialogue), you will realize that it consists mostly of thoughts about the past and future. Thoughts about the past evoke feelings of shame and embarrassment – hatred of your looks, your actions, and your feelings – which you try to hide from other people. Thoughts about the future evoke fantasies of glory, in which you revel in other people's approval, approbation and vindication.

Shame and glory are the carrot and stick which motivate people in our society. We are all taught to hide our shame from other people, and to seek glory in their eyes. Hiding shame and seeking glory is the engine which drives all our social striving. It is our constant inner dialogue of thoughts of shame and glory which makes us believe that we are separate and unique and special. Glory and shame are two sides of the same coin: the me-me-me coin.

This is what the Mercury cycle reveals in the horoscope: people's inner dialogue of shame and glory thoughts; that is to say, their self-images and beliefs (about themselves and other people) which evoke shame and glory. The Mercury cycle shows different people's inner dialogues – not so much the content, as the how: how people compare themselves to others, feel superior to others, judge and criticize others, and expect things from others. Mercury's synodic cycle shows the ways in which different types of people manage (balance) their shame and glory.

Astronomically speaking, Mercury's synodic cycle of phases reflects its (approximately) 116-day cycle of revolution around the sun, as this is viewed from the point of view of the earth. This cycle is delimited by two conjunctions: Inferior Conjunction, in which Mercury is retrograde and is on a direct line between the earth and the sun; and Superior Conjunction, in which the sun is on a direct line between the earth and Mercury; and also by two elongations (varying from 18° to 28° in separation between Mercury and the sun): Greatest Western Elongation when Mercury rises in the east before the sun; and Greatest Eastern Elongation when Mercury sets in the west after the sun. The elongations can be recognized in an ephemeris as the points where Mercury's daily travel in longitude equals the sun's daily travel in longitude.

When Mercury is near the sun, the solar principle has dominance over the Mercurial principle. Mercury conjunction natives thoroughly repress their shame: they are all force, fortitude, stick-to-their-guns bullheadedness – making knee-jerk decisions and then sticking by them forevermore. On the other hand, when Mercury is relatively distant from the sun, the Mercurial principle dominates the solar principle. Mercury elongation natives flaunt their shame: although they are thoughtful and analytical about their decisions, they are also trifling, flighty, and well aware that everything they say and do is phony.

Mercury's Conjunctions

Natives born with Mercury conjunct the sun (within two days of IC or five days of SC) tend to operate on instant, gut-level impressions and responses rather than on reflection and thinking things through. They rely more on intuition and cunning rather than logic: they have an unerring sense of where their own advantage and other people's weaknesses lie. They possess powerful concentration and focus: once they have made up their minds about something, they are indomitable. They have the greatest personal force of any of the Mercury types because they stand by their decisions and opinions come hell or high water.

The problem with Mercury conjunction natives is that the decisions they stand by are usually not their own, but rather their parents' and society's choices made for them and imposed upon them when they were little. Mercury symbolizes the child within who can never get very far away from its parent, symbolized by the sun. Natives with natal Mercury conjunct the sun cling tenaciously to those self-images which they created as children. Even in adulthood they hew very closely to the images their parents and society inculcated into them. They are the "good" and obedient children who later on become "good" and obedient citizens. Mercury conjunction natives don't examine or question their motives or reasons, but rather charge ahead in the sure and certain knowledge that "God" – their parent – is on their side. Mercury conjunction natives are the backbone of society.

Actually, what we are saying here about Mercury conjunction natives is true of everyone to one degree or another; the other types are variations on the theme of the basic conjunction type. The conjunction represents the extreme case, and thus epitomizes the entire cycle. No one ever escapes parental conditioning; however, greater separation between Mercury and the sun in the natal horoscope permits greater freedom of choice.

Often one or both of a Mercury conjunction sun natives' parents was a harsh, dominating, and repressed individual who gave the native very little in the way of true love – acceptance of the child's feelings. Because they had no model of true acceptance when they were growing up, these natives are intolerant of other people's feelings; and they take any sort of criticism, or even disagreement, as a personal attack. They have themselves under tight control, and try to control everyone around them as well.

Mercury conjunction natives project an idealized, exalted image of themselves, and then work like hell to live up to it. The image is of a good and honorable person; but in their own hearts, they don't quite believe it. On a subconscious level doubt gnaws at the image: perhaps underneath it all they are really killers, perverts, uncontrolled savages! They don't dare take a chance on letting their true feelings out of the cage without a whip and a chair.

Mercury conjunction natives express their shame as a supercilious contempt for other people, whom they force to live out their own shame openly even as they contemn it. They are terrified of being unmasked by other people, of being confronted with their shame; hence they adopt a mask of shamelessness, closing their ears and closing their hearts.

Mercury's Elongations

When Mercury is located at either one of its elongation points (within five days of exact GWE or GEE) it is furthest from the sun, so the natives' inner dialogue is developed to a high degree of refinement, embellishment, and decadence. Instead of relying upon what was drummed into them when they were little, these natives must puzzle everything through for themselves, and convince themselves (and other people) through logic and reasoned argument. Where Mercury conjunction natives tend to sleepwalk through life, focusing all their attention on those areas in which they have some degree of superiority or control and ignoring everything else, the elongation natives tend to overuse mind – they are utterly taken by their own cleverness and perspicacity, and refuse to act on the pure promptings of their hearts without first thoroughly rationalizing them.

Where the Mercury conjunction natives are ashamed of sharing their real thoughts and feelings (indeed, they have a horror of sharing their thoughts and feelings, and thereby making themselves vulnerable), elongation natives tend to think out loud. Where conjunction natives rely on immediate, knee-jerk responses – or immediate dismissal of ideas to oblivion (once they've decided something, their minds are made up forever); elongation natives rely on continual self-analysis, sifting and refining their thinking, over and over and over and over. The conjunction natives operate on blind faith; the elongation natives on lack of faith, which in turn tends to sap their decisiveness. The question that the conjunction natives never ask themselves – which elongation natives never stop asking themselves – is: "Suppose I'm wrong?"

Elongation natives have a more realistic picture of their relationship with their parents – and a more objective view of them as people – than the conjunction types do. On the other hand, they have more self-doubt than the conjunction types, because their mind is further removed from the ultimate source of self-assurance.

Both conjunctions and elongations strive for glory, but the conjunctions cut off the other side of the coin – the shame – until it piles up and up to a crisis. Elongations, on the other hand, can see the shame as well as the glory. They analyze a lot of their shame as they go along; don't repress as much pain and hurt in the moment; and therefore are less surprised in the end. It is their conscious awareness of their own shame which weakens their conviction, their inability to make a stand, and feeds their self-doubt (their awareness of the falseness of their own images). The Mercury conjunction types don't have this problem because they repress their shame completely and rarely permit themselves a moment's conscious doubt – hence their forcefulness and unshakeable conviction of rectitude.

Elongation natives tend to be far more open sexually than the conjunctions – not because they are any "sexier" per se (which is a matter of personal planets posited in certain signs, such as Scorpio and Capricorn) – but rather because they are less emotionally and sexually repressed; more relaxed within themselves and at home with their impulses; less inhibited by parental and societal fiat (what the neighbors might think). They are also more tolerant of variant behavior – both sexual and nonsexual – in other people (unlike the conjunctions, who cannot bear to see anyone else acting out openly that which they themselves are taking great pains to repress).

If the requisite data could be obtained, it is probably possible to prove (or disprove) statistically that people classified as "disordered personalities" (shameless) are more likely have Mercury near the sun; and people classified as "neurotic personalities" (overburdened with shame) are more likely have Mercury elongated from the sun.

What the Mercury cycle actually reveals is the natives' response to toilet training. As Sigmund Freud pointed out, toilet training is the main technique by which our society inculcates hiding shame and seeking glory. In our society toilet training is instilled with a sense of shame. The most important result of toilet training is that children learn to feel ashamed of themselves before their parents and to hide (repress) their shame. What children are learning is not so much how to control their sphincters as how to feel ashamed of themselves. After children learn how to clench up their bodies, clenching up their feelings – particularly their sexual feelings – is the next logical step. Feces symbolize feelings: learning to hold one's feces inside is a symbol for learning to hold one's feelings inside, so as not to make oneself smelly (vulnerable) to others.

A lot of personality traits are a direct product of individual experience with toilet training, which is as severe an exercise in concentration as any advanced mind training technique – not only is it the root of societal shame, but also the constant, moment-to-moment focus of attention upon not soiling oneself becomes the cornerstone for constant, moment-to-moment focus upon an inner dialogue– except that it is imposed upon people when they're two years old. Indeed, this is fundamentally what is symbolized by Mercury's synodic cycle – different ways that different types of people respond to toilet training (see drawing below).

In a general kind of way, Mercury conjunction natives are toilet trained at an earlier age than are elongation natives (it might be possible to prove or disprove this point statistically). Mercury conjunction natives are usually toilet trained the same way as puppies – their mothers rub their noses in it – not literally, perhaps, but with the same indelicacy and force. Their mothers wash their genitals similarly: roughly, rudely, contemptuously. This is why these natives find it difficult to be soft and vulnerable to others – their first model of an intimate relationship was usually rough and disrespectful of their feelings, and they thus learn to be disgusted by their own feelings and intolerant of the feelings of others. Mercury conjunction natives become the "good" children who shut their mouths, hold their feelings inside, and do as they're told.

By contrast, elongation natives are usually toilet trained rather late since they tend to be fascinated by and proud of their feces, so it's more difficult for them to take toilet training seriously. Elongations are naturally looser and more relaxed than conjunctions, and not as awed by their parents. Because they are never "properly" toilet trained, elongations never learn how to hold their feelings inside; even into adulthood they tend to hold their feces (feelings) up for public display and admiration, and at their worst spew them over other people.

Shame and glory are what are meant by ego – they are how all of us are trained as children. We can say that the Mercury cycle as a whole symbolizes how different types of people handle their shame: shame hides things (conjunctions); turns aside from what it doesn't want to face (elongations); or closes up into itself (stations).

Probable Realities

The theory of probable realities can provide us with a good intuitive idea of how astrology works, and what its limitations are. The idea of probable realities, if not the term itself, has become a common theme in popular culture in recent years. For example, the novel *The French Lieutenant's Woman* and the films *The Family Man* and *Sliding Doors* can be considered allegories for how events happen to the same protagonist in different probable realities.

Gary Zukov's book *The Dancing Wu Li Masters* summarizes the theory of probable realities as follows:

"The orthodox interpretation of quantum mechanics is that only one of the possibilities contained in the wave function of an observed system actualizes, and the rest vanish. The Everett-Wheeler-Graham theory says that they all actualize, but in different worlds that coexist with ours! ...

"According to the Everett-Wheeler-Graham theory, at the moment the wave function 'collapses,' the universe splits into two worlds. ... There are two distinct editions of me. Each one of them is doing something different, and each one of them is unaware of the other. Nor will their (our) paths ever cross since the two worlds into which the original one split are forever separate branches of reality."[1]

It might be argued that even if probable realities do exist on a level of subatomic particles, that doesn't necessarily imply that they exist for humans – at least not in any consciously accessible or meaningful way.[2] However, this is precisely what astrology is all about. Astrology doesn't seek to examine and measure accomplished events (although sometimes it can do this) so much as tendencies and potentials.

Probable realities are not a question of the size of the particle involved. Rather, they are a question of the nature of time itself. Time is not how we perceive it to be in our normal, everyday consciousness.[3] Although human perception and cognition make sense to humans, the universe itself doesn't make sense in a way that humans believe.

Where materialistic science sees time as linear, astrology sees time as rhythmic, as an emanation consisting of birth – death – rebirth. What we see as linear time is but one way of apprehending this emanation, which is useful for certain purposes but is a terrible distortion of what time really is. We apprehend time as linear because our thinking is linear, and we are constantly thinking-thinking-thinking from the moment we wake up in the morning until the moment we go to sleep at night. Animals and human babies don't apprehend time in this fashion, and neither did ancient human hunter-gatherers. Time is not linear, but to see this directly one has to stop thinking.

Materialistic science measures points and intervals along a well-ordered continuum, whereas astrology measures cycles upon cycles. The moment of birth can be viewed as a point along a linear continuum, as it is in materialistic science; or, conversely, it can be viewed as a stage in the unfoldment of potentialities on various levels – i.e. as the intersection of many different interpenetrating cycles, as it is in astrology. Astrology can identify decisive points in which things could go – or could have gone – this way or that.

A good intuitive description of what probable realities are all about is found in the Seth books by Jane Roberts:

"In your daily life at any given moment of your time, you have a multitudinous choice of actions, some trivial and some of utmost importance. ... It seems to you that reality is composed of those actions that you choose to take. Those that you choose to deny are ignored. ... If you wanted to be a doctor and are now in a different profession, then in some other probable reality you are a doctor. If you have abilities that you are not using here, they are being used elsewhere. ... These probable selves, however, are a portion of your identity or soul, and if you are out of contact with them it is only because you focus upon physical events and accept them as the criteria for reality."[4]

Practically everyone has experienced bleed-throughs from other probable realities into this one at one time or another, without realizing what they were experiencing. Wistful longings; quasi-memories or presentiments; events which produce a deja-vu-like sense of connectedness to another "me" in a similar but different reality; are often feeling connections with other probable realities. Once when I was deeply in love with a certain person, I went to a party expecting and hoping that she would be there. While she never came physically, I could feel her presence there beside me the whole time. My guidance later explained this sensation to me as follows:

"What keeps you glued into one track or lifetime is the sense of familiarity. To break that track is to feel all your lifetimes and probable realities at once, just like you felt C.'s presence at that party in another probable reality. That's an example of how you can have two different memories of the same event: going to the party with C., and going to the same party without her."

Me: "Did the same things happen at both parties?"

"Yes. Eduardo sang at both parties, but not the same songs. What do you think, stupid? Of course different things happened at both parties. That's not the point. The point is that life consists of feelings. You can only get to those feelings directly by getting past the screen of thought forms of importance and familiarity that hide them. There was a feeling at that party. Remember when you suddenly felt that you had to return immediately, and you jumped up and raced out of the party without even saying goodbye to anyone, and when you got to the pier – by a weird turn of events – you missed the last boat back to Panajachel? And the next day you learned that it was at that precise moment that C. had left for Mexico?"

Me: "How will I ever forget it?"

"You were dreaming then, you know. That event didn't occur in normal, waking consciousness. Or rather, it did, but didn't. Does that explain it? You know that things like what happened to you that day don't occur in real life. They only occur in dreams. You were dreaming that day."

According to the theory of probable realities, every single desire and memory that we have or have ever had creates unto itself an entire probable reality. Every feeling is an entire universe. Everything we desire creates an entire world in which that desire is realized – i.e., every desire creates its own future. We don't desire something for the future, or in the future; but rather the future only exists as there is a desire reaching out to it and creating it. And our minds choose which possible future to go with, out of all the possible futures.

Similarly with memories. Every memory is a thought form record5 of an entire universe (a decision we have made). We believe that we have had a linear personal history – a series of events which began at birth and led up to where we are right now – and from here we will have a linear future. And there is one "me" who has had this personal history and who is going to have this personal future.

In fact, there are infinite number of "me's" who had an infinite number of probable pasts, and there are an infinite number of "me's" who will have an infinite number of possible futures. The action of mind is to select a path going backward and forward: it selects one particular set of memories going back, and one particular set of desires going forward, out of the culture and Zeitgeist (i.e., thought forms) it finds at hand.

All of the thought form material that's left over – all of the "could have beens" and "might have beens" and "should have beens" – are the probable realities for a given lifetime (and are in fact consciously accessible via a technique similar to past life regressions).[6] Probable realities are parallel lifetimes which branch off from this one at each point where a decision, large or small, is made. That is why we must stand by our decisions; otherwise we are draining the energy we need in this lifetime to realize our true desires off into other probable realities. Probable realities are no more nor less real than this lifetime. There are always probable realities in which we get (or got) what we want (or wanted). Mind picks which probable reality to go with from the smorgasbord of possibilities.

      For example, consider a person diagnosed as having some fatal disease (e.g. AIDS). The person chooses a moment in which a doctor says to him, "You have AIDS; you're going to die", and he makes that thought form of fear into an overwhelming belief when he could as easily – after the initial fear – just laugh it off and refuse in his heart to believe it. But instead, he makes the thought form into an overwhelming belief by assigning tremendous importance to it, and he then carries that belief through the rest of that probable reality.

      At the moment the doctor said, "You have AIDS", another probable reality branched off in which the doctor said, "You don't have AIDS". These two probable realities interact on each other: in the AIDS branch, there is a wistful longing for the non-AIDS branch; and in the non-AIDS branch, a constant fear of the AIDS branch. The wistfulness of the AIDS branch may send messages to the non-AIDS branch like: "Enjoy your health! Appreciate what you have!" And the non-AIDS branch may send messages to the AIDS branch saying, "Cheer up! Life has its bright side too!"

      If at any moment the AIDS patient realized that the AIDS is just a belief he could change – only a reality that he is creating by believing it every moment – then at that instant it would collapse and the person would be cured. But this becomes harder and harder to do as the person becomes "sicker and sicker"; i.e. believes more and more in his sickness, thus making it into an overwhelming reality (of course, this is a greatly oversimplified example; what is really going on out there in the universe is far more complex and infinitely ramified than anything the human mind could ever conceive of).

      Which probable reality we find ourselves in at any given moment is largely a function of what conscious choices we are making for ourselves, or else what conceptual thought forms we are letting live our lives for us.

      Consider, for example, a desire for joy. Suppose our mind has attached to that desire the thought form of "getting a raise". Since most of us have thought forms working at cross purposes, there are various probable realities in which that basic "getting a raise" thought form could be physically realized. If we truly feel in our hearts that we deserve the raise because we've done a good job and we want our world to reflect our joy in accomplishment, then we'll take a probable reality branch in which we receive the raise and are joyous about it. However, if in our hearts we know we don't deserve the raise but are only desiring it for our own glory, then we can either take a probable reality branch in which we get the raise and feel false joy about it, or else we don't get the raise and feel disappointed about it. In the latter two cases our true feelings are trying to steer us to true joy by making us feel shame (false joy or disappointment). Just because we block the natural action of the feeling with our thought forms doesn't mean that the feeling isn't still operative and calling all the shots; all it means is that we experience the joyous impulse as shame rather than joy.

In the above example, all three probable realities are equally real. Which one we choose for this lifetime (this personal history) is a function of which choice of the three we decide to make for this lifetime: one choice we make by going along with our true feelings, and the other two we make by going along with our glory thought forms, at the moment when the universe pops the possibility of getting a raise up before our eyes.

A child's anger at a deceased parent for having abandoned him; a woman's feeling of guilt for having been raped; a parent's self-recrimination for an unavoidable accident suffered by her child; are all valid feelings because those probable realities were indeed chosen in preference to happier ones. For example, the parent whose child died in an accident, who spends weeks thereafter ruminating on "If I hadn't done this … " and "If I'd only done that …" is actually reviewing all her decisions (branching points into other probable realities) which led up to this reality.

Some psychologists believe that it is infantile for a child to blame himself when his parents divorce; yet the child is absolutely correct: he chose that probable reality. This is what is meant by "taking responsibility for our already-made decisions" or "taking responsibility for the situation in which we find ourselves"; because that is what we have chosen for ourselves: that is our intent – the place we have to start from. In Viktor Frankl's book about his experiences in Auschwitz, *Man's Search for Meaning*[7], he described the various opportunities he had to leave the concentration camp or to obtain advantages which, had he accepted any one of them, would have led to his death. And the chain of events – the miracle – which led to his ultimate survival was the decision he made at each branch point to consider the needs of his patients above his own needs.

The sum total of all the probable realities which branch off from a person's present lifetime is what William Butler Yeats termed the "Body of Fate."[8] This is what the astrological horoscope shows. Attempts to use the natal horoscope to describe what Yeats termed "Will" – the precise series of events which occur and occurred in this present lifetime – often lead to incorrect predictions. The person's birth horoscope is valid for all of his or her probable realities rather than for any particular one of them. The birth horoscope shows tendencies, propensities, possibilities; but not facts. Exact prediction is sometimes possible when there are lots of indications pointing the same way – e.g. lots of Uranus transits and directions happening about the same time, which indicates sudden and unexpected shakeups in the life. But the only way to make exact predictions in the normal course of an astrological reading is to use intuition. This is the only way to cut across all the possibilities and get down to the one that will be chosen for this present life history. And this is done by reading the client – by psychically anticipating his or her already-made subconscious decisions – not by astrology.[9]

All probable realities for a particular lifetime start from the same birth moment: they are all variations on a theme begun at the same moment in time. Astrology merely suggests; it doesn't command. All astrology per se shows or ever can show is the wind speed and direction at a given moment, but not where the leaf will land. There is always a greater or lesser element of chance involved. Astrology doesn't have the mechanistic surety of physics or chemistry, and it never will. All claims of exact astrological prediction that I have investigated have proven false.[10] Exact prediction is only possible by using inspired intuition or psychic ability.

The existence of probable realities means that even physics and chemistry are not and can never be as mechanistic as materialistic scientists would like. We astrologers must not make the mistake of the materialists, falling for their incorrect assumptions about the nature of reality (in particular that time is linear).[11] We are not unitary beings who live our lives in linear sequence, but rather infinitely ramified "waves" who can only remember one single line of personal history at a time (although our memory can be expanded to include probable realities using a technique similar to past life regressions).

I am a devotee of zodiacal primary directions to angles equated to time with the Placidian True Solar Arc in RA measure (the MC is moved in Right Ascension – both forward and conversely – at the same rate that the progressed sun is moving in RA. The Ascendant is dragged along at the same rate in Oblique Ascension). I've always found these directions to be pretty accurate, particularly the conjunctions, and therefore I've always been puzzled about why the converse direction of Neptune to my Ascendant in the fall of 1980 produced no event whatever.

About the only thing that was happening in my life then was that I was eleven years into an unhappy marriage which was progressively deteriorating and would end nine years later; and I had a three-year-old son. Then an extremely attractive (Leo rising), single, hard-working and dedicated, witchy Scorpio woman, whose natal moon precisely conjoined my natal sun and who fulfilled every image I had of what I wanted in a woman, moved into town.

Looking back it's kind of funny: my wife met her before I did and, being very psychic, she immediately picked up the vibe – meeting this woman really raised her hackles. Anyway, from the beginning this woman and I were super turned-on by each other. She came onto me big-time and made little effort to conceal her feelings. I was torn to pieces, since although I would readily have dumped my wife in a second – even if this woman hadn't appeared – I couldn't justify to myself abandoning my son. It got so bad that I purposely avoided this woman whenever I could because being in her presence forced me to stifle impulses that were raging out of control. I have never had to clamp down upon myself so hard in all my life. Eventually, a few months later, she moved away and that was that. The marriage continued downhill, two more kids were born, and in the end we split up.

So, not much of an event that I can point to happened at that time to correspond to the Neptune direction to my Ascendant. But my guidance has told me that there is another probable reality in which I did abandon my son and leave with this other woman. This present probable reality, in which I stayed with my wife and son, is no more nor less real than the probable reality in which I left with the other woman. And the birth horoscope is an indicator of all possible probable realities: the chart of the "me" who stayed with my wife is the same as the chart of the "me" who left with the other woman. So, if this is true, then at least the Neptune conjunct Ascendant direction worked in the probable reality in which I left (if not in this one, in which I stayed).

Then recently I was channeling to ask the question of whether I'd made the right decision in staying with my wife, since the thing fell apart in the end anyway. And this is what my guidance told me: "It wouldn't have mattered. That's something you still haven't figured out – that there's no 'right' or 'wrong'; all there are, are different decisions, different lessons to learn, none of which ultimately matter in the least. That was a great sacrifice you made for your son, which he'll never understand or appreciate, but which definitely made you a far more selfless person – hence a better father and husband, and a more spiritual person. You lost a lot of selfishness on that one. And, if you'd left with K., it wouldn't have been any bed of roses either. That's what the Neptune conjunct Ascendant – which you've never understood – means. In some probable realities you left with K. In this one you made a tremendous sacrifice for the sake of another person, which put you squarely on the spiritual path. Or another way of putting it is: splitting with K. may or may not have destroyed your chances for spiritual advancement, just as leaving the ranch (a job I hated but which I sensed was a spiritual test); or leaving during the guerrilla war (another test: a situation in which I never knew from one day to the next who would show up to kill me, but which my guidance told me to stick out) might or might not have destroyed your spiritual aspirations. But staying in your marriage – honoring the commitment you had made to your son (and wife) – definitely moved you forward on the spiritual path. Shirking your responsibilities and taking the easy way out would have left you right where you were. And that's what Neptune conjunct Ascendant meant."

Will the human race be able to save itself in the coming century, let alone prosper? Or will it self-destruct and drag the planet down with it? There are probable realities which go either way. Which one of these we find ourselves in – or place our children in – depends upon which one we choose for ourselves.

We call the outer circumstances of our lives – the situations and relationships in which we find ourselves – for some reason; and we can also change that reason if only we don't lose sight of (feeling for) the ultimate goal. This means reaching out to probable realities in which there is joy, no matter how improbable they may seem at the moment, rather than to ones which will only reinforce our self-pity and self-hatred. Hope is the fuel that propels desire forward. This means faith not in ultimate success, but in ultimate self-worth.

Notes

[1] Gary Zukav, *The Dancing Wu Li Masters*, Bantam 1980 page 83
[2] Gary Zukav, op.cit., page 87
[3] Our normal, everyday consciousness is a highly distorted view of how things actually are. Our sense of the passage of time, for example, is a socialized phenomenon, whose distortions become apparent when we enter altered states of consciousness. Indeed, the slowing down of time is a good definition of "altered state of consciousness." For example, in life-threatening situations, such as while we are having an automobile accident or during a big earthquake, time slows way down. We can see everything that is happening with great clarity, in great detail, as if it were unfolding in slow motion. This slow motion perception of time is closer to the truth. It is closer to how babies experience time: more like dream time perception and less like our adult, gloss-over-things-quickly-and-superficially-and-not-pay-much-attention-to-what-is-going-on-around-us perception of time. However, we are incapable of acting in the normal way in this slow motion perception of time because we can't think. If we are going to act or

react in this frame of mind, we can only do so on intent, on our gut-level instinct, not on thought. Therefore the slow motion perception is not as useful in performing all the humdrum tasks of everyday life as is adult time perception.

[4] Jane Roberts, *Seth Speaks*, Bantam NYC 1974 page 256

[5] "Thought forms" can be defined as monads or homunculi of awareness; momentary observer / observed dualities. There are two kinds of thought forms: "sensory thought forms" which consist of sights, sounds, smells, tastes, and feelings; and "conceptual thought forms" which consist of thoughts. We are born with sensory thought forms (we are born knowing how to see, hear, smell, taste, and feel); conceptual thought forms are everything we have learned since birth from our parents and society. Conceptual thought forms are similar to what some cognitive theorists have termed "memes" (cf. Richard Dawkins' *The Selfish Gene*, Oxford NYC 1976 p 192 ff, and Daniel Dennet's *Consciousness Explained*, Penguin London 1991 p 200 ff); and other theorists have termed "schema control units" (cf. Michael Gazzaniga-Richard Ivry-George Mangun, *Cognitive Neuroscience*, Norton NYC 1998 p 458 ff).

[6] The past life regression entry technique can be adapted to viewing probable realities as well. When you are "up in the sky", intend (ask) to come back down into whatever probable reality you wish to examine. This technique can also be run off into the future, to view the probable result of making a decision. For example, to see what it would be like if you married a certain person, use the past life entry technique to access the probable reality in which you are married to this person. This technique is really, really easy to do.

[7] Viktor Frankl, *Man's Search for Meaning*, Beacon Press Boston 1963

[8] William Butler Yeats, *A Vision*, Collier NYC 1966 page 83 ff.

[9] You can psychically probe a client at a distance; even one you've never met. But this is intuition, not astrology, although the practice of astrology sharpens intuition.

[10] Bob Makransky, *Inexact Astrology*, appendix to the book *Primary Directions*

[11] Time is not linear. Rather, everything that has ever happened and ever will happen, in all past and future lives and probable realities (what William Butler Yeats termed "Mask"), is all going on at once, in an eternal now moment. Linear time is an illusion, similar to the illusion of motion produced by the series of still pictures which make up a movie. Babies (and even young children, who sometimes talk about memories from other lifetimes) are not as centered in a one-track existence as adults are. Babies and young children are consciously impinged upon by influences from other lives and probable realities which most adults have learned to ignore. The same socialization process which props up a baby's sense of being a unitary, abiding, separated individual also imprisons that individual in a furrow of inexorable linear temporality. For more information see Bob Makransky, *Thought Forms*, Dear Brutus Press 2000.

Saturn Return Readings

No matter how grown up we think we may think we are in our twenties, life doesn't usually challenge us seriously until our Saturn return. We skip merrily through our twenties as if life were some kind of a picnic, as if we were charmed and invulnerable; and then suddenly, at age 29-30, a gauntlet is thrown down at us and we are forced to pick it up. Seemingly insuperable difficulties and obstacles pop up, everything we've been relying upon and taking for granted gives way, and we are faced for the first time with intimations of our mortality. This frustration and sense of being blocked or defeated usually occurs the year or two before the Saturn return is exact.   It is a time of isolation and anguish.

Whether this sensation is pleasant (challenging) or unpleasant (oppressing), and which specific areas of life are affected, depend upon the condition of Saturn by sign, aspect, and house in the natal chart. But there is usually a sense that time is running out on us; we are getting older and still haven't even begun to get a firm grasp on life; and how we've been handling ourselves up until now just isn't going to cut the mustard. We are called upon to work hard, to truly dedicate ourselves, rather than to get by passing over our experience lightly and half-heartedly.

Life is serious business: decisions count, decisions can be irreversible. Life is like a vortex that can suck you down, down, down and trap you helplessly unless you take a stand. And the Saturn return is one of those times when we must take a stand and show life that we mean business. Something difficult, daunting, and oftentimes disagreeable has to be faced up to and dealt with. Of course, people have the option of ducking out of this responsibility and running merrily off to play; but if they do this – if they refuse to make the commitment which the time demands of them and try to stay loose and carefree – then they will spend their thirties, and perhaps the rest of their lives, drifting aimlessly.

If the Saturn return is difficult, it is nonetheless also an opportunity. It calls for a tour de force – we have to go beyond ourselves, beyond what we thought we were capable of – and therefore it teaches us how to accept more responsibility for our lives and destinies. In forcing us to come to terms with our own limitations, Saturn teaches us the true meaning of freedom.

Finally, in the year or so after the Saturn return passes, a sign is given to us. We are shown that, yes, we are on the right track in life; yes, our suffering does have a purpose; yes, we can control the direction our life will take by using our own volition. We may have lost the nervous, eager expectations of our youth, but in their place we have discovered forbearance, discipline, and wisdom.

What each of the people in the following six examples had to do during their Saturn returns was to deepen – or seriously reexamine – their commitments. That's what the Saturn return is all about: deepening one's commitment to life instead of running off merrily to play.   It's not about the specific choices; it's about the decision to start choosing

Miyamoto Musashi – samurai swordsman

"From youth my heart has been inclined toward the Way of strategy. My first duel was when I was thirteen. I struck down a strategist of the Shinto school, one Arima Kibei. When I was twenty-one I went up to the capital and met all manner of strategists, never once failing to win in many contests.

"After that I went from province to province dueling with strategists of various schools, and not once failed to win even though I had as many as sixty encounters. This was between the ages of thirteen and twenty-eight or twenty-nine.

"When I reached thirty I looked back on my past. The previous victories were not due to my having mastered strategy. Perhaps it was natural ability, or the order of heaven, or that other school's strategy was inferior. After that I studied morning and evening searching for the principle, and came to realize the Way of strategy when I was fifty." < From *A Book of Five Rings* by Miyamoto Musashi. Translation copyright 1974 by Victor Harris. Published by the Overlook Press, Woodstock NY 12498.>

Beverly Sills – opera singer

"The 1958 spring season of the City Opera would be devoted to contemporary American operas, sponsored by the Ford Foundation. The showpiece opera was to be *The Ballad of Baby Doe* by Douglas Moore.

"I loved the role (of Baby Doe). I read everything that had ever been written about her. I copied her hairdos from whatever photographs I could find. I absorbed her so completely in those five weeks of studying the opera that I knew her inside and out. I was Baby Doe.

"At every performance Walter Cassel, as Horace, made me cry. When Horace was dying he would look up at me and sing, 'You were always the real thing, Baby' and I would sing, in reply, 'Hush, close your eyes. Rest.' Then I would take him in my arms and howl like a baby. It was difficult to do the final aria after that scene. Walter and I lived those roles when we were on stage; there was never a moment during the performances when I didn't believe he was Horace Tabor. And even offstage he never called me Beverly or anything else, just 'Baby.'

"The morning after the opening night I grabbed the New York Herald Tribune away from Peter (her husband) before he had a chance to look at it. But there was no review on the regular review page. 'Look at that,' I said to Peter, 'they didn't even cover it, can you imagine?' 'Well,' Peter said, 'do you mind if I read the rest of the paper?' He turned to the front page and there – on the front page! – was the review.

"*The Ballad of Baby Doe* is one of the great contemporary American works. I will always be grateful to Douglas Moore for having written it and for the opportunity it gave me to play opposite someone like Walter Cassel. Baby became an integral part of my operatic experience; it was difficult to shake her off even after I left the opera house. If I have ever achieved definitive performances during my career this far, Baby Doe is one of them. The other three would be *Menon*, Cleopatra in *Julius Caesar*, and Queen Elizabeth in *Robert Devereux*. They have been the only times in my entire career when I have walked out of the theater feeling that I have done everything I wanted to do with a role and that nobody else could have done it better." < From *Bubbles* by Beverly Sills. Warner, NY 1976.>

Charles Darwin – biologist

"During these two years (ages 28-30) I was led to think much about religion. Whilst on board the Beagle I was quite orthodox, and I remember being heartily laughed at by several of the officers (though themselves orthodox) for quoting the Bible as an unanswerable authority on some point of morality. I suppose it was the novelty of the argument that amused them. But I had gradually come, by this time, to see that the Old Testament from its manifestly false history of the world, with the Tower of Babel, the rainbow as a sign, etc. etc., and from its attributing to God the feelings of a revengeful tyrant, was no more to be trusted than the sacred books of the Hindoos, or the beliefs of any barbarian.

"But I was very unwilling to give up my beliefs; I feel sure of this for I can well remember often and often inventing day-dreams of old letters between distinguished Romans and manuscripts being discovered at Pompeii or elsewhere which confirmed in the most striking manner all that was written in the Gospels. But I found it more and more difficult, with free scope given to my imagination, to invent evidence which would suffice to convince me. Thus disbelief crept over me at a very slow rate, but was at last complete. The rate was so slow that I felt no distress, and have never since doubted even for a single second that my conclusion was correct. I can indeed hardly see how anyone ought to wish Christianity to be true; for if so the plain language of the text seems to show that the men who do not believe, and this would include my father, brother, and almost all my best friends, will be everlastingly punished.

"And that is a damnable doctrine."
< From *The Autobiography of Charles Darwin*, W.W. Norton, NY 1958.>

Albert Schweitzer – theologian

"One morning in the autumn of 1904 I found on my writing table in the college one of the green-covered magazines in which the Paris Missionary Society reported every month on its activities. That evening, in the very act of putting it aside that I might go on with my work, I mechanically opened this magazine. As I did so, my eye caught the title of an article: 'The needs of the Congo Mission.'

"The writer expressed his hope that his appeal would bring some of those 'on whom the master's eyes already rested' to a decision to offer themselves for this urgent work. Having finished the article, I quietly began my work. My search (for a way of serving others) was over.

"My thirtieth birthday a few months later I spent like the man in the parable who 'desiring to build a tower, first counts the cost whether he have wherewith to complete it.' The result was that I resolved to realize my plan of direct human service in Equatorial Africa.

"My relatives and my friends all joined in expostulating with me on the folly of my enterprise. In the many verbal duels which I had to fight, as a weary opponent, with people who passed for Christians, it moved me strangely to see them so far from perceiving that the effort to serve the love preached by Jesus may sweep a man into a new course of life. They thought there must be something behind it all, and guessed at disappointment at the slow growth of my reputation. Unfortunate love experiences were also alleged as the reason for my decision. I felt as a real kindness the action of persons who made no attempt to dig their fists into my heart, but regarded me as a precocious young man, not quite right in the head, and treated me correspondingly with affectionate mockery.

"What seemed to my friends the most irrational thing in my plan was that I wanted to go to Africa, not as a missionary, but as a doctor, and thus when already thirty years of age burdened myself as a beginning with a long period of laborious study. And that this study would mean for me a tremendous effort, I had no manner of doubt. I did, in truth, look forward to the next few years with dread. But the reasons which determined me to follow the way of service I had chosen, as a doctor, weighed so heavily that other considerations were as dust in the balance." < From *Out of My Life and Thought* by Albert Schweitzer, trans. C.T. Campion, Henry Holt, NY 1949.>

Bertrand Russell – mathematician

"About the time that these lectures finished, when we were living with the Whiteheads at the Mill House in Grantchester, a more serious blow fell than those that had preceded it. I went out bicycling one afternoon, and suddenly, as I was riding along a country road, I realized that I no longer loved Alys. I had had no idea until this moment that my love for her was even lessening. The problem presented by this discovery was very grave. We had lived ever since our marriage in the closest possible intimacy. I had no wish to be unkind, but I believed in those days (what experience has taught me to think possibly open to doubt) that in intimate relations one should speak the truth. I did not see in any case how I could for any length of time successfully pretend to love her when I did not. I had no longer any instinctive impulse toward sex relations with her, and this alone would have been an insuperable barrier to concealment of my feelings.

"Although my self-righteousness at that time seems to me in retrospect repulsive, there were substantial grounds for my criticisms. She tried to be more impeccably virtuous than is possible for human beings, and was thus led into insincerity. She was malicious, and liked to make people think ill of each other, but she was not aware of this, and was instinctively subtle in her methods.

"During my bicycle ride a host of such things occurred to me, and I became aware that she was not the saint I had always supposed her to be. But in the revulsion I went too far, and forgot the great virtues that she did in fact possess.

"The most unhappy moments of my life were spent at Grantchester. My bedroom looked out upon the mill, and the noise of the millstream mingled inextricably with my despair. I lay awake through long nights, hearing first the nightingale, and then the chorus of birds at dawn, looking out upon the sunrise and trying to find consolation in external beauty. I suffered in a very intense form the loneliness which I had perceived a year before to be the essential lot of man." < From *The Autobiography of Bertrand Russell*, Little, Brown and Co., Boston 1967.>

Dylan Thomas – poet

Poem in October

It was my thirtieth year to heaven
Woke to my hearing from harbour and neighbor wood
And the mussel pooled and the heron
Priested shore
The morning beckon
With water praying and call of seagull and rook
And the knock of sailing boats on the net webbed wall
Myself to set foot
That second
In the still sleeping town and set forth.

My birthday began with the water-
Birds and the birds of the winged trees flying my name
Above the farms and the white horses
And I rose
In rainy autumn
And walked abroad in a shower of all my days.
High tide and the heron dived when I took the road
Over the border
And the gates
Of the town closed as the town awoke.

A springful of larks in a rolling
Cloud and the roadside bushes brimming with whistling
Blackbirds and the sun of October
Summery
On the hill's shoulder,
Here were fond climates and sweet singers suddenly
Come in the morning where I wandered and listened
To the rain wringing
Wind blow cold
In the wood faraway under me.

Pale rain over the dwindling harbour
And over the sea wet church the size of a snail
With its horns through the mist and the castle
Brown as owls
But all the gardens
Of spring and summer were blooming in the tall tales
Beyond the border and under the lark full cloud.
There could I marvel
My birthday
Away but the weather turned around.

It turned away from the blithe country
And down the other air and the blue altered sky
Streamed again a wonder of summer
With apples
Pears and red currants
And I saw in the turning so clearly a child's
Forgotten mornings when he walked with his mother
Through the parables
Of sun light
And the legends of the green chapels

And the twice told fields of infancy
That his tears burned my cheeks and his heart moved in mine.
These were the woods the river and sea
Where a boy
In the listening
Summertime of the dead whispered the truth of his joy
To the trees and the stones and the fish in the tide.
And the mystery
Sang alive
Still in the water and singingbirds.

And there could I marvel my birthday
Away but the weather turned around. And the true
Joy of the long dead child sang burning
In the sun.
It was my thirtieth
Year to heaven stood there then in the summer noon
Though the town below lay leaved with October blood.
O may my heart's truth
Still be sung
On this high hill in a year's turning.

< From *Poems of Dylan Thomas*, copyright 1945 by the Trustees for the Copyrights of Dylan Thomas.>

Terrestrial State

"*First: the four angular Houses (1, 10, 7, and 4) are inherently more powerful than the other Houses.*" "*Next in strength to the Ascendant comes the Midheaven, then the Descendant, and finally the Imum Coeli.*" "*The angular Houses take precedence* [in strength] *over the succedent ones, and these in turn over the cadent Houses.*"

-- Jean Baptiste Morin de Villefranche, *Astrologia Gallica Book 18*

The disposition of the planets with respect to the circle of the houses gives rise to the dignity of Terrestrial State, or propinquity to one of the four angles of the birth chart: Ascendant (ASC), Midheaven (MC), Descendant (DESC) and Nadir (or Imum Coeli, IC). Terrestrial state refers to the natives' approach to social relationships. A planet posited in an angular house (1st, 4th, 7th, 10th) tends to find social relationships stimulating; a planet posited in a succedent house (2nd, 5th, 8th, 11th) tends to find social relationships challenging; a planet posited in a cadent house (3rd, 6th, 9th, 12th) tends to find social relationships overwhelming. Angular planets do not indicate favorable relationships (which is shown by being well-aspected) so much as an easy control of relationships – an ability (symbolized by the particular planet) to land on one's feet and dominate the proceedings. Cadent planets, by contrast, are more in thrall or in bondage to their social relationships – these planets bring a schooling in self-denial or renunciation.

Terrestrial strength – more than any other type of dignity – is a measure of adaptation to social conditioning. Where celestial strength is inborn – a gleam in the eye – terrestrial strength refers to learned strategies of social dominance. Angularity is not merely a matter of social skill. It also implies a certain take on everyday society – thoroughness, leaving nothing to chance or happenstance, enforcing one's own will rather than just crossing one's fingers and hoping for the best (as most people do). Therein inures the real strength of an angular planet: taking complete responsibility for the proceedings.

In general, society trains people to shut up and obey blindly; to take as little initiative and personal responsibility as possible. However, some people – at least in some areas of their lives (shown by their angular planets) – come to the realization that it's all just a game; and that the game does have rules; and that those rules can be manipulated to advantage. Often this knowledge is learned from rather singular parents, who tended to make or break the rules themselves. This is perhaps why Gauquelin found that "children tended to have the same angular planets as their parents, especially if the latter's were just past the Rising Point or MC." (Geoffrey Dean, *Recent Advances in Natal Astrology*, Astrological Association 1977, page 391).

"Observe whether a planet is in the angular, succedent, or cadent houses; for planets in the angles indicate effects which are continuous – especially when also in the fixed signs ... But in cadent houses and moveable signs the planets indicate things which are unstable; in the succedent houses the effects are intermediate." -- Morin, *Book 21*

In any given area of life, most people are milling around aimlessly, waiting for someone to tell them what to do, and there's a small minority of people giving all the orders. These latter people are symbolized in astrology as those who have angular planets. Actually, angular-planet people don't know much more about what's happening than anyone else, but they seem to: they have a facility for projecting the impression that they know what they're doing. There's a self-assurance and economy to their actions that induce other people to defer to them and cede them the lead.

Angularity symbolizes a sense of belonging, of being in the know, on the inside track. Angular types are not unconventional, but rather are above convention. They go through the motions of meeting – indeed, exceeding – social expectations; but they put very little importance upon appearances. They are aware (as most people are not) that social conventions and expectations are wholly arbitrary and not to be taken too seriously. Therefore, they are able to make social role-playing a joyous, fulfilling, fruitful activity, rather than an onerous or daunting enterprise (as it seems to cadent planet people).

Practically everyone is personally ambitious; what distinguishes angular types from the rest is their understanding that there is a science to life – a technology for getting what you want. They don't sit around waiting for their "lucky break" to drop down from heaven; nor do they just put in the time while slowly moving up the ranks. They intuit that life is a game, with definite rules – definite steps and decisions that can be made to succeed in the game. Where most people obey the rules, or more accurately, stumble around in the dark trying to figure out what the rules are, angular types make the rules.

Angular types possess a talent for self-promotion, not in an officious way, but with a definite noblesse oblige. In contrast to the strength conferred upon planets by virtue of their being posited in their ruling or exaltation signs, angular planets exhibit little exuberance or effusiveness. They possess a natural self-control which arises not so much from discipline as from a sense of ease, patience, and forbearance – a sense that life is at one's service, so there is no need to be pushy or overreaching. There is nothing blatant or indelicate about angular planets; their energy is not expended needlessly in demonstrativeness or attitudinizing, but is conserved, held back in reserve until needed. All angular planets make for a hard, cold practicality – even the so-called "nice" planets (moon, Venus, Jupiter) are nice only because that is the easiest way to manipulate people and get one's own way with them.

People with angular planets are the winners in life because they make that assumption – that they are winners. And because it's lonely at the top, angular planets also indicate a certain solitude and isolation. If those with angular planets quite consciously manipulate people and make decisions for the group, they also understand the responsibility that this entails.

Angular planets give people that sense of easy self-assurance associated with being a member of the ruling class. In earlier ages this meant membership in the aristocracy; in today's meritocracy it shows the educated and upwardly mobile as well as those born in the upper classes of society. People born in the upper classes have a winning attitude inculcated into them from birth (that they "belong", that they are destined to rule), which is why angularity is associated with high social class and success in life. The members of the upper classes were historically the people who were "bred" to lead and succeed.

Of course, there are always wealthy and upper-class natives who have no angular planets. These are the ones on whom this born-to-command-and-control-one's-destiny attitude doesn't stick or fit properly. They turn it into an attitude of snobbery, or one that says that life owes them a living. In other words, although exposed to the "angular" attitude by virtue of their upbringing, they fail to catch the meaning of what a natural sense of prowess, adequacy, and leadership actually entails. They understand the superficial trappings of angularity (success) without grasping its essence (personal responsibility).

By the same token, there have always been instances of people born in the lower social classes who by sheer gumption raised themselves up in life in spite of all handicaps. The people with no angular planets who "make it" on their own in a big way don't contradict the theory; all this means is that these people made it even without a native sense of fitness to command. Perhaps they stumbled into the limelight; or maybe they did it through driving ambition, determination, and force of will. In any case, this success will be found to have been accomplished as a freak of nature, or else as a tour de force, rather than as the end result of a natural process of unfoldment. It means that these natives' success in life was not the end result of a conscious sense of fitness but rather was the result of extraordinary talent, effort, or luck. In other words, success can come in spite of an absence of angular planets, but in that case the native has to work harder, or hit the right combination of fortuitous circumstances, in order to get the same effect.

It must also be noted that angularity shows nothing of the degree of success attained in life – whether the native set his or her sights high, or aimed for a comfortable niche; whether big success was attained with little pother, or at the cost of great sacrifice and suffering; indeed, whether success was actually attained, or whether the native went crashing down in flames. This sort of information is shown by benefic / malefic angular planets, and by how well-aspected or afflicted they are.

The angular houses are houses of action, whereas the cadent houses are houses of thought. Angular planets do; whereas cadent planets hold back and watch rather than jump in and stir things up. Thus, being cadent isn't as bad a debility for mental planets such as Mercury and Jupiter as it is for active planets like the sun and Mars. What is shown by terrestrial state is how the native interacts in social groups – as a leader or follower, and in what ways. Angular planets are puppet masters, or Pied Pipers, who have everyone dancing to their tune. In one fashion or another (shown by the particular planet) angular planets maintain the upper hand: their POSITION is DOMINATING, whereas that of cadent planets is REACTIVE. The particular planet involved indicates how the native interacts (e.g. in a Mercurial, Jovial, Saturnine fashion); and the particular angle involved indicates in what type of social group the native interacts in that fashion.

Angular planets symbolize strategies of control, and the four angles symbolize four different types of social relationships: casual, face-to-face relationships (Ascendant); formal and group relationships (Midheaven); intimate relationships and partnerships (Descendant); and standing alone (Nadir). Here we are only concerned with the dignity of angularity as a strength factor, not with what individual angles or planets conjunct the same mean in terms of personality factors, which will be discussed at the end of this chapter.

As an example, I have Jupiter rising in my natal chart and I am very generous with and appreciative of people, and I am always able to understand their viewpoint (whether I agree with them or not). However, this is just a conscious tactic to disarm people, win their trust, and make them dependent on me, rather than being a truly heartfelt and sympathetic impulse of benevolence. Sometimes people who have tried to tell me what to do have been blown away by how cold, hard, and utterly ruthless I can be (since I also have sun, Saturn, and Pluto conjunct on the MC); but they foolishly believed my Jupiter-rising mask of being the nice guy. And, that stellium of planets on the MC is just another mask – a violent temper thing designed to scare people off (which it does), to force them to back down and leave me alone (since I also have moon on the IC).

"Saturn, when unfortunate by its celestial state in the 1st or the 10th House, because of that [House placement], will be much more noxious for the essential significations of those Houses. Thus, when Ptolemy said that planets in the angles are greatly fortified, this must be understood as being strengthened either to benefit or to do harm." <Morinus, *Book 18*>

Take Saturn as an example: Saturn controls by fiat and fear – by sheer adamancy. Thus when on the Ascendant, Saturn is cold, gruff, and forbidding. Saturn conjunct the Midheaven moves unerringly into power vacuums to seize command. Saturn on the Descendant makes for obstinate or absent partners and difficult partnerships (planets conjunct the Descendant project their nature onto the partner – i.e. describe the type of partner chosen). And Saturn on the Nadir closes up into itself and goes its own way. Thus the ASC and MC can be considered active and the DESC and IC passive in their operation. The planets other than Saturn operate similarly, according to their respective natures: Sun on any angle disarms by self-assurance and forthrightness; moon conjunct an angle is vulnerable and puts all its cards on the table; Mercury on an angle is glib and convincing; Venus conjunct an angle is gracious and accommodating; Mars conjunct an angle butts ahead and insists on its own way; Jupiter plays the impartial arbiter. All of these are bids for control; and the particular arena of control is shown by the particular angle (ASC = superficial, tête-à-tête relations; MC = formal and group relations; DESC = intimate relations; IC = solitude).

Let us, for present purposes, define a planet to be angular if it lies within a range of 5° of longitude before that angle to 15° after it. We will define a planet to be cadent if it lies within a range of from 15° before an angle to 35° degrees before it. This tactic – defining "cadent" in terms of distance in longitude before the succeeding angle – sidesteps the problem of defining which house system to use (although it could be argued that this defaults to the Equal House System). Also, by specifying 20° rather than 30° ranges, we sidestep the question of the exact point where cadent turns into angular, and thus can keep distinctions as distinct as possible.

Angular planets have an angle: they have a come-on, a spiel. They are like used-car salesmen – in one way or another, they are selling themselves. Angular planets show a technique of self-promotion (depending upon the particular planet). Angular planets usually manage to land on their feet, and to dominate or capitalize on their situation.

If you have a preponderance of angular planets (4 or more) then you have an air of sublime self-assurance and a quiet bravado. You are shrewd, calculating, Machiavellian. You project the sense that you are in possession of yourself; can handle yourself in any circumstances; and you want everyone to know it. You can be unduly self-absorbed at times and affect an aloof benevolence, but you possess a unique point of view and love to demonstrate your skill. In the context of an afflicted chart this usually means that you feel a constant need to prove yourself and demonstrate your prowess and superiority – you play to the gallery. In a well-aspected chart it means you tend to insulate or isolate yourself – to go your own way and do your own thing, making as few waves as possible.

Having no angular planets means that you have no angles, no come-ons. You are not trying to set the world on fire or impress anybody. This is not to say that you are particularly humble or self-effacing; but there is a certain hesitancy about you, a willingness to just go along. You are low key, bland, easy-going, hail-fellow-well-met. You lead a conventional life, don't get ruffled, or make waves; and tend to be content with your lot. On your positive side you are artless, unaffected, unvarnished, and plainspoken. You're a straight shooter; a simple person; what people see is what they get. You're not trying to sell anybody anything; nor are you driven by a need to have other people see you as successful. You tend to conform to what is expected of you by your social milieu; you do your job as well as you can; and you do not call special attention to yourself.

Keywords for Terrestrial State of Planets

Planet	Strengthens/Weakens	Angular	Cadent
		DOMINATING	REACTIVE
SUN	PURPOSE	SELF-POSSESSED	DEFENSIVE
MOON	ASSURANCE	POISED	SOLIPSISTIC
MERCURY	MENTALITY	CONVINCING	AWKWARD
VENUS	ENJOYMENT	SPONTANEOUS	CALCULATING
MARS	ACCOMPLISHMENT	PLUCKY	MALCONTENT
JUPITER	UNDERSTANDING	ENTHUSIASTIC	CAUTIOUS
SATURN	RESPONSIBILITY	FIRM	VAGUE
URANUS	INDEPENDENCE	OUTSPOKEN	CAGEY
NEPTUNE	INTUITION	CERTAIN	WORRIED
PLUTO	CLARITY	UNCOMPROMISING	DOUBTFUL

* * * * * * * * *

Mayan Shamanism:

The REAL Mayan Prophecy

It is such a joy to live Guatemala, and to have the privilege of participating in an ongoing spiritual tradition which has continued uninterrupted for five millennia. I have met many Mayan priests, and have sometimes been asked by them, "What is all this about a Mayan Prophecy for 2012?" – for after all, even Mayan priests read newspapers and see the television now and then; so some of our kwashru (craziness) filters down to them. I explain that it's just New Age silliness by people exploiting the Mayan cachet to make money; not anything to take seriously.

Indeed, it is true that the Mayan Long Count calendar, a 5,000-year cycle, does come to an end and reset itself on December 21, 2012. But this has no more significance for the Mayans than Y2K did for us. There are a lot of so-called "experts" on the Mayan Prophecy out there now; but not one of them is Mayan, not one of them speaks a Mayan language or has studied with a Mayan priest; and as far as I know, not one of them has even set foot in Guatemala. What this "Mayan Prophecy" is really all about, is how easily New Agers fool themselves.

Unlike the self-appointed Mayan Prophecy "experts", true Mayan priests (Ajk'ihab' or daycounters) are chosen by the Mayan spirits themselves. Then they study for decades under the tutelage of accomplished Ajk'ihab's. The Mayan priests whom I have met are very humble (most of them are subsistence maize farmers from the countryside), and yet they have a commanding presence. When they put on their headbands and begin ceremonies they become filled with the Spirit (Ahau) and are completely self-effacing – not there, and yet utterly real and masterful in a way which makes most of our religious and spiritual leaders seem, by comparison, phony and ugly.

The point is that the Mayans (unlike the "experts") are making a connection with the spirit world. Connecting and communicating with the Mayan spirit world is an everyday part of Mayan life, just as the telephone and internet are for us. This connection is made principally at Mayan ceremonies, where priests channel messages for participants and also perform healings. This connection is also made in daily life – by respecting the natural world and propitiating its guardian spirits.

This is difficult for us First Worlders to understand, since we are so used to empty, formulaic church services which are basically just social functions. Mayan ceremonies, on the other hand, are magical invocations in which spirits are contacted to obtain useful information and healings from the spirit world. The spirits actually do come; their presence can be felt; and their answers are very right on. For example, once during a ceremony my teacher, Don Abel Yat, stopped and told me, "You are about to have an enormous land problem." Sure enough, two weeks later a land dispute began which dragged on for the next three years and cost me a boodle of money and a lot of grief. The point is that the predictions which are channeled by Mayan priests are very specific and to the point (not vague generalities).

By contrast, this "2012 Prophecy" thing is being touted by the non-Mayan "experts" as a kind of New Age version of the Rapture: a miraculous transformation of human consciousness which sweeps humanity up into the Pleiades to escape the coming tribulation. But things don't happen that way in real life. If there is a fundamental transformation in human consciousness, the way it will probably occur is that the environment and civilization will deteriorate over the next few decades. And in the crisis people will draw together and open their hearts to one another, as they do in the face of any natural catastrophe such as an earthquake or flood. When people lose their faith in the system and start listening to their own hearts is when the system will change.

Our society is in spiritual crisis. We have a great deal more wealth and freedom of choice than the Mayans do, but to what end – to buy this instead of that? To be robotic producer / consumers trapped in an endless spiral of insatiable desire? Where our society has lost all sense of spiritual purpose, Mayan society has not. The Mayans had the highest civilization in the New World at the time of the Spanish conquest, and they have maintained it in spite of five centuries of oppression and persecution. Mayans possess the dignity of a people who know where they belong in the universe. They have a sense of connectedness and rootedness which contrasts sharply with the empty materialism of our society. Mayans know in their hearts that nature is sacred; they are capable of feeling awe and wonder; they are broken and humble. Viewed through Mayan eyes, our behavior seems boorish, crass, and profane – utterly lacking in culture and manners.

We can learn from the Mayans, not by mindlessly aping the outward shibboleths of their cultural traditions, but rather by taking a hard look at our own personal behavior and assumptions. If the human race is to survive the coming crunch, it is going to have to find some other way to motivate people besides capitalistic greed and selfishness; and it is going to have to provide people with a truer sense of connection to the divine than that which is offered by most conventional religions. This is a more viable path for human salvation than silly, irresponsible "prophecies", or the short-sighted avarice and pipe dreams offered by materialism. This is the REAL Mayan Prophecy – what we really should be learning from the Mayans – which is found in the Christian Bible as well: "Blessed are the meek, for they shall inherit the earth."

Mayan Ceremonies

Mayan religion, philosophy, jurisprudence, medicine, agriculture, hunting, intimate relationships, etc. etc. completely revolve around a 260-day almanac known as the Chol Qij, or count of days (the term Chol Qij is Kiché – central Guatemala – Mayan. Academic archeologists and anthropologists prefer the Yucatec – Mexican – Mayan term Tzolkin). The Chol Qij consists of twenty naguals, which can be thought of as archetypes roughly analogous in significance to our twelve zodiacal signs; except they are considered to be alive and petitionable. A nagual is preceded by a numerical coefficient ranging from one to thirteen which modifies its underlying meaning. Thus twenty naguals x 13 numerical coefficients = 260 days. The Chol Qij commences on the day 8 Batz. The Chol Qij is the basis of Mayan invocational magic; that is to say, the order of a Mayan ceremony follows the order of the twenty naguals, beginning with the nagual of the day of the ceremony.

For a nominal fee a client hires a Mayan priest, or spiritual guide (Ajk'ihab' = day counter, or katok utzuj = candle burner), to perform a ceremony for a particular purpose: to heal an illness; to bring prosperity in business or a suitable mate in marriage; to fecundate a sterile woman; etc. Certain naguals are favorable for hunting, others for planting, others for asking a woman's hand in marriage, others for launching business enterprises. Initiating activities, as well as performing prayers or ceremonies to petition blessings for such activities, are done on the correct day.

The priests wear their uniform of office: bandanas on their heads, sandals on their feet, seashell necklaces, and long cloth belts. The priests lay out the fire: first a circle is described in a pit with sugar, and the four quarters are delineated with a cross within the circle. On top of this 260 cylinders of incense are laid; then a cross of many small candles, whose colors correspond to the four directions, is built in the center of the circle: red candles to the east, black to the west, white to the north, and yellow to the south. Chunks of copal pom incense are placed at the four corners, and more colored candles, dried herbs, cinnamon sticks, and cigars are arranged around the circle. Finally the circle is delimited by sprinkled dried romero herb around its circumference; and a tower of twenty candles bound around a cigar, symbolizing the Tree of Life, is placed in the center. The overall impression of the fireplace is quite decorative and colorful.

After the fireplace is laid out the head priest and his assistants make offerings to

Counting to 13 (Don Domingo Bolon)

the four cardinal directions in a sing-songy chant. The words sung-spoken by Mayan priests aren't as important as the rhyme and rhythm, the hypnotic patter of the litany. The priests invoke the earth god Kawa Tzul Taka (Lord Mountain-Valley). The priests also call for blessings from the 166 sacred mountains and ceremonial sites in Guatemala: Uaxactun, Ceibal, Tikal, Aguateca, Chajompec, Pecmo, Beleju, Chicoy, Chiajxucub, etc. Then the priests ask the participants to name their deceased ancestors, and the ancestors are called upon to come and witness the ceremony.

After the invocations are finished, a handful of twenty small candles is given to each participant; and then the tower of candles in the center of the fireplace is lit by the client (the person who has commissioned the Mayan priests to perform the ceremony). The tower of candles will slowly burn down and eventually ignite the other candles, incense etc. laid out in the fire pit, creating a large blaze which dances in the breeze. The flames are regarded as being alive, as representing the presence of Kawa Tzul Taka, and as such the priests watch the fire very carefully for omens throughout the ceremony. If the fire swirls around in a counterclockwise vortex, then this is a good omen; but if it swirls clockwise then it's a bad omen. If the fire divides in two then it's an omen that the present company will divide into factions and dispute. Similarly, the behavior of the fire in response to petitions (e.g. for health, or economic prosperity, or when individuals are journeying around the fire) made during the course of the ceremony is a sign of whether and how the wish will be granted.

After the fire is lit the head priest sacrifices a chicken. This payment is made to Kawa Tzul Taka to ask for blessings. The priest first offers the chicken to the four cardinal directions, then he dances around the fire with the chicken draped around his neck. Finally he kills it by hand by stretching the chicken's neck until the head tears off. The still-beating heart of the sacrificial chicken is torn from its breast by the priest, who hands it to the client to make a wish on until the heart stops beating, at which time it is offered to the fire.

After the payment is made to Kawa Tzul Taka, the order of the ceremony follows that of the twenty naguals of the Chol Qij. The twenty Lords are called upon in serial order to bless the "great-grandchildren," (mam inmam) which is how the Mayans refer to themselves. The first nagual is the nagual of the day the ceremony takes place. Often the day Batz is chosen for ceremonies since it is considered to be the noblest of the Lords, and is the initial nagual in the 260-day cycle. In a sing-songy litany the chief priest explains that Batz symbolizes a ball of thread, which is the Mayan metaphor for time. Batz is the weaver of the family and community, the ties which bind people together. The priest asks this Lord that his client be able to roll up family, children, wealth.

At the end of Batz the priest counts up to thirteen for the thirteen powers (gods of the upper world): hun (1) Batz, kwib (2) Batz, oshib (3) Batz, kayib (4) Batz, ob (5) Batz, kwakib (6) Batz, kukub (7) Batz, kwashakib (8) Batz, beleb (9) Batz, laheb (10) Batz, hunlahu (11) Batz, kablahu (12) Batz, oshlahu (13) Batz. After the count to thirteen is made for each nagual, the participants in the ceremony make a wish on one of the twenty candles they were handed at the outset and then throw the candle into the fire. The portion of the ceremony devoted to each individual nagual varies in length, but typically lasts five to ten minutes. At intervals there is ritual dancing of the slow son dance around the fire by the priest alone, and sometimes by participants as well. Participants are cued by the high priest as to what to do next.

When a nagual's turn ends the next nagual becomes "host" of the ceremony: after Batz comes Be (road), and the priest sing-songs a litany asking this Lord to protect his client's journey, that no matter where he goes he should have no accidents and live a long life; that he should have good roads, beautiful roads, level roads. During this invocation the priest and client journey (dance the son as they slowly circle the fire) three times. The invocation of Be ends with the count up to thirteen: hun Be, kwib Be, oshib Be, etc. to oshlahu Be; and then the participants make their wishes and throw a candle into the fire.

The Lord Aj, the maize plant, is then invoked. Where the great-grandchildren have forgotten their traditional ways, Aj reminds them of their inheritance and culture – how to count the days and to remember their forefathers and their past. Then the count is made to thirteen: hun Aj, kwib Aj, oshib Aj, etc. to oshlahu Aj, and the participants make wishes and throw candles into the fire.

Hish is the jaguar, who roams the earth and sees everything under his domain. Hish represents strength and fertility, so clients seeking to have children might commission petitioning ceremonies on the day Hish. Then the count is made to thirteen: hun Hish, kwib Hish, oshib Hish … and candles are thrown into the fire.

Tzikin (bird) is the guardian and messenger of the supreme deity Kawa Tzul Taka. It is this Lord who brings money, wealth, livestock, and property. The participants will approach the fire and wave their wallets or purses above it; and the head priest asks this nagual for abundance for his client. After counting to thirteen this time the head priest and participants each give the fire a handful of sesame seeds as an offering, since sesame is the food of Kawa Tzikin; then they wish for prosperity and throw their candles into the fire.

Ajmak is the Lord of sinners. The head priest and participants now kneel down around the fire and call upon Kawa Ajmak to forgive them their faults; to pardon wherever they have made errors, wherever they have committed sins, wherever they haven't done as they should. The head priest and participants prostrate themselves, touching their foreheads to the ground and kiss the earth, and humbly beg forgiveness. Then the count is made to thirteen Ajmak and candles are thrown into the fire.

Noj is the Lord of intelligence and wisdom. The head priest asks this Lord to bless his client with wisdom and divine guidance. Kawa Noj is also asked to bless children who are studying in the ladino school system: at this point in the ceremony the children come forward and the priest blesses them by touching them with candles on the head (where ideas are born) and hands (with which they write), and then he throws the candles into the fire. Then the priest counts hun Noj, kwib Noj, oxib Noj, to oshlahu Noj.

Tihash represents the obsidian blade, and it is the Lord of danger. This day is used for rituals to avoid evil influences for people and sickness in domestic animals, and to remove curses. On the other hand, sorcerers use Tihash to perform witchcraft. After calling upon this nagual to protect his client from injury, the head priest counts to thirteen Tihash.

Kawok is the thunder. Its power is fire; its lightning illuminates the darkness. The priest prays to the lightning gods not to hurt the great-grandchildren, but to strengthen their spirit; then he counts to thirteen Kawok.

Ajpu is the sun. This Lord represents the hero of the Popul Vuh creation myth, who triumphed over the Lords of Hell and became the sun. The priest prays to this Lord to overcome sorrows – all the tribulations which the Mayan people have suffered at the hands of their conquerors. This is the day created by the ancestors to make a balance between the good and the evil; their teachings show us that good will always triumph over evil. Then the priest counts to thirteen Ajpu.

Imosh is the rabbit. It is the Lord of those who are crazy, confused, or have lost their way. Rituals are done on this day to help people with mental problems, to cure illness, and to pray for the return of a strayed or missing spouse. The invocation is completed with a count to thirteen Imosh.

Ik is the wind. Rituals are done on this day to bless all that exists in nature and to give thanks; and so that the wind will take away all suffering and evil influences. The priest petitions Ik not to blow troubles or illness the client's way; but to blow away what problems he does have. Then the count is made to thirteen Ik.

Akabal is the dawn. Rituals are done on this day to give thanks to the light and to avoid calumny and lies. The priest gives thanks for our awakening each day, and invokes this Lord to give us good ideas and good thoughts. Then the count is made to thirteen Akabal.

Kat is the net, like the net bags in which maize is stored. It is the day of payment to the ancestors. The priest invokes this Lord to bring the people together like nets bring together the ears of maize. Then he counts to thirteen Kat.

Kan is the snake, the plumed serpent which ties together the Heart of Heaven and the Heart of the Earth. Rituals are done on this day to ask for justice, wisdom, strength, equality and to avoid disequilibrium with Mother Nature. The priest petitions this Lord not to bite, not to send dangers. Then the priest counts hun Kan, kwib Kan, oshib Kan, kayib Kan, … up to oshlahu Kan.

Kemé is the Lord of death. The priest prays to this nagual to guard against the powers of the night which steal people's souls, and against the dangers of the daytime. Participants in the ritual who have come for a healing are now called forward one at a time. When healing someone the head priest gives the person a handful of candles to hold and then stands behind the person with one hand on the person's shoulder and the other held above the person's head. The priest prays over the person, then takes candles in both of his hands and traces the person's body from heart to feet; then he grinds the candles into the person's hands and throws them into the fire. Next the priest raises a bottle of aguardiente liquor, takes some into his mouth, and spit/sprays a forceful cloud of aguardiente over the person's body four times, once from each of the four cardinal directions, to burn away the person's illness. After the healings he counts hun Kemé, kwib Kemé, oshib Kemé … up to oshlahu Kemé.

Kej is the deer. It also symbolizes the four cardinal directions. The priest petitions this Lord to bring strength to the great-grandchildren, to lift their legs and backs and heads, to give them the strength of a deer, to overcome weakness and tiredness, to grant them power and success. Then he counts to thirteen Kej.

Qanil is Venus. Qanil is the nagual of the farmer, the day to pray for a good harvest. The priest calls upon this Lord to bless the maize seeds, the bean seeds, the seeds of every cultivated plant; also to bless the leaves of all plants. This Lord is asked to bring forth bounteous harvests of grain and fruit to feed the hungry. Then he counts to thirteen Qanil.

Toj is jade, or payment. The nagual Toj symbolizes offerings, the payment of what is due, and the leveling of justice. The priest begins the ceremony by offering payment (the chicken), and now he asks Kawa Toj to accept the tribute of candles, copal incense, etc. to protect the lives and roads (journeys) of his client and all the great-grandchildren. Then he counts up to thirteen Toj.

The final nagual is Tzi, the dog. On this day offerings are made so that negative forces won't triumph and so that the authorities will use wisdom and vision to administer justice. The priest petitions Kawa Tzi to influence and win over judges, lawyers, police, and the military on behalf of the great-grandchildren; to guide and protect them in the legal system and with all governmental authorities. Then he counts to thirteen Tzi.

After all twenty of the naguals have been invoked, the priest thanks them for bringing the great-grandchildren together on this occasion, and to bless everyone. Then all the participants are given a candle and instructed to kneel down around the fire and pray for whatever they desire; then the candles are thrown into the fire. The participants stand and clasp their hands behind their backs, and everyone dances a slow, rhythmic son dance in a circle around the fire. The priest closes the ceremony as he began it, by thanking the four cardinal directions. In toto the ceremony lasts about five hours.

K'ekchi Mayan Paganism

In contrast to the Abrahamic religions (which include rationalistic-materialism: academic "science"), paganism isn't a matter of beliefs, but rather of cognition. Paganism seeks to operate on an altogether different guidance system than thinking – namely, feeling; intuition; direct knowing. Paganism isn't learned from books, but rather from relaxing, turning off the thinking mind, and tuning in to the messages of the plants; the wind; and the world around us.

Direct knowing is a more functional operating system for hunter-gatherers than is thinking (which became predominant when agriculture was invented). As the earth continues to turn against us humans; and our materialistic society collapses as its short-term profit- (rather than long-term survival-) oriented mechanisms are increasingly unable to adequately respond to the crisis; this original form of cognition will revindicate itself. Either we humans will relearn how to rely upon feeling (direct knowing) rather than thinking to make our moment-to-moment decisions; or else we won't survive as a species. We will either relearn how to listen to what the earth, our mother, is telling us; or else she will spit us out. This is what the much-vaunted coming transformation in consciousness is all about.

In this regard it can be fruitful to take a look models of present-day pagan societies (of which a few remain on the earth), for indications of the possible forms and directions which can be taken by societies which emphasise feeling and intuition over thinking and believing. Although the Mayan Indians of Central America are, for the most part, subsistence maize farmers (i.e., agriculturalists); and for over three millennia their noble and priestly classes have evolved one of the most complex and sophisticated intellectual systems (mathematical, astronomical-astrological) which the human race has ever devised; nonetheless their everyday cognition is decidedly pagan (not materialistic).

Anyone trying to make head or tail of Mayan stories (such as the Mayan "Bible", the *Popul Vuh*); or trying to interview Mayan priests with a view towards understanding the taxonomy of their systems of deities and worlds and astrology; soon runs up against a wall: there is no way of classifying anything. You can't get the same answer about anything from two different Mayan priests; nor the same answer from the same priest on two different days. When performing ceremonies Mayan priests recite sing-songy litanies which don't really mean anything per se, but instead have a lyrical, evocative, poetic quality rather than any kind of literal meaning. In other words, to the Mayans thinking is not really the point.

In making major decisions, Mayans rely upon one form or another of what we would call channeling spirits. Everyday life in a Mayan home is governed by a set of ritualized behaviors which serve to remind people that everything – plants, animals, rocks, mountains, possessions – have feelings which must be respected in order to live in harmony with Ahau (The Spirit of the Universe), of which everything that lives is a manifestation.

There are at least two dozen Mayan tribes in Guatemala, who speak related but mutually unintelligible languages, and who possess differing cultural and religious traditions. In this article we will examine some features of K'ekchi Mayan (north-central Guatemalan) paganism; but K'ekchi traditions are similar in kind to those of their neighboring tribes.

To the Mayans, everything is alive; everything is watching; everything cares. A person's health, wealth, and well-being are very much dependent upon maintaining a correct balance in this world of living entities, many of whom are malevolent, or at the very least super-sensitive to being slighted. Some entities must be scrupulously avoided; others worshipped or propitiated.

Although there is a host of spirits – mostly malevolent – in the Mayan worldview, the principle deity of the K'ekchi Mayans is Kawa Tzul Taka (Lord Mountain Valley), who has power over – and takes care of – the earth, trees and plants, rocks, animals, and humans. Although usually referred to in speech as a male being, Mayan priests, if pressed, will aver that Kawa Tzul Taka has no sex; or perhaps is a dual deity partaking in nature of two of the nine Mayan gods of the earth (namely the Creators-Formers Gucumatz, the feathered serpent; and his consort Tepeu, the Conquerer).

Kawa Tzul Taka can mete out punishment to those who offend him; and he confers blessings upon those who worship him. He is invoked at ceremonies which take place several times yearly, at the times of the planting (April), cultivating (July), and harvesting (October) of the maize crop.

During the prayers at these ceremonies the altar will sometimes appear to "light up" – a palpable presence fills the room – and a group of female channels are ready to receive Kawa Tzul Taka's messages, and then pass them on to the attending priests.

It is normal for Kawa Tzul Taka to appear in the dreams of leaders of religious brotherhoods to tell them whom to appoint to which offices in the brotherhood (appointments should not be made in the absence of such dreams).

Unlike the ceremonies of other Mayan groups (which take place in daytime, around an open fire), K'ekchi ceremonies take place at night or in caverns (k'ek means dark or night, and the word K'ekchi means "of the darkness"). These ceremonies go on all night long, prayer alternating with dancing to slow, rhythmic, haunting son music accompanied by musicians on homemade harp, guitar, violin and drum.

After the prayers conclude at 2:00 am, everyone shakes hands and eats. At dawn the men scatter to nearby caves to invoke Kawa Tzul Taka's blessing on the maize crop and the community. The following noon the participants gather again for a luncheon and prayer session.

Kawa Tzul Taka is associated with the mountains, and the thirteen principle peaks in the K'ekchi area are regarded as especial manifestations of Kawa Tzul Taka (and they are considered to communicate with one another through the lightning and shooting stars). All mountain tops – and also cave entrances, crossroads, and entrances to villages – are marked by wooden crosses, which represent the presence of Kawa Tzul Taka. To the K'ekchi's, many (but not all) man-made objects are considered to possess souls; but crosses (Mayan crosses which, unlike Christian crosses, are equilateral) are unquestionably the most sacred of man-made objects. When people come to one of these crosses they must give offerings of incense, candles, flowers, or pine boughs as a sign of veneration for Kawa Tzul Taka. A slow dance might also be dedicated to the deity, and a prayer made thanking Kawa Tzul Taka for his protection. A stone is often left at a cross as a substitute for the person's soul. Before continuing on their journey, people will switch their legs and feet with small branches to ensure that their feet do not get tired.

Before cutting a tree, moving a boulder, or clearing a site for planting or building, permission for injuring the earth must be sought from Kawa Tzul Taka at a cross or in a mountain cave. This often involves sexual abstinence, and observance of food taboos, for a period of thirteen days prior to the ceremony. As in most K'ekchi ceremonies, Kawa Tzul Taka is propitiated with offerings of turkey soup, cacao, candles, flowers, and copal pom incense, as well as prayers of petition. At especially important rituals, such as planting ceremonies, a chicken might be sacrificed as well, and its blood sprinkled on the seed maize and the cross.

If permission is not sought or is not properly requested (if sexual or food taboos were not observed), then Kawa Tzul Taka will retaliate: hunters are punished with a dearth of game, or are bitten by snakes; farmers find their crops attacked by animals or destroyed by winds and rain; or the people might suffer illness or lose their souls. Besides fulfilling ceremonial requirements, it is necessary to propitiate Kawa Tzul Taka by leading a good life. Arrogance, marital fighting, and lust can bring punishments or soul loss. Whenever an offense against Kawa Tzul Taka has been committed, counteracting rituals must be performed.

Soul loss can either be permanent (resulting in death) or temporary (manifesting by physical or mental illness, or being struck dumb). The souls of the dead are considered dangerous to the living, since they are considered to linger on, and can steal the souls or frighten the survivors with noises and manifestations if they are not propitiated. Candles or maize stalks are placed in the coffin as substitutes for surviving relatives, so that the dead soul doesn't return to take its loved ones with it; and when the family leaves the home for the cemetery, an old woman remains behind to sweep the house and bid the dead soul to depart with the body.

If people fall into a river, their souls are considered to remain trapped in the water until they provide a ritual substitute – an image of themselves fashioned from copal pom incense, which includes bits of the people's hair and fingernails. Incense is burned at the spot where the people fell into the river and their souls are coaxed to return.

Besides humans and spirits, certain objects possess souls, and become sad (rather than malevolent) if not treated respectfully. Some of these sacred objects are foodstuffs, particularly maize, beans, and sugar cane; and religious objects such as the cross, incense, candles, and harp. If the soul of one of these sacred objects is lost (through disrespect) then the well-being and happiness of the family suffers as a result. If maize is insulted (by being wasted, for example) then it loses its power to protect itself against mice and weevils, and it won't germinate when used for seed. Besides disrespectful treatment, the soul of the maize can be lost by leaving a ladder standing against the house in whose rafters the maize is stored (the soul of the maize will slither down the ladder and get lost).

As mentioned previously, special all-night propitiatory ceremonies are done to bless the seed maize, which is fed with turkey soup, cacao, and boj (fermented cane juice), and the blood of sacrificial chickens. Besides seed maize, religious objects such as the cross, harp, and shakche (decorated arch of liquidamber boughs placed at the entrance of the house) must be ceremoniously fed with boj liquor, or else they lose their protective power (for example, the harp won't play properly and the arch will permit disruptive people and influences into the house).

Other objects which possess souls and can punish disrespect are trees, which must never be cut and left to rot without being used; and the house itself, which is considered to be greater than the sum of the souls of the trees which were cut down to construct it, and which can sicken and kill the family within if it is not treated respectfully. This propitiation begins when the first corner-holes for the house are dug, by feeding the holes the blood of a sacrificial chicken. When the construction is completed, candles are burned in the four corners and another chicken is sacrificed so its blood can be used to feed the rafters and door, to propitiate the spirit of the house. Bridges also have souls, and pigs (formerly, humans) are sacrificed at ceremonies to feed the spirit of a newly-built bridge so that it won't take human victims (take the souls of people passing over it by occasioning their fall).

A person's walking stick is considered beneficent to the person, but malevolent for anyone else. Walking sticks are stuck in the ground at night near the pallets where they sleep to waken the owners in case a thief breaks into the house. Hammocks must not be left hanging up when not in use; nor must brooms be left outside overnight, else the spirit of the night will desecrate them and bring illness to the owner. The spirit of the night is dangerous, and indeed K'ekchis who go abroad at night do so in trepidation. Pregnant women avoid going out at night for fear their fetus might become sick or deformed; and men must avoid lustful thoughts when they are outside at night else they be accosted by temptress spirits who can steal their souls.

The point here is not that we modern pagans should mindlessly ape the Mayans' particular cultural traditions (as so many New Agers seem to be doing), but rather that we understand how the Mayans sanctify their everyday lives; and perhaps emulate the essence of what they are doing (not the outward shibboleths) in our own fashion – and perhaps with less of the irrational fear (which is also a staple of the Abrahamic religions). Mayans have a connection to the world about them which we moderns, in our materialistic society, have largely lost. The Mayans make this connection by instilling a sense of humility (rather than self-important hubris) in people – by making people aware that they are not the centre of the universe – and also by restoring a sense of the sacred to the routines of everyday life.

In our decadent, materialistic society we don't have as much of a feeling of relationship with the things about us the way Mayans do. This is why so many people feel a need to keep obsessively buying and buying and buying, to fill the emotional void they feel inside themselves. Feeling connected means, that instead of treating things as insensible objects, treating them as if they were as capable of feeling as we are. A sailor knows that his ship loves him; a child knows her dolls are alive; and most of us have at one time or another felt emotionally intimate with our automobiles. These feelings are no mistake – this is true mingling with the objects in our environment, relating to the world on a basis of true feelings, as Mayans do, rather than on a basis of thought forms (concepts and beliefs, such as that a car is just a "car", and any feelings we are picking up from it are just our imagination). This is where each of us must begin again to learn to love, because if we can't love inanimate things, which have no malign intent, there's no hope of our ever learning to love something as bewilderingly complex as a human being.

Besides the deep respect which most of us modern pagans feel for nature, we can do this by paying attention to what we're doing when we are touching or handling things; by being grateful to our tools for the help they give us; by lifting things gently and placing them where we want them; by dealing with things with the same delicacy and respect with which we ourselves would prefer to be treated. We toss things about carelessly or leave things in a mess, and then wonder why we feel that life is tossing us about like an insensible object, and why our life is a mess. We can't make that connection in our minds, of where those feelings are coming from.

Our society teaches people not to care about the fate of our mother earth or future generations; and then it wonders why the earth has turned against us. We modern pagans have to point out that it is possible to feel the world rather than conceptualize it; to follow our own intuition rather to mindlessly obey societal fiat; to base our actions on the assumption that we are not the most important thing going. This is the lesson we can learn from the Mayans.

Barack Obama's Mayan Horoscope

By Don Abel Yat Saquib and Bob Makransky

The purpose of this article is to give some predictions made for Barack Obama by traditional Mayan astrology, as interpreted by Don Abel Yat Saquib, a Mayan Ajk'ihab' (daycounter: a priest/astrologer/healer) from Guatemala. At the same time, this article will serve as a simple introduction to the rudiments of Mayan astrology.

The important thing to remember about Mayan astrology is that it is inseparable from the invocation of Mayan spirits. In other words, there is no book you can read or workshop you can take which will make you a Mayan astrologer.* To become a Mayan astrologer you need, first of all, to be chosen by the Mayan spirits themselves. Then, you must study for decades under the tutelage of an accomplished daycounter.

Mayan daycounters use their astrology loosely, as a point of departure. That is to say, their interpretations, whether obtained from the "natal chart" of the 9 nagual diagram (described below); or whether obtained (in what we would term "horary" fashion) by manipulating 260 red tzinté beans to obtain an answer to a specific question; or whether obtained by direct knowing during a Mayan ceremony; are all channeled from the Mayan spirits. Mayan daycounters sometimes receive their information in the form of channeled thoughts; or by observing the behavior of the fire during a ceremony; but more often, they receive this information as pulses in their veins, which they learn how to interpret with experience (e.g. a pulse in the left shoulder means such-and-such; a pulse in the right wrist means something else; and so on). The Chol Qij thing – the astrology part – is regarded as an aid to intuition. But the basis is communication with the Mayan spirits; and the daycounter knows he is on the right track when he gets the pulses.

Unlike Western (Greek) astrology, which is based upon a zodiac of twelve signs, Mayan astrology is based on a calendar of 260 days. This calendar is called the Chol Qij or "Count of Days" (the terms given in this article are Kiche Mayan; in Yucatec Mayan the Count of Days is termed Tzolkin). The Chol Qij consists of twenty "naguals" represented by glyphs, which are roughly analogous to our twelve zodiacal signs in significance (except these change every day instead of every month; so every 20 days the same nagual comes up again). Everyone is born under the influence of one of these naguals, which determines the person's character and destiny. Prior to the Spanish conquest it was normal for a person to be named for their birth nagual: thus the hero of the *Popul Vuh* legend (the Mayan bible) is named Hun(1)Ajpu. Moreover, unlike our zodiacal signs, these naguals are considered to be alive, and petitionable. One invokes one's birth nagual for protection, guidance, and blessing. Traditional Mayans still do special propitiatory rituals every twenty days when their birth nagual repeats; and especially every 260 days when the nagual and its numerical coefficient coincide.

Each nagual is preceded by a numerical coefficient between 1 and 13 which modifies its meaning. The lower numbers (1 – 3) are considered timid, immature, or hesitant; the higher numbers (11 – 13) are considered stronger or more extreme. 8 is the ideal number, and 8 of any nagual – even a purportedly unfavorable nagual – becomes fortunate. Thus, 20 naguals x 13 number coefficients = 260 days in a complete cycle.

The first day of the Chol Qij is 8 Batz (which in 2010 occurred on February 6th and October 24th); then comes 9 E, 10 Aj, 11 Ix, 12 Tzikin, 13 Ajmak; then the numerical coefficients begin again with 1 Noj, 2 Tijax, etc. until all twenty naguals have been paired with all 13 numbers.

Barack Obama was born on August 4, 1961 at 7:24 pm, which corresponds to the Chol Qij nagual 9 Aj, or maize plant. Many of the naguals of the Chol Qij have symbolism which is related to the creation story given in the Mayan bible, the *Popul Vuh*. Here Aj symbolizes the maize plant in the house of the grandmother of Hunajpu and Ishbalankej (twin heroes of the *Popul Vuh* legend). In this story, Hunajpu and Ishbalankej journeyed to the underworld to avenge the murder of their father; but before leaving they planted two maize plants in their grandmother's house, saying that if these plants should dry up, it would mean they had died. When the plants dried up the grandmother was stricken with grief; but when the plants resprouted (when the twins were reborn from a fire in which they had perished) she knew they had triumphed in the end.

The nagual Aj thus symbolizes the spirit of joy, of the victory of good over evil. It signifies home, family, corn field (practically all Mayan men are subsistence maize farmers), offspring, stability, renovation, and the staff of power. People born on Aj have a good character and live contentedly. They have much spiritual energy and are lucky in love, business, and family life. Men born on this day make good Mayan priest-shamans since they are very psychic and perceptive. Women born on Aj are responsible wives and mothers, and are especially lucky with raising children and animals. Aj people are intelligent, knowledgeable, and studious; they tend to be conservative and are very decisive. Where we have forgotten our traditions, Aj reminds us of our cultural inheritance, how to count the days, how to remember our forefathers and past. Aj symbolizes command and success in public office (the maize plant or cornstalk also symbolizes the scepter of command which is the mark of office of Mayan community leaders). Thus people born on Aj make good leaders if they stand straight (do not permit themselves to be dominated by others). Thus Barack Obama will make good decisions for his country and be a strong leader and administrator. Aj commands obedience and brings good fortune to others. The President's triumph will be to bring many positive changes to his country. Some famous people born on 9 Aj include: Horatio Alger, Giovanni Casanova, Deng Xiao Ping, Judy Garland, William Penn, and Dionne Warwick. In one way or another, these people were definitely leaders and innovators.

Although Aj gives much spiritual energy, it nonetheless inclines to sickness and physical limitation or debility. However, the coefficient 9 gives strength, since it is one of the two key Mayan numbers (the other being 13), which symbolizes the 9 moons of gestation and the 9 Mayan gods who created and protect the human race. This augments Barack Obama's luck – he carries the blessing of the gods. 9 is in the middle of the range 1 – 13: the coefficients 12 or 13 Aj would make for a real dictator (whereas a 1 or 2 Aj would be too dilatory and vacillating).

Nine and thirteen are the sacred Mayan numbers: the nine nagual diagram reveals the connection between God (Ahau) and the earth as manifested in this person. That is, the diagram shows how the person fits into the cosmic scheme of things. The positions in the diagram refer to parts of the body; and the naguals which occupy them are obtained by adding or subtracting a certain number of days from the birth nagual:

Right arm -14 days	Head - 8 days	Left arm - 2 days
Right waist - 6 days	Heart = birthday	Left waist + 6 days
Right leg + 2 days	Feet + 8 days	Left leg + 14 days

In Barack Obama's case, the nine nagual diagram is as follows (see also graphic version with the actual Mayan glyphs):

8 Kawoq lightning	1 Kan snake	7 Batz monkey
3 Kej deer	9 Aj maize plant	2 Kawoq lightning
11 Tzikin bird	4 Imox rain	10 Kej deer

    The nagual of birth stands in the position of the heart – in this case, 9 Aj shows what is in the President's heart: home, family; and also the strength to command others.

    The nagual above the heart in the diagram is the head – the person's mind; how he is thinking, and what he thinks about – in this case, 1 Kan (snake), which occurs 8 days before the birth nagual (9 Aj). The head nagual is also considered to be the nagual of conception (the day upon which the person was conceived); and thus it is also very important in determining the person's character and destiny. Kan is the snake, the plumed serpent (symbolized by the rainbow) which ties together the Heart of Heaven and the Heart of the Earth. Kan tends to be variable in its thinking – not so much indecisive as mutable; changeable; fickle; it is also rather short-tempered and impatient. But what these people desire, they get: they are cunning; they slither their way around obstacles and opposition to avoid being trapped; and they can bite like a snake if need be. Snakes are omens – and Kan in the place of the head gives President Obama intuitive (psychic) ability to anticipate (intuit, predict) the future. Like Aj, Kan symbolizes strength and authority. Although 1 tends to be a weak coefficient (indicating he can be easily misled), nonetheless President Obama will obtain what he wants, by outmaneuvering his opponents.

    In the place of his right arm – 14 days before the birthday – stands 8 Kawoq, lightning and thunder. This is also a very angry nagual; and the right arm is the person's force of achievement, the person's motivation and power; the strength of his personality to reach out and take what he wants. Kawoq people are outspoken and direct, and can be quite intolerant; they do not accept being fooled or lied to. Also Kawoq moves around and travels quite a bit; so one might expect President Obama to make many journeys and visit many countries in pursuing his policies and objectives.

    The place of his left arm – 2 days before the birthday – is occupied by 7 Batz, the monkey. This is actually the holiest and most fortunate of the naguals, and is considered to bring joy which radiates confidence, hope, and staying power to overcome difficulties. The left arm symbolizes the person's worries and problems, that which impedes or weakens him; and since Batz also symbolizes "ball of thread" – the ties which bind people together – then what weakens the President is the people he is (politically) tied to. The president's family and political associates will create major problems and embarrassments for him. But with 7 Batz here, the President will have the spiritual vigor and élan to overcome all obstacles and tribulations. His weakness is his pride and stubbornness (misguided loyalty to associates); but Batz grants a stability which serves as a model for many people. He overcomes all difficulties and shines – always comes out on top.

The position of the right waist – 6 days before the birthday – is held by 3 Kej, the deer. Both right and left waist symbolize duties and obligations: the right side is positive energy and the left is negative. Since Kej is very agile and quick, the President moves fast to discharge his responsibilities and is alert to grasp opportunities and to spring out of the way of harm. It also makes him headstrong and dominating. Kej gives lots of springy vigor to the President's mind and to his entire body.

The left waist – 6 days after the birthday – is the person's negative obligations: how the person is burdened; held back, or loses what he has won. The left waist here is 2 Kawoq, which shows anger, an anger which holds the President's right arm back from achieving everything it could. He has trouble controlling his temper and can be overly precipitate in his reactions; so the President's left waist sometimes dissipates the power of decision which his right arm achieves. At times he is too quick on the trigger for his own good; oversteps himself and makes enemies needlessly.

The legs symbolize the transformative force which moves the person forward through life; some people take big, bold steps, others take small, cautious steps. The right leg – 2 days after the birthday – symbolizes how the person steps forward in life, initiates action: his enthusiasm and motivation. Here 11 Tzikin (bird) is very fortunate for money, especially with such a high numerical coefficient. The president has, or will acquire, money very easily to realize all of his projects and endeavors. He will always be able to come up with the money, and muster the financial resources, required to put his plans into action. And when he retires, he will be a very rich man.

The left leg – 14 days after the birthday – shows obstacles which hinder him or keep him from his true path; how he trips over himself. Here 10 Kej – the deer – is a fortunate nagual, so his right waist gives positive energy to his left leg to enable him to move forward out of impasses, problems, and illness. Nonetheless, Kej's willfulness and impulsiveness can trip the President up. Kej always springs forward, lets nothing hold him back, and gives him reserves of force and energy to kick obstacles aside – sometimes a little too vigorously.

The feet – 8 days after the birthday – symbolize what the person seeks; also where the person is going: his destiny, the end of his life, and his death. It reveals the qualities the person has as he ages. Here 4 Imox (rain) is not a fortunate nagual, symbolizing anger and craziness (anger which makes him do crazy things). Many of Barack Obama's nine naguals happen to signify anger, which is his greatest failing. However, since here the feet lie between two auspicious naguals (Tzikin and Kej), the President is able to dominate his anger and craziness (keep them beneath his feet). Nonetheless the feet indicate the end, which is why the President may experience serious illness or physical or mental debility at the end of his term of office or his life.

Adding up all of the numerical coefficients in the nine nagual diagram yields a sum of 55. This is a favorable sum since it's not too high (the range of possible sums is

53 – 73). A sum over 60 is angry; and over 70 is extremely angry. By contrast, 55 is low enough to be laid-back, relaxed, and able to take things as they come. This is going to be a cooled-out presidency in which the people trust their leader; because Obama is sure of himself.

* On the other hand, if you are looking for a book, then I recommend *Time and the Highland Maya* by Barbara Tedlock (U of N.M. Press, 1992), who is an initiated Mayan daycounter. And, for interpretations (albeit based upon his intuition rather than Mayan training), I recommend *Day-Signs* by Bruce Schofield (One Reed Publications, 1991).

Short Stories:

Acapulco Gold

The summer of '68. There had been a shortage on for months, and all we had to smoke was this crappy Mexican weed that they cut with sugar for weight, and which was so sticky and gooey that you could scarcely light it, much less smoke it.

Then one day Ace came in and told me, "Hey man, I got a line on some genuine Acapulco Gold! This friend of mine scored ten keys last night, and he just told me on the phone he'll sell me a pound of it if I come pick it up right now!"

Well that was groovy news, and brightened my day considerably. I marveled at my luck in being the only one in my circle who owned a car, since Ace would not have been so eager to share such a find had he not needed the means to transport it.

The friend, it turned out, lived in a large Victorian era apartment building in Germantown. In accordance with the etiquette of scoring, I waited outside in my VW sedan while Ace went in and made the buy. About half an hour later he came out clutching a package, his big red face beaming with joy. He even jumped and clicked his heels together as he approached the car, making his long, sandy hair fly in all directions.

"Just look!" he cried, as he climbed in and shoved the package towards me. I opened it and beheld the radiant golden brown leaves shining up at me from the Spanish-language newspaper in which they were nestled. A whole pound! It was truly a transfixing sight! I wondered how much Ace would be willing to sell to me. He reached into his shirt pocket for cigarette papers, and I handed him the package so he could twist up some numbers for the journey home.

He lit one up and it smelled great. He passed it to me and it tasted great. Maybe it was my imagination, after the long famine, but I really felt like I was flying from that one toke.

"Better drive, man." Ace told me. "I feel safer on the move."

I pulled away from the curb, and we drove leisurely through the balmy Germantown summer, passing the joint back and forth. It was a beautiful day. Little black kids played in an open fire hydrant, squealing with delight over the gush of the water. Lovers made out on the lawn of a funeral parlor. A Little League baseball team was cheering in the park. Everything felt pretty groovy.

We stopped for a traffic light and I was toking deeply on the remains of the joint when I became aware of honking going on behind me. I looked in the rear-view and saw a dark blue Plymouth with only one occupant, an older woman apparently, who was honking her horn like crazy and signaling me with her hand. I thought maybe she was trying to tell me that something was wrong with the car, so I put out the joint, and when the light turned green I pulled over to the curb across the intersection. She followed and stopped behind me, and then got out of her car.

She came up to the window on my side and looked me in the eye. I didn't like her look. She was sixty or so, nattily attired, with an American flag pin in the lapel of her suit. She had steely blue-gray hair and mean, steely blue eyes.

"You went through the stop sign back on Upsal Street without even pausing!" she shrilled at me. "That's a dangerous intersection: there are always children playing around there. Thank God you hippies didn't kill anyone!"

"Sorry, lady." I said. "I didn't see it." Which was true. I guess I was passing the joint at the time and didn't notice it.

"You tell that to the police!" she demanded. "I'm making a citizen's arrest. You are both under arrest! You can follow me to the police station."

"Hey lady, I said I was sorry. Okay? I won't do it again."

"Why'm I under arrest?" Ace put in. "He was the one who was driving."

"You're under arrest, young man. And your friend too. I have your license number, and you'll follow me right now if you know what's good for you."

"Come on, lady, get serious. Who do you think you're messing with?" I thought it was time to get tough. I mean, for all she knew we were killers or something – long hair, beards, pierced ears. Ace had tattoos up and down his arms. We looked like hell. I narrowed my eye at her and snarled, "I don't want no trouble; you just flake off, okay?"

"Your kind don't impress me." She pulled an umbrella she'd been carrying out from its sheath and flourished it like a sword. "Are you resisting arrest then? That's a felony!"

"Come on, man!" Ace whispered to me. "Quit jawing and get the hell out of here."

I turned the ignition and gunned the accelerator, giving the lady a sneer as I shot away. Since a VW sedan is not match for a Plymouth, I thought it prudent to put some distance between us, and I turned corners at random until I thought we'd safely eluded her.

"You know, Ace," I observed. "I wonder why this kind of stuff only happens when you're stoned?"

He replied with a stoned grin, reached into his pocket, and pulled out another joint. He lit it up and we passed it back and forth, cruising leisurely towards home, when I noticed in the rear-view, barreling down on my tail like a Messerschmidt, the dark blue Plymouth with its honking, raving occupant.

"Oh Jesus!" I exclaimed. I jammed on the accelerator but was too slow: she was up to me on my left side, smiling like a death's head, forcing me to the curb before I could get any momentum. As I screeched on the brakes she sprang from her car yelling, "Help! Police! Help!" and brandishing her umbrella for the attack. I shifted into reverse and backed up, with her beating the hood of my car with her umbrella, then I executed a tight U-turn which almost grazed her, but she didn't flinch.

"Criminals! Criminals! Police! Police!"

I didn't look back, but Ace said she'd jumped back into her car and was following.

"I don't see how we can get away." I said, rounding a corner. "She's got the faster car. Ace, you're going to have to ditch the weed."

"No way, man. You kidding? This is Gold! She's just a nut. Hey look! Look there!" He pointed towards an open garage attached to a duplex. "Pull in there fast!"

I turned into the driveway and pulled into the garage. Ace jumped out as I stopped and pulled the garage door down.

"I think we made it!" he said with a grin. "She didn't see us."

"I wonder whose garage this is?" I asked. My tummy was still tumbling and my adrenalin pounding.

"Some black, probably. It's a black neighborhood."

That made me feel better. We sat down in a corner of the garage next to a door that apparently led inside, and we waited. We couldn't hear anything happening inside the house. Maybe no one was home. Ace pulled his package out and began rolling some more joints. He lit one and handed it to me.

"Well, my friend," he observed. "a fruitful and adventurous afternoon."

The grass was good grass. After a few tokes I began to relax and calm down. We joked about the lady.

"A typical fascist." Ace said. "Low link on the Great Chain of Being. Complete lack of *Dasein*."

"*Dasein*?"

"Yes, *Dasein*. Being there. Don't you read Heidegger? Like that lady, she just ain't there, you know what I mean? No *Dasein*."

We sat passing the joint back and forth for about fifteen minutes while Ace enlarged on the subject of ontology. When the joint was gone he lit another one. As he passed it to me he must have flipped the match into a pile of gas-soaked rags, because all of a sudden, WOOMPH! – a sheet of flame leaped up the wall next to us. We jumped up and stomped on the rags to put the fire out. Finally we got it under control.

"We'd better get out of here." Ace suggested. He made for the garage door and opened it, and we both stuck our heads out and gulped fresh air, as smoke poured out around us. Then, suddenly, Ace pulled the garage door shut again.

"What's the matter?" I asked.

"Eva Braun's coming down the street in her Plymouth. We'd better wait 'til she goes by."

The place was still smoky, so we lay down on the floor where the air was better. There was still no sound from inside the house. Ace picked up his joint where he'd dropped it and lit it up again. He passed it to me.

"What we need more of, especially at times like this," he observed, "is *Dasein*." He went on for a while, and I became aware of the sound of sirens off in the distance.

"You hear sirens?" I asked him.

"Fire sirens. Don't worry." he replied. "You can tell fire sirens from police sirens. Fire sirens are the voice of the fireman, which has more Dasein than the voice of the policeman."

"Ace, they sound to me like they're coming this way!"

Suddenly the door next to us flew open and a huge black woman with horn-rimmed glasses and a broom in one hand and a pail of water in the other burst into the garage. She caught sight of us; froze in an attitude of total indignation; and shrieked in a booming, gravelly voice, "Bums! Bums! Hippie bums!"

She threw the pail of water in our faces and attacked us with the broom.

"It ain't no fire! It's just bums! Hippie bums!"

I made for the car door with my hands over my head to fend off blows from the broom, turned on the ignition, and backed out as Ace went for the garage door. As soon as he opened it a wail of sirens poured in. Ace jumped in as I backed down the drive. The lady was yelling her head off, but we couldn't hear her over the screams of sirens. I hit the street, turned, and took off, passing a police car and two fire engines coming the other way a block up the street.

"Why does this kind of stuff only happen when you're stoned?" I asked forlornly, wiping my wet hair and face with my shirttail.

"Because it augments the *Dasein*. Here, have a hit." he offered.

"I think I've had enough, thanks." I replied. "Are they after us?"

"Nope. We're safe. Just relax, you're all tense."

I was trying to go as fast as I could without actually speeding, turning corners every time I came to one. When we stopped at a red light I hunched over the steering wheel and closed my eyes for a second.

"Don't look now," Ace said. "but guess who's staring at us from over there across the intersection."

I looked up and saw a dark blue Plymouth stopped at the light coming the other way. And although I couldn't hear anything, I saw a face behind the wheel contorted with anger. When the light turned green I shot through the intersection and sped straight away.

"She's made a U-turn." Ace reported. "She's coming after us."

"Ace, ditch the stuff, man!"

"You're kidding. You've got to be kidding."

I raced down Johnson St. and reached the turn for the Wissahickon Drive. The traffic light was red, but I didn't see any traffic coming on the Drive, so I plowed right through and made the left turn. Then I saw a cop. He was on the opposite pavement, waving at me and whistling his whistle. I smiled and shrugged at him, and kept going.

"She ran the light too. She's about 400 yards back." Ace reported. "Come on, man, come on! Don't let her run us off the road again!"

She gained on us fast, and bore down on my tail, so I opened the car door on my side and began swerving back and forth across the two lanes to keep her from passing us. She was honking and zooming right up on my tail as if to ram me, and at one point she did hit us because I felt the bump. She kept trying to get around me on the left, feinting to the right and then zooming back, but I didn't let her get around me.

"I see a flashing light back there." Ace said.

"Ace, get rid of the stuff, man! Please! Get rid of it!"

"Don't panic, there's time. They might nab her. Just hang a right into the park."

I saw the park entrance up ahead on the right – a bridge over the creek – and when it was still 200 yards away I let her get around me. She started to bear down on my left again to force me off the road – I could see her smile of impending triumph – but just before the bridge I slammed on my brakes and made a screeching turn over the bridge while she shot on ahead.

"Now what? Burn the bridge?"

"No, man, just head up into the woods. She won't be able to follow on those bridle trails."

"Let's ditch the weed, man!"

"No way, man! This is Gold, man! Just head into the woods. She's backed up and is turning over the bridge, and some cops are coming up the Drive behind her! Come on! Come on!"

I headed for the woods on a bridle trail. The road got narrower and muddier, and I felt a ray of hope that the Plymouth and cops wouldn't be able to follow. In fact we did seem to be eluding our pursuers, though we could hear sirens shrieking through the treetops, when the car hit a big slough, bogged down, and stalled.

"Come on, man! Come on!"

I turned the ignition over and over, but the engine wouldn't start. I opened the door and saw that mud was up to the axles.

"Come on!" Ace shouted, jumping out. "Let's get out of here! They'll never find us in the woods!"

"What about my car?"

"What's more important – your car or your ass? Tell 'em somebody stole it. Come on!"

We raced through the woods, Ace clutching his package and leaping like a gazelle through the underbrush. We could hear sirens in different directions now: they seemed to be all around us.

"Ace, you'd better ditch the stuff, man! Hide it somewhere – we'll come back for it."

"You kidding? We'd never find it again. Could you find where we are again? Don't worry, they won't find us. We'll hang out here 'til dark. Look there!" He pointed to a thicket. I followed him as he crawled through the shrubs and down into a depression in the middle of the thicket.

"Just look at this!" He gestured around with his hand. "A perfect hiding place! Just relax. Here, don't worry." He handed me a joint.

We lit up and he leaned back against a stump and relaxed. We passed the joint back and forth, and I began to relax my tense vigil. Even the scream of the sirens seemed to recede into the distance. The sunlight streamed down through the trees and made beautiful speckled patterns on the variegated forest litter and the clumps of mayapple which shared our burrow. I looked up and saw the sun dazzling though the shimmering veil of leaves. The wind whispered through the trees and blew away the buzz of the sirens.

"I wonder why this kind of junk only happens when you're stoned?"

"It's the *Dasein*, man. It's the *Dasein*."

Then I became aware of movement in the bushes in front of us, and suddenly a head with blue hair and steely blue eyes was facing us.

"Aha! I thought I smelled smoke! Here they are! Police! Police!"

She jumped for us, waving her umbrella, and I felt a blow glance off my back as I scooted up and through the bushes, a hair behind Ace.

"Get rid of the stuff, man!" I yelled at him as we darted out of the thicket and panted up a hill. "Get rid of it!"

"No way, man! She's just an old lady. Come on, up here!"

We ran up a hill towards a highway embankment. The sirens shrieked behind us. I glanced back and saw the lady, maybe a hundred yards behind us, pointing her umbrella at us and gesticulating madly at a bunch of cops maybe two hundred yards behind her. We raced up the embankment and came out on a wide highway with traffic zipping by in both directions. We could hear sirens in the distance, both ways. Ace stopped running and nonchalantly stuck out a thumb towards oncoming cars, as if to hitchhike. No one stopped. I glanced down and saw the cops starting up the embankment. I grabbed the package from Ace and ran to the bridge over the Wissahickon Creek, tearing at the paper as I went. Ace took off after me, yelling, "Hey, man! Wait, man!"

I reached the bridge and turned the package upside down and shook it. Ace reached me with a look, first angry and then resigned. We looked down from the bridge. The golden leaves were falling down gently in the breeze, barely rippling the water as they joined the leaves of the oaks and tulips on their journey to the sea. I wadded the

Spanish language newspaper into a ball and threw it into the creek. It floated for a while, then began to sink. I felt Ace pulling urgently at my sleeve. I turned around, and all I could see was cops.

Well, we had a good lawyer, and he got us a reduction from possession to disturbing the peace, since all they really had on us was some seeds they found on the floor of the car, although I did have to pay a good, stiff fine. But damned if I didn't get my operator's license suspended for passing a stop sign.

A Love Story

My name is Henry. First off, I want to say that I slobber when I talk. I can't help it. I've always done it. I can't control it. The children sometimes follow me home and mock me. It's their way of being more grown-up, I guess. It's their way of asserting themselves. You know how kids are. It used to bother me, but it doesn't anymore. Kids are kids. Please forgive my slobber when I talk, I'll try not to do it too much. I can't help it, it just comes out when I talk. I've tried to control it by not talking to people, but that just made me feel really frustrated. I went to a doctor once, but he couldn't help me. No one can help me. My mother often tried to get me to stop. She would put a bib under my neck and make me wear it all day long, so I wouldn't spoil my clothes. She thought she was being helpful, but it made me feel awful. My mother was a kind woman in many ways, but she never understood me. Just because I slobber is no reason to assume I have no intelligence. In fact, I am quite intelligent. All the kids would cheat off my exams in school. But I never got good grades, I don't know why. Everyone assumed I was stupid, I guess, because I slobbered; and the teachers gave me poorer grades than I had really earned. And the children taunt me. It's okay, they're just children. They have to taunt someone, and it may as well be me instead of someone who would really feel hurt by it. That makes me happy, to know that someone else isn't being taunted because I am. Maybe I can't help them, but I can slobber for them.

Actually, I'm pretty happy now that I'm married. Oh yes, I am married. What happened was that one day I was sitting outside on the front steps of my rooming house, and a girl I had seen around the neighborhood came up to me, crying. She was in her twenties, and was very pretty. She sat down on the stoop next to me.

"What's the matter?" I asked her.

"Oh Mister!" she said in a Spanish accent. "I don't know what will happen to me. I in this country not legal. I so afraid they catch me and send me back to my country!"

It turned out that she was from Salvador. She had had a very sad life in Salvador. Her father had been killed in the war, her family had no money, so one day she ran away and came here to live. She was crying while she told me this, and I felt like hugging her but I didn't want her to misunderstand. I thought maybe she wanted some money, so I offered her some, but she just shook her head.

"Isn't there anything I could do for you?" I asked her.

"Yes. You can marry me."

"Marry you?"

"Yes. If you marry me, then I can stay here. Will you marry me?"

Well, I was taken aback, but I thought about it. It seemed very unlikely that anyone else would ever marry me, and if that would make her happy, then why not? So I told her I would do it.

"Oh Mister!" she cried, overjoyed. "You so nice!"

She hugged me in joy, and even went to kiss me, but I was afraid I would slobber on her, so I just hugged her. I was happy that she was happy. We made a date to get a license the next day, and then we made an appointment to be married by a Justice of the Peace the next week.

That was a happy week. Actually, I didn't see her at all that week, but I thought about her all the time. I took some money out of the bank and bought a wedding ring. Then I thought maybe I should buy her a wedding dress too, so I went to a bridal shop and bought a dress. Truthfully, I bought the cheapest dress they had because I hadn't realized how expensive wedding dresses were, but I thought it was the thought that counted.

As my wedding day approached, I was so excited that I couldn't sleep at night. I thought about how beautiful Carmen would look in the dress, and how happy she would be. The morning of the wedding she came over to my room. I hadn't seen her since the morning I proposed to her. She was even more beautiful than I remembered. She went into the bathroom down the hall and tried on the ring and dress. Unfortunately, I must have bought a dress several sizes too big because it sort of hung on her like a shroud, and the ring was too small to fit her ring finger, so she'd had to put it on her pinky. She wanted to take them off, but I guess I looked sad when she said that, so she decided to wear them. That was nice of her. She even went up to me and hugged me and thanked me for them.

Well, the wedding was a nice wedding. We got married in the office of the J.P. It was rather business-like and was over in five minutes, but I was really happy, except that on the way out Carmen tripped over her dress and fell down the steps, but luckily she wasn't hurt. Then I realized we should have a real wedding dinner to celebrate, but I didn't have much money left, so I took her to a diner. I was so happy, I wanted all the world to see us, but in the diner all the people stared at us and laughed. That's okay, I guess we were pretty funny-looking.

When we got back, she kissed me on the forehead and thanked me and went to her apartment, and I went back to mine. I lay on the bed for long time. I guess I should have been really happy, but for some reason I felt sad. I felt sad for a long time after that. I tried to make myself happy by thinking about how pretty Carmen had looked on our wedding day, but truthfully she had looked sort of funny in that saggy dress. But at least now she could stay here legally, and that made me happy.

About a month later there was a knocking on my door, and I got up to answer it, and it was Carmen. She was so beautiful, but she was crying again.

"Carmen, what's the matter?" I asked her.

"They throw me out of my apartment!" she wailed at me. "I have nowhere to live!"

"Carmen, don't you worry, you can stay here." I told her. I told her that without thinking, because actually my apartment is just one room, with a bathroom down the hall, and it's kind of small even for just one person. But after all, she was my wife, so I was responsible for her. And when I told her she could stay, she became happy at once.

"Oh Mister Henry, you so nice!" She hugged me and it made me feel sort of embarrassed, but I was happy that she was happy.

Later that day she moved in. She didn't have many belongings, just a big suitcase with clothes, so we weren't too cramped. I offered her the bed, and I bought another mattress so I could sleep on the floor. Those days were very happy for me. Actually, it was the happiest time of my life. She worked nights and would come home around nine o'clock, and I would greet her with dinners I prepared in the communal kitchen downstairs and brought up to her. In the morning I would make breakfasts and take them to her.

One night I was napping and was still asleep when Carmen came home from work. I was so sleepy, I just lay there as she tiptoed in and began to undress, it kind of embarrasses me to say this, but I want to tell the truth. I watched her undress. I know that was wrong, but after all, she was my wife (or at least that's how I justified it to myself). You know, she was so beautiful, I can't tell you. I've never seen a more beautiful woman, although to be truthful I'd never seen a woman undressed before.

I could barely sleep that night. I was in a strange state of mind. The next morning when I brought her breakfast, I tried to act normal. I tried not to look her straight in the eye, but I think she must have known that something was the matter. Maybe I was slobbering more than usual. For the next few days, I tried not to look at her as I served her her meals.

"Something is the matter?" she asked me. "You don't look at me anymore. Maybe you don't like me?"

I assured her that I liked her, but something was the matter with my eyes.

"Maybe you don't like me because I so much trouble for you."

"Oh no!" I told her. "I like you a lot. My eyes have been bothering me, that's all."

"Oh poor Mister Henry!" she said and went to hug me. "You better go to eye doctor."

"No, it's okay. Sometimes my eyes bother me, that's all. It'll go away."

"You better go to a doctor to be sure. I take you. Maybe you no see where you going and a car runs into you."

So I let her take me to a doctor. Actually I have very good eyesight, but there in the doctor's office I pretended I couldn't see the last lines on the eye charts. The doctor told me it wasn't a major problem, but that I ought to have corrective lenses, and he wrote me a prescription. When we left the doctor's office, I thought that was that, but then Carmen said,

"Well, let's get the glasses."

"I don't have enough money right now." I told her. "I'll buy them next month."

"Oh poor Mister Henry." she told me. She looked in her purse and counted her money. "I buy you glasses."

So we went to a store that sold glasses and I tried on a lot of different frames until I found a pair that she approved of. "You look handsome in those." she said. So we ordered them, and she went to pay the deposit, but I tried to stop her.

"Carmen, I can't let you pay for them."

"Oh please, Mister Henry. I make money. Let me do it!"

So I let her pay for them. I felt sort of ashamed of the whole thing, but what could I say? A week later she picked them up and brought them home.

"Now put them on!" she said proudly. I tried them on, and they weren't too bad except they made things look kind of woozy.

"Now your eyes feel better?" she asked. I assured her that now my eyes felt great. After that, I always had to wear the glasses whenever she was around. I got used to them, but I had to be more careful going down the stairs.

A few days after that, there was a knocking on the door. I answered it, and there at my door was a fat man with a dark woman and three children.

"Here where Carmen Sanchez live?" he asked me in a Spanish accent. Actually her name was now Carmen Peachus, but Sanchez had been her maiden name. I answered him in the affirmative.

"Good. She my sister." He offered me a hand, and beckoned to his family to come on in. They walked in and sort of flopped down on the bed and mattress. They must have been very tired. I was taken a bit aback, but after all, he was apparently my brother-in-law; and these were apparently my sister-in-law and nephews and niece, so I told them to rest while I fixed something to eat in the kitchen.

When I returned they must have rested, because the kids were running around the room yelling at each other, and my sister-in-law was poking into the drawers of my dresser, and everyone was talking but I didn't understand what they were saying because it was in Spanish. I spent the rest of the afternoon trying to entertain them, hoping that maybe Carmen would come home early that night.

Carmen got back late. When she saw the family, she laughed for joy and ran and embraced the children and her brother, and then the two of them carried on a long conversation in Spanish. However, she didn't talk to her sister-in-law; actually it seemed to me that after the initial glance, she ignored her. Then she came to me and explained,

"This is my brother Carlos and his family. He my only family. He has nowhere to go."

Well, the ball seemed to be in my court. It was a pretty small room, but they were after all my family now too. So Carmen slept on the bed, her brother and sister-in-law on the mattress, the kids on some pillows, and I dozed off on a chair. We bought some more mattresses the next day.

Truthfully, it was pretty crowded in there for a few weeks. Also I wasn't getting much sleep, what with all the cooking to do and the cleaning up after the kids. But at least it took my mind off of Carmen and my confused feelings for her. Also, in the beginning, Carmen was really happy that her brother was there, so that made me happy.

But after a while it got kind of hard. The brother couldn't find a job, and he used to come home in the afternoons really disappointed, and then he started drinking. He borrowed money from Carmen to buy drinks, and he even borrowed money from me a couple of times, but I didn't have much left from my pension to lend him, after paying for rent and food. I didn't mind lending him the money because I could see how unhappy he was, and at least the drinks made him happier.

Also, it seemed that Carmen didn't get along too well with her sister-in-law. In the beginning they didn't talk to each other, but after a time, especially after her brother started coming home drunk every night, they snapped at each other. I didn't know what they were talking about because they spoke in Spanish, and even after I bought a Spanish dictionary I couldn't tell what they were arguing about because they talked faster than I could look up what they were saying, and I found it hard to read the small print with glasses on.

Also, the children seemed to grow more and more unhappy. They were sort of mean kids, but maybe they were just bored. I took them to the park a few times, but it always seemed to wind up with them getting into fights with the other kids. I didn't really understand them. They would point at me and call, "Baba! Baba!" and laugh, while I was happy that they called me papa, it seemed like they were teasing me. I guess I didn't speak their language well enough to understand them.

It was during this time that Carmen and I would sometimes go out for long walks together at night after she got home from work, and on weekends. It was nice that she asked me to go with her. She would tell me about her life in Salvador, and about how nice her brother was to her when they were growing up. She told me she felt really sad seeing him so unhappy now.

"He changed so much. I no like being with him now. It very hard for me, and it very hard for you, too." she said.

Then she cried sometimes. She would walk hugging me close or holding my hand. That made me happy, that I could comfort her. But it also made my confused feelings for her come back.

Truthfully, I think I was in love with her. But I wasn't sure, because I didn't know what being in love felt like. Once we sat on a bench in the park and she snuggled up to me and hugged me, and I hugged her back. Then she looked up at me, and I thought that maybe she wanted to kiss me even, but I wasn't sure, and I was sort of scared, and that made me start to slobber, so I turned away. Poor Carmen, to be married to a slobberer.

Anyway, after that she spent whatever time she could down in the kitchen with me helping to cook and clean up. That was fun. She didn't know how to use American utensils, like pressure cookers, so I taught her how to cook. We had lots of fun in the kitchen making meals together in the middle of the night.

Well, the situation with my in-laws got worse and worse. One Saturday afternoon her brother was drunk and was lying on the bed. Carmen said something to him which I didn't understand, but the sister-in-law jumped up and got really mad at Carmen. They both cut loose and began yelling at each other in Spanish, and then the kids joined in and started yelling and crying too. All of a sudden the sister-in-law slapped Carmen on the cheek. Carmen's eyes blazed, and I saw that real trouble was brewing, so I stood up and moved in between them. Then the sister-in-law turned on me and began yelling at me in Spanish. I tried to calm her down and explained I couldn't understand what she was saying until I got my dictionary out, but I must have started slobbering because the next thing I knew the brother was there too, yelling at me:

""You spit on my wife! You pig! Don't you spit on my wife!"

"I'm sorry, I'm sorry." I apologized. "I can't help it, it just comes out when I talk."

"You pig! You spit on me! Don't you spit on me, you dirty cheat!"

Cheat? That was an odd thing to call me. I don't think I'm a cheat, but then his English wasn't very good. Maybe he meant "slobberer" or something.

"You spit on me, you cheat, I spit on you!" he yelled, and he began to spit on me. "You cheat! You cheat!"

He grabbed my glasses and threw them to the floor and stomped on them. At least now I could see him clearly, but Carmen became enraged. She threw herself at him, screaming in Spanish, and he backed away from me. Then there was all this screaming and yelling that I didn't understand at all, and finally Carmen said something which produced a dead stillness. Everyone looked at one another. Then they all looked at me. I felt like smiling or waving or something, but I thought maybe I'd better just keep still. Then the sister-in-law and the kids started crying, and the brother gathered them all together and hugged them. Carmen started crying too, and came to me, and I hugged her.

After a while the in-laws quieted down and moved apart and began to silently pack up their belongings. When they had everything together they stood for a moment looking at Carmen and me, and then they left, banging the door behind them. Carmen began crying again, and hugged me tighter. When she had calmed down I asked her,

"What did you say to him?"

"I told him to go." she said. "He no can act like that with my husband."

She looked up at me, and then she reached up and pulled me to her and kissed me on the lips. I was afraid maybe I would start to slobber again, and I tried to turn away, but she pulled me back and kissed me again. And then, well, it doesn't matter what happened then. But I knew I was really in love with her.

Anyway, we have a little baby now. She's really cute, she looks just like Carmen. The only thing that worries me is that she slobbers a lot, but Carmen says that's okay, it's perfectly normal. I guess she's right. I hope she's right.

It was a cool, clear, moonlit night in the springtime of the guerrilla war. Chico Xol and Cu Tut were doing their monthly civil patrol duty in the thatched-roof guardhouse on the Coban road – their country's first line of defense against the growing guerrilla insurgency. They were huddled over a little fire they had started to warm themselves, when suddenly they heard a clatter of footsteps outside, and someone stumbling and falling with a crash, and a yell,

"Mierda!"

Startled, they jumped up and grabbed their rifles.

"Is anyone here?" a voice asked.

"Yes, we're here." Chico replied.

A shadow reeled into the guardhouse. It was Jorge Fernandez, one of San Juan's half-dozen full-time drunks. He grabbed Chico's arm to lift himself and exclaimed with a waft of alcohol breath,

"The guerrillas are here! The guerrillas are here!"

Chico felt a jolt in his stomach.

"What do you mean?" he asked.

"I had stopped to pee by the side of the road," Jorge Fernandez explained patiently, "and I was looking across the barranca towards Barrio San Luis, and I was looking at the corn, when all of a sudden I saw all these men moving in the corn! I couldn't believe my eyes!"

"How many men?" Chico asked apprehensively.

"Maybe thirty, maybe fifty, maybe more, I don't know, it was hard to tell. But they all had guns and knives!"

"What were they doing?"

"They were sneaking through the corn, as quiet as could be!"

Chico and Cu were stunned. They tried not to look at one another. They stared at the ground.

"And so … ?" Chico asked.

"And so I peed as fast as I could and then I came running back here to tell you that the guerrillas are here!"

Having accomplished his mission, he plopped himself down on the bench and began warming his hands over the fire.

"The guerrillas?" Chico asked wanly. But he knew. He had known all along that the day the guerrillas finally decided to come would be the day that he was doing civil patrol. He knew that, so he wasn't surprised, only he had hoped that maybe it wouldn't happen quite yet. He felt numb in the pit of his stomach.

"Are you sure it was guerrillas?" he asked. Jorge Fernandez was a bit tipsy and unsteady on his feet. On the other hand, he was a ladino – the mayor's brother-in-law, no less – whereas Chico and Cu were only Indians.

"Yes, guerrillas!" Jorge Fernandez was positive. "They're here!"

They all stared in frozen silence at the fire. Then a thought occurred to Chico, and he asked Jorge Fernandez,

"Did you see the guerrillas near the pasture of Catalina Caal?" Catalina Caal's pasture was where Chico had tethered his new little bull.

"Yes, that's where they were!" Jorge Fernandez replied. "They were by Catalina Caal's land."

"Did you happen to see a little black and white bull tied up in the pasture? By the big avocado tree in the corner?"

"No, I didn't see any bull." Jorge Fernandez replied.

So that was it! That's what the guerrillas were up to! Chico jumped to his feet and grabbed up his rifle and jerked Cu's sleeve.

"Come on, hurry!" he said, and raced out of the guardhouse.

"Where are we going?" Cu called, struggling to catch up.

"To Barrio San Luis!" Chico called back.

"No, Chico, stop!" Cu commanded, grabbing Chico's arm forcibly to wheel him around.

"Come on, Cu, there's no time!"

"We can't go to Barrio San Luis, Chico! We have to tell the commissioner first. Do you want him to report us to the Military Zone?"

No, Chico didn't want that. He stopped for a moment to think. Something in him wanted to go straight to Barrio San Luis, to see about his bull. The little bull had cost him 150 quetzales just the month before, and it was Chico's pride and joy. Chico didn't really want to report to the commissioner, who in his civilian life was a butcher, and one of the town's chief sons-of-bitches; but he certainly didn't want to get into trouble for not reporting to the commissioner. Perhaps the commissioner would send men to see about the bull.

They walked across the plaza to the commissioner's house, and Chico rapped softly on the door. Immediately a fierce dog began barking within. They waited, and the dog barked and whined and rattled a chain, but no one answered the door.

Chico knocked again, louder this time, and the dog went into a frenzy of howling. There was a loud crash, and then a shout,

"Mierda!"

Chico winced. A light came on in the window. In a moment the door opened and the dog was there snarling up at them and the commissioner was there snarling down at them, and tucking his undershirt into his trousers. Chico and Cu removed their hats.

"Well?" the commissioner demanded indignantly.

"Buenas noches, commissioner." Chico said politely.

"Well?" the commissioner scowled at him.

"Commissioner, there are guerrillas in the corn."

The commissioner stopped to think about this. He had only just gotten to sleep after a night of heavy drinking, and he had awakened with a splitting headache, and he couldn't remember if he was supposed to be angry or not.

"Guerrillas?" he asked.

"Yes, guerrillas."

"Where are they?"

"In the corn."

"In the corn?"

"Yes, the corn."

"What corn?"

"Over in Barrio San Luis."

The commissioner thought about this.

"Who saw them?"

"They saw fifty of them, commissioner."

The commissioner tried to think. He had been trained for this very moment, but he was having difficulty concentrating. He knew that the first thing to remember, which they had reiterated over and over during the week-long workshop for military commissioners which he had attended at the Military Zone, was to stay calm. It was most important to stay calm. He took a deep breath. He looked out the doorway, past Chico and Cu, to the moonlit cobblestones of the street. He felt nauseous and his head hurt him. He knew he had to summon the deputy commissioner.

"You!" he barked at Cu. Cu jumped. "Go get the deputy. Now!"

Cu turned and raced down the street towards the deputy's house.

The commissioner remembered that there were three important things to remember besides staying calm, but his head throbbed and he could only remember the third one: "Wipe them out!" He couldn't remember the two things you were supposed to do between "Stay calm" and "Wipe them out!"

"What are the guerillas doing?" he demanded of Chico.

"Maybe stealing our bulls, commissioner."

"Our bulls? What bulls?"

"They're stealing our bulls. For beef."

"Ah, for beef." Him being a butcher, this made sense. "What bulls are they stealing?" He thought of his own bulls.

"All of our bulls, commissioner!"

"All of them?" This made the commissioner very angry. He stepped back into his house and retrieved his pistol and jacket, then beckoned to Chico to follow him to the armory, where the rifles and ammunition were stored.

When they arrived the commissioner reached into his pants pocket for the key, but he couldn't find it, and he realized that he must have forgotten it.

"Mierda!" he shouted, kicking the door. Chico winced. Well, nothing for it but to wait for the deputy, who also had a key. The commissioner tried to think. Stay calm, he told himself. He thought about his bulls, but since he had no bulls in Barrio San Luis, his own bulls were probably safe for the moment. He gave out a little grunt of satisfaction. Then he thought about dispatching a messenger to the Military Zone for help, though it would be hours before they could arrive, and he wondered if they would commend his alertness or reprimand his presumption. He wondered where the guerrillas were. Then he got a sudden inspiration:

"Listen!" he said to Chico. "Remember this: stay calm; observe their movements; something else; and then wipe them out! Have you got that?"

"Could you say it again, commissioner?" Chico asked, anxious to comply correctly.

"Stay calm! Observe their movements! Then something else."

"Check our bulls?"

"No, not check our bulls. Something else; and then wipe them out! Now, repeat that."

"Not check our bulls. Something else; and then wipe them out."

"No, fool!" the commissioner said angrily. "What came before that?"

"Before what, commissioner?"

"Before 'wipe them out!'"

"Something else."

"I know that, but what was it?"

"Not check our bulls?"

"No, not not check our bulls, stop saying 'not check our bulls', fool!" His head throbbed and he felt like punching Chico. Chico winced. "Just get out of here! No, stay here!" Idiot! Now he couldn't remember any of it, except "Wipe them out!"

The deputy commissioner raced up breathlessly, with Cu at his heels.

"Buenas noches, commissioner." The deputy saluted.

"The key!" the commissioner demanded of the deputy. "Where's the key?"

"Don't you have it?" the deputy asked.

"Oh, this is wonderful!" the commissioner threw up his arms. Open the door now!" he screamed at the universe, rubbing his temples.

The deputy examined the door. It was fastened with two screw-eyes held together by an old padlock. He would have to smash it open somehow.

"Go get a rock!" he commanded Cu. "A big rock." he added, so there would be no mistake.

Cu took off in search of a big rock. Meanwhile the commissioner briefed the deputy:

"There's a band of fifty guerrillas over in San Luis!" the commissioner informed the deputy. "We have to stay calm!"

"And observe their movements." continued the deputy. "Then encircle them with superior forces, and wipe them out."

"That's right!" the commissioner was pleased. He had forgotten that the deputy had attended the workshop with him.

"Also we should send a message to the Military Zone." the deputy continued. "I can borrow my cousin Guicho's car and be there in half an hour."

"All right." agreed the commissioner. "But don't leave yet. So, the first thing to do, in order to observe their movements, that is … ." His head hurt him.

"Who saw the guerrillas?" the deputy asked.

"They saw fifty of them stealing cattle over in San Luis."

"Has the San Luis patrol reported?" the deputy asked.

"No." the commissioner replied. "Maybe the guerrillas captured them."

"Probably sleeping when the guerrillas came." the deputy conjectured.

"Cowards!" muttered the commissioner indignantly.

"Surrendered without firing a shot." added the deputy.

"Cowards!" exclaimed the commissioner angrily, balling his hands into fists. "Have them sent to the Military Zone immediately!"

"Maybe they're dead already."

That thought brought a chilling sense of peril.

"Maybe I should report to the Zone," suggested the commissioner. "while you observe their movements."

"No, no." protested the deputy. "Guicho won't lend you his car. He won't lend his car to anyone but me. Moreover, I should leave immediately. 'The Military Zone must be notified immediately of any … .'"

"All right." grumbled the commissioner. "But what message are you going to give them?"

"I'll tell them to send help; that the situation is desperate."

"It is desperate." agreed the commissioner. "But they should also know that we are staying calm. Staying calm, and observing their movements, and encircling them, and wiping them out."

"But if I tell them that, they won't send help." protested the deputy.

"Well, then, maybe … ."

"I could just say that you are staying calm and observing their movements."

"But what will you tell them if they ask if we are encircling them?"

"I'll say that you are in the process of encircling them, but don't have them quite encircled yet."

"And we desperately need help to finish encircling them."

"No, I think you are supposed to encircle them by yourself. I don't think it's the Zone's job to help encircle them."

"We'll encircle them! Tell the Zone we'll encircle them, not to worry! But although we don't need any help encircling them, we desperately need help anyway, in order to, um … ."

"Collect the bodies." suggested the deputy.

"That's a good idea!" agreed the commissioner. "But don't mention it unless they bring it up. Just say that the guerrillas are here! And we are desperate, but staying calm!" The cold air was helping his headache.

"Okay!" the deputy saluted, and turned to go.

"No, wait a minute!" called the commissioner. He looked at the door to armory, and then down the street. "Where is that Indian?" he screamed in frustration, banging the door with his fist, and even starting to consider the idea of going to get a rock himself. Then he remembered Chico.

"You! Go get a rock! Now!"

Chico ran out the door in the direction he saw Cu go, and he spied a man a block away staggering under a heavy load. Getting closer he saw it was Cu carrying an enormous boulder cradled in his arms.

"Come help me!" Cu grunted. Chico took a hand. The thing must have weighed sixty kilos, but between them they hustled it down the moonlit street to the armory, where the two ladinos were still discussing the plan of battle.

"At last!" the commissioner snarled. He pointed at the door. "Smash that lock!"

Chico and Cu looked at one another; heave-ho'd; and hurled the boulder against the door, tearing one of the screw eyes out of its socket. The commissioner threw open the door and raced to the arms closet, and started passing rifles out to Chico and Cu until they had eight or ten each. Then he barked at the deputy,

"All right, go to the Zone now. Tell the commander that we are desperately calm. Okay?"

"Okay." the deputy saluted smartly, turned, and left.

"Wait!" called the commissioner. "What do we do first?"

"Send out a patrol," the deputy called back without stopping, "to observe their movements."

The commissioner grabbed a rifle for himself and raced out of the armory towards the plaza, with Chico and Cu stumbling under their loads behind him. When he reached the plaza he took up his rifle, aimed it at the sky, and cut loose with a volley of shots, to summon all the men of the town together.

Now when the commissioner fired the shots to summon all of the men, all of the women heard the shots and sat up straight in their beds and crossed themselves and thought about their babies and listened intently; but strange to say not one man in the town heard the shots. All the men to all appearances continued sleeping soundly. So after a few minutes of impatiently stomping around the plaza waiting for the men to come, the commissioner fired another volley of shots.

"Cowards! Where is everybody?" he shouted, stumbling around in circles and kicking the ground. He wasn't about to face the guerrillas with just two men.

"You say there were fifty guerrillas?" he asked Chico.

"Fifty, commissioner. Maybe more."

That settled it. The commissioner knew that the Indian was probably exaggerating; but even if there were only fifteen guerrillas he'd be outnumbered five to one. If any other man were to be captured, the guerrillas might or might not kill him; but if he, the commissioner were to be captured, there would be no question. The situation was indeed desperate; yet he had to encircle them and wipe them out. Well, the first thing to do was to observe their movements by sending out a patrol, and then he could rouse the men and start the encirclement later.

"You!" he barked at Cu, who jumped. "Head out on the back path to Sotzil, and then double back towards the San Luis guardhouse. And you," he pointed at Chico, "take the main road to Barrio San Luis. The guerrillas captured the guardhouse. Those cowards in the San Luis patrol were asleep and surrendered without firing a shot!" The very thought made his blood boil. "Find out where the guerrillas are now. Go!"

Chico and Cu were dumbfounded. They dropped their rifles. The blood pumped in their temples. They stared at the ground, and tried not to understand.

"Well? Get going!" The commissioner gave Chico a rude shove in the right direction.

"But, commissioner … ."

"Go!" the commissioner shrieked at them, and made as if to kick them, but Chico turned, grabbed up his rifle, and marched off; and Cu followed.

"Faster!" the commissioner yelled at them, "Or I'll … ."

He pointed his rifle at them. Chico and Cu scurried off as the commissioner cut loose with another volley of shots in the air.

When they were out of the plaza they slowed down again.

"Chico, I'm just going to run home quickly and tell my wife where we're going. I'll be right back." Cu said.

"You can't do that. The commissioner would kill you."

They walked slowly towards San Luis. At the point where the footpath branched off for Sotzil they stopped and looked at one another in the moonlight. Then they looked at the ground.

"You're supposed to go that way." Chico said.

They looked up at each other. Cu had a tear in his eye which glistened in the moonlight. He looked down at the ground again, and then crossed himself. He stood there.

"Goodbye, Cu." Chico said softly.

Cu looked up again. His eyes were full of tears. He said nothing, but heaved a deep sigh, and then he turned and walked slowly towards Sotzil.

Chico took a deep breath. He turned and faced San Luis. He crossed himself and then started walking. He thought of his wife. He saw her face, and his children's faces. They were laughing. They were all seated on the ground around the fire laughing up at him, and he was laughing too. They were all laughing together.

Then another volley of shots came from the direction of the plaza, and dogs started barking. Chico snapped to attention. The road ahead of him was deserted. A gust of wind blew in his face and he felt a chill run up his spine.

Then he thought about his little bull, and what the guerrillas might have done with it. That thought made him angry, and he forgot all about his fear and began to trot, keeping to the side of the road where the shadows of the trees blocked out the moonlight.

A hundred paces from the San Luis guardhouse he stopped and listened. Dogs were still barking back towards town. He could see the guardhouse silhouetted in the moonlight, but there was no sign of movement either in it or around it.

He dropped to the ground and crawled slowly towards the guardhouse on all fours, gripping his rifle in one hand, and keeping to the shadows. Ten meters from the guardhouse there was a large pine by the side of the road. He crawled to it and took up a position behind it. He stared at the thatch-roofed guardhouse, frosted in the moonlight, and while he saw nothing moving, he thought he could hear voices murmuring urgently within. He felt another chill. He didn't know what to do. He was supposed to find out where the guerrillas were. Well, he had found out. Now what? He strained to listen. There were voices all right, but he couldn't tell what language they were speaking.

He shivered as he crouched behind the tree, waiting and wondering what to do. Report back to the commissioner? That idea had its attractions; but he didn't want to get into trouble for returning without having fired a shot. Fire a shot? He was trying to consider what the possible consequences of that might be, when all of a sudden he remembered his little bull, which had been tied up not two hundred meters the other side of the guardhouse.

He felt a surge of anger. He felt angry at these guerrillas, who came into a peaceful town like San Juan to attack poor people and to steal their little animals. The little animals never hurt anybody.

He involuntarily stood up, braced himself against the tree, took aim squarely at the guardhouse door, and called loudly:

"Guerrillas! Surrender!"

His own voice startled him. His heart was pounding in his chest and head. He heard a moan, "Jesus Maria!", come from the guardhouse. The blood pulsing though his temples made the guardhouse seem to ripple in the moonlight. He strained to listen.

"Guerrillas! Surrender!" he called again. Waves of nausea flushed through his body. He felt like crying, but was too stiff. Dogs were barking; they seemed very far away. There was a rustling sound coming from inside the guardhouse, and the thwacks of a machete. He felt a surge of impatience.

"Guerrillas! Surrender!" He raised his rifle up and fired a shot into the air. A scream, "Aiyyyyyyy!", came from the guardhouse, which sent a shiver through his heart. Dogs were howling, and he strained to hear what was going on in the guardhouse. He could hear rustling and banging sounds, and then loud thumps on the ground behind the guardhouse.

He had a moment of uncertainty, and then an angry realization. He rushed into the guardhouse with his rifle pointed forward, but it was empty. They had escaped! He felt cheated. He looked up and saw the moonlight streaming down through a large hole in the thatch, illuminating a pile of straw on the floor beneath. He jumped up on a bench and peered out of the hole to see which way they had gone. He could only see stalks of corn, waving in the moonlight. His heart was still pounding and his legs were shaky. He wondered what had happened to the San Luis patrol – whether the guerrillas had killed them or captured them. He was angry at those cowardly guerrillas, who only pick on innocent people and little animals, and then run away the moment they're caught.

Then he remembered his bull. He ran out of the guardhouse with his rifle in his hand, down the moonlit road to Catalina Caal's pasture. He crawled through the barbed wire and raced panting towards the big avocado tree. And there, under the tree, was his little black and white bull. It looked up at him and gave a low "moo" of recognition.

Chico was overjoyed. He dropped the rifle and ran to the bull and embraced it and petted it, and scratched it behind its ears. It licked his hand. He wished he had brought some salt, and made a note to do so first thing in the morning. He crossed himself, and gave thanks to Jesus and Mary and St. John the Baptist for having saved his bull, and for having chased the guerrillas away from town.

It was getting on towards dawn by the time he got back to the plaza. There was a small crowd of people and dogs milling around. As he approached the group a flashlight played upon his face and the commissioner's voice rang out:

"You! There you are! Where have you been? Where are the guerrillas?"

"They left, commissioner."

"Left? Where did they leave to?"

"Who knows?"

"How many of them were there?"

"Who knows? Maybe fifty."

"Yes, that's about what I figured too." agreed the commissioner.

"They must have captured the San Luis patrol." Chico ventured.

"No, I just saw those cowards myself. They ran away without firing a shot the minute the guerrillas showed up!"

Later that morning it was reported to the Military Zone that a band of fifty guerrillas had been observed, encircled, and routed.

The commander of the Military Zone placed a red pin on the map on the wall behind his desk, and nodded thoughtfully to himself.

In the newspapers in the capital the next day it was reported as a "massacre", but it was difficult to determine from the published accounts precisely who had massacred whom.

Our Lady of Compassion

When Chepe awoke he realized, in succession, that he was cold, wet, miserable, and surrounded by a group of gargoyles who were peering down at him like hyenas drooling over a carcass.

"What? What? What?"

He struggled to raise himself from the ground but got only up to his elbows when a splitting pain shot through his head. He grabbed his temples and fell back to the ground and tried to go back to sleep, but it was no good, he was awake. He rolled over and groaned, and then felt a nudge on his back.

"Hey, you! Wake up! Time to get up!"

He groaned some more and rolled back on his back and opened his eyes.

"Leave me alone."

"Time to get up, boy." said one of the gargoyles, a wizened old man with a stubble beard. "Breakfast is ready."

This provoked laughter from the other men.

"Where am I?"

"Where you're supposed to be. Welcome home!"

This produced more laughter. Chepe sat up and his head began to throb. He rubbed his temples and blinked his eyes. He was in a courtyard, with groups of men scattered around here and there. He smelled something foul. He looked down at himself and saw that he was covered with vomit. He dropped back to the ground and rolled over. Again he felt a nudge.

"Come on, you! Get up! It's time to eat!"

"I don't want to eat."

"I don't blame you. Looks like you haven't even finished your dinner yet."

All the men laughed and moved away. The wizened old man moved around behind him and grabbed him under an armpit.

"Let's go, up, up!"

Chepe stumbled to his feet and almost fell. He rubbed his eyes and temples and felt like throwing up.

"Just leave me here."

"Can't do that, boy. Come on."

He tugged at Chepe's sleeve and moved off, and Chepe stumbled after him.

"Where am I?" he asked.

"Our Lady of Compassion."

"Our Lady of Compassion?"

"Our Lady of Compassion Home for Inebriates."

"How did I get here?"

"I don't know. You weren't here yesterday. I guess they brought you in last night."

"Who brought me in?"

"I don't know."

"How do I get out of here?"

"I don't know."

"Where's the director?"

"I don't know."

Chepe followed the old man in silence to the far end of the courtyard, where some Indian women were making tortillas and stirring something in a large garbage pail over a fire. The old man stopped and gestured like a maitre d',

"Breakfast!"

They joined a line of men queued up behind the women. When it was Chepe's turn he was handed two tortillas, and then some amorphous substance was ladled onto the tortillas from the garbage pail. It looked like vomit, and Chepe thought it smelled like it too, but it could have been his clothes. He felt nauseous.

"Good appetite! the old man called cheerfully as he bit into his portion.

Chepe looked at the mess and threw it to the ground in disgust.

"Now, now, that's no way to act. You have to keep up your strength. You don't want to get old before your time like me."

"How old are you?"

"Twenty."

"How long have you been here?"

"All my life. I was born here."

The old man went back to his tortillas. After breakfast he got to his feet and strolled to the middle of the courtyard, and Chepe followed after him.

"You know, boy, you ought to wash up. You stink."

"So do you."

"That's no way to talk. I'll show you to the lavatory."

They walked to the other end of the courtyard. The old man indicated a door, and Chepe pushed it open. A stench of piss and shit wafted into his face and brought back his nausea. The floor was half an inch deep in piss, the two toilet bowls were overflowing, and the urinals were brimming with piss and vomit. Chepe tiptoed to the sink and turned on the tap. A trickle of water dribbled out. He cupped his hand and sloshed water over his face, and then he removed his shirt and tried to wash it in the trickle. He tried not to breathe through his nose. He wrung out the wet shirt, then moved to the urinal and pissed into it from a distance. That made him feel better, even though his head still hurt. He went back out into the courtyard, but the old man wasn't there. He wanted to go back to sleep, but he didn't want to lie down on the ground again. His head was still throbbing. He felt like a drink.

"You, there." a voice called from behind him. "You have a cigarette?"

"No." Chepe turned. A man of about fifty was there.

"Pity." The man moved off.

"Wait a minute." Chepe called. "Where can I lie down?"

"I don't know."

"Aren't there beds here?"

"Yes."

"Then where can I lie down?"

"I don't know. You'll have to ask the director."

"Where's the director?"

"I don't know."

"Where's his office?"

"Over there." the man pointed.

Chepe made his way across the courtyard to the door. Actually, it wasn't just his clothes, the whole place had a smell of something like piss and vomit. He arrived at the door and saw a small sign saying: "Director. Please Knock." He knocked, but got no answer. There was a bench next to the door, so he sat down on it to wait. After a few minutes he began to get sleepy, so he lay down on the bench and went to sleep.

He woke again to someone shaking him.

"You! You there! What do you mean by sleeping on the bench?"

"Sorry. I was waiting for the director."

"This is the director." The man who was shaking him pointed to a large, dignified man with a handlebar mustache standing behind him.

"Ah, Director, may I speak to you a moment?" Chepe asked.

"You'll have to wait your turn." the director stated, going on into his office.

Chepe waited, perhaps an hour, sitting on the bench. He didn't dare go back to sleep, but he wasn't as sleepy now anyway, and his head didn't hurt as much; but he sure felt like a drink. In that hour no one else came, but neither did the director call him into the office. Thinking that maybe the director had forgotten about him, he stood up and knocked on the door. After a moment it was opened by the director's flunky.

"Yes?"

"I'd like to see the director."

"He's occupied at the moment. You'll have to wait your turn."

Chepe went back to waiting. After another half hour the door opened and the flunky came out and beckoned Chepe to enter. Chepe went in and stood before the director's desk. There was no place to sit. The director stared at him and said nothing.

"Director, my name is Jose Alvarez." Chepe stated.

"What of it?"

"I would like to leave, please."

"No doubt. Let me see." He beckoned to the flunky, who brought a sheaf of papers. The director leafed through them, found the one he was looking for, and studied it a moment.

"Jose Alvarez Garcia. Age forty-six. Clerk." he said.

"That is correct. I would like permission to leave."

"Permission denied. Is there anything else you would like?"

"Yes. I would like to know why permission is denied."

"Because your wife signed you in here, and she has to be the one who signs you out."

"My wife?" Chepe asked incredulously.

"Yes. You were found last night lying in the gutter by the National Police. They took you in and called your wife, and then they and she brought you here, and she signed you in. Since she is the one who is responsible for you, you can only leave when she signs you out again."

"My wife? Peta stuck me in here?"

"Mrs. Jose Alvarez."

Peta, the bitch! The filthy bitch! No doubt she and her mother were having a good laugh over this one right now. The bitch! The filthy bitch!

"Thank you, director."

"Good afternoon."

The director turned to some papers on his desk. Chepe left, taking care not to slam the door. Once outside he kicked the ground. The bitch! The bitch! He stomped around and cursed. The bitch! He beat his fist against the post at the edge of the patio. The bitch! The bitch! Oh God, I want a drink!

He saw some feet in front of him and looked up. It was the wizened old man.

"What do you want?" Chepe snarled at him.

"Nothing." the old man replied.

"Go away." Chepe said.

The old man said nothing, but neither did he move away. Chepe rubbed his temples. Then he turned to the old man and asked,

"Look, where can you get a drink around here?"

"From the porter."

"From the porter?" Chepe asked in disbelief.

"Yes. I think he makes it himself. You have any money?"

Chepe felt in his pockets.

"No."

"That's life." the old man said, and started to walk away.

"Wait a minute!" Chepe called. "Will he give credit?"

"Hah!" the old man said, and kept walking.

Chepe sat down and stared at the concrete. Peta! Would he wring her filthy neck when he got the chance! Her and her mother both! The bitch!

Lunch that afternoon seemed to be a repeat of breakfast, and dinner an encore of lunch. But Chepe was hungry at both meals, so he forced himself to eat, and by not breathing as he ate he managed to get the stuff down, but he chewed Peta with every bite.

He cursed Peta with every breath he took that day, and he stomped on her with every step he took in his aimless wanderings around the yard. And as he lay awake on the pallet they assigned him that night, shivering because he didn't have a blanket, he plotted Peta's demise. He was torn over the question of strangling Peta first while her mother watched, or strangling the mother first while Peta watched. He wished he had a drink. Finally he slept.

The next day he had calmed down somewhat. In between rages at Peta, he considered his position calmly. The little bitch had the whip hand, he had to give her credit. Now what? Eventually she'd have to come to see him, probably today or tomorrow at the latest. He couldn't beat her up then and there, not if he wanted out. He'd have to stay calm. Smile at her. Take her in his arms and kiss her. Peta, dear Peta. You've certainly taught me my lesson! Very clever of you. Once he got her home, then the bitch would pay!

In between such musings he thought about how nice a drink would be. At one point he decided to seek out the porter, and through inquiries he found the man asleep in a chair by the door.

"Are you the porter?" Chepe asked, awakening him with a start.

"Yes." the man answered with annoyance.

"You sell liquor?" Chepe asked.

"Who told you that?" the man snapped at him.

"Never mind who told me. I would like to buy an eighth."

"Oh, you would. Where is your money?"

"I haven't any at the moment, but my wife is coming today or tomorrow at the latest, and I'll be able to pay you then."

"I think you're mistaken." said the porter, and he went back to sleep. Chepe felt like cursing that bastard too, but he thought better of it. He walked back into the courtyard. God, how he wanted a drink!

Peta didn't come that day; nor did she come the next day. Or the next, or the next. Chepe's rage did not abate, no indeed. With every passing day it waxed and took new forms, and new ideas for torture and vengeance came into his mind. The problem was that there was really nothing to do all day except to think about vengeance on Peta and to wish for a drink. His companions in Our Lady of Compassion were not the most sparkling conversationalists: the chief topic of discourse was the wish for a drink. Some of them apparently could afford to drink, judging by their smell, but these certainly were not disposed to share their bounty.

One of them was a dapper old man of about sixty, who lived in a room by himself which was fitted out like an office, with diplomas on the wall and a desk and filing cabinet. This was Licensiado Ruiz, a lawyer, who continued to practice law even though his family had committed him to Our Lady of Compassion. He had a runner who worked for him taking messages back and forth to the outside world, and on occasion he would see a client through the grill of the main door. The runner brought him his meals, and every afternoon at 2:00 p.m. he would close his office, walk across the courtyard to the porter's chair, return to his office, and not be seen again until the next morning.

Chepe had heard that on occasion Licensiado Ruiz had even succeeded in winning liberation from Our Lady of Compassion for some of her wealthier inmates. Why then, Chepe had asked, couldn't he liberate himself? He had nowhere to go, was the answer. His family didn't want him back, and besides, he had gotten used to it. He had been there twenty years.

"Twenty years?" Chepe exclaimed in horror.

"Yes, twenty years." was the reply. "Some of us have been here even longer."

Chepe was flabbergasted! Where, oh where, was Peta? What the hell was she doing?

Exactly one week after Chepe arrived in Our Lady of Compassion, the little old man came up to him and said,

"The porter has a message for you. There is a woman here to see you."

Aha! At last! Stay calm, take deep breaths, don't lose your temper. He went to the porter who escorted him to the main door and opened the grill. Chepe looked out the grill. It wasn't Peta, as he'd expected, but Rosa, his little sister.

"Rosa!" he called with delight. "Rosa! Sweet Rosa!"

"Chepe! Poor Chepe!"

They tried to kiss through the grill, but couldn't make it.

"Rosa, you've got to get me out of here!"

"We can't, Chepe. Mama and I spoke to the director. Only Peta can sign you out."

"Peta, the bitch!"

"Mama went to talk to Peta. She told us you were here. She said it was good for you, that they would cure you of drinking."

"How long is she going to keep me here?"

"She says until you're cured."

The bitch! The bitch! I'll cure her!

"Rosa, tell Mama she's got to get me out of here."

"She tried, Chepe. We went to the lawyer. He said only Peta could sign you out, since she's the one who signed you in."

Peta! I'll strangle her!

"Listen, Rosa. You've got to get me some money. Have you got any money?"

"I have a little." She counted it out and handed it through the grill.

"Fifty cents? That's all?"

"That's all. That was to be for my lunch."

"Okay, Rosa. Thank you. Listen. You've got to take a message to Peta."

He tried to think of a message for Peta, one that would bring her down there to sign him out.

"Tell her I want to see her." He could figure out the details later on. Then, as an afterthought he added, "Tell her I love her." though he almost choked getting the words out. "Tell her I love her and I want to see her, okay?"

"Okay, Chepe."

"Thank you, Rosa. When will you come back?"

"Tomorrow."

"Thank you, Rosa. I love you. Listen, Rosa, can you bring me a blanket? I freeze to death every night."

"Of course."

"Thank you."

They tried to kiss again through the grill.

"Come back tomorrow. And if you can bring any money … ."

"Chepe, you know … "

"I know, I know, but if you can."

"I'll try."

He watched her descend to the sidewalk and cross the street. Then the porter was there, shutting the grill. He wished he could kick the man! But instead he said,

"Here is fifty cents. Give me a drink."

"Where is your glass?"

Glass! Glass! He felt like slapping the insolent dog. Instead, he turned and went into the courtyard and found the old man.

"Have you a glass? Lend me a glass."

"A glass? What would you be wanting with a glass?"

"Don't you worry, just lend it to me."

"Give me a gulp."

"A sip."

"All right, a sip then."

"All right."

These swine! Such craven beggars! The old man returned shortly with the glass. Chepe grabbed it with joy and raced to the porter.

"Here is my glass. Fill it."

The porter took the glass and the fifty cents and went into his room. He returned with the glass about two-thirds full.

"What is this? Where's the rest?"

"That is fifty cents." the porter said curtly.

"What? Is this fine imported rum, then? Fill it!"

"That is fifty cents. You don't want it?"

"I want it filled, dog!"

"Don't you call me a dog. You want your fifty cents back?"

Chepe scowled at him but said nothing. He turned towards the courtyard holding the glass to his breast so no one would notice it, but the old man was right there.

"My sip, please."

"If you don't mind, I haven't even had a sip myself."

"I don't trust you."

"Take your damn sip, then." Chepe snarled.

He handed the old man the glass, watching him like a hawk. The old man took a judicious sip.

"That was more than a sip!" Chepe cried.

"The hell it was. It was just a little sip."

"It was more like a gulp!"

These swine! These petty, cheating swine!

"Here, give me it!"

He grabbed the glass, almost spilling some, and walked over to a corner of the patio and sat down. He would do this right, his first drink in a week! He would savor it, in little sips. He raised the glass to his lips and took the tiniest of tastes. It was delicious! He let the warm liquid roll around his tongue before swallowing gently. He took another delicate sip, then another. With each sip he closed his eyes and concentrated upon his taste buds. What delight! Towards the end of the glass he took half sips; and when it was all gone he placed the glass lovingly beside him and lay back against the wall. The first warm buzz from the alcohol rose into his head. He felt so relaxed, so peaceful. He waited for a stronger feeling of intoxication to come. He waited patiently for five minutes, but no stronger feeling came. That was it. He looked up and saw the glass. There were a few drops left in the bottom. He picked it up and thirstily drank them down, and then licked the inside of the glass. No more. That was all. He felt cheated. His first drink after long deprivation, and that was all there was to it! He wanted more. He picked up the glass and went back to the porter.

"Fill it up again." he told the man.

"And the money?"

"My sister's coming back tomorrow. I'll pay you then."

"Okay, then I'll fill it up then."

Swine! Chepe walked back into the courtyard and gave the old man his glass back. If only he hadn't given him that sip! Oh well, tomorrow he'd ask Rosa to bring him a glass.

The next day he was again called to the main door, and there was Rosa.

"Dear, dear Rosa! Did you bring me … ?"

"A blanket, Chepe, here it is. I couldn't bring more than my fifty cents lunch money. You know Mama hasn't any money."

"I know, I know, thank you, Rosa. I really appreciate this. And Peta? Did you talk to her?"

"I talked to her, but she said that she's not coming until you're cured."

"Until I'm cured! Until I'm cured! What do you mean, until I'm cured? Rosa, do you know what it's like in here? It's a prison!"

"I know, Chepe, I know. I tried my best. What more could I do? She won't listen to me."

"The bitch! The bitch! I'll kill her! I'll break out of here and kill her!"

"Don't do that, Chepe! I'll come every day. Mama couldn't come. No, actually she could have come, but she was ashamed to come. She said you wouldn't want her to see you like this. She sent you a cake."

"A cake. How nice. A cake. And meanwhile I'm supposed to stay here and rot?"

"What can we do? Peta won't listen to us."

Chepe summoned the porter, who opened the door sufficiently to pass the blanket and cake and fifty cents through, and then locked it again.

"Listen, Rosa, I'm sorry I yelled. Really, I appreciate this. Tell Mama I appreciate it. Listen, Rosa, go back and tell Peta I'm cured. Okay? Tell her I hate myself for having been such a drunk, and that I really love her and want to see her. Okay?"

"Okay, Chepe."

They tried to kiss through the grill but couldn't touch. Only after Rosa had left did Chepe remember he'd forgotten to ask her to bring a glass. He turned to the porter and showed him the fifty cents.

"And your glass?"

"I don't have a glass. Lend me a glass."

"I can't lend you a glass. I can rent you a glass."

"How much is the rental on the glass?"

"Five cents."

"Five cents? I've only got fifty cents."

"I can rent you a glass, and give you forty-five cents worth of liquor."

The swine! But Chepe handed the man the fifty cents. The porter returned in a moment with a glass about half full.

"That's all?"

"That's forty-five cents."

Chepe glared at him and took the glass. He went back to his corner. Today he would drink it all down in one gulp, and see if that gave him more of a lift. He raised the glass and toasted,

"To Peta!"

And he swallowed it down in two gulps. He glared around. He felt like smashing the glass on the floor, but thought better of it. He returned to the porter, and then he remembered the cake.

"Would you like a piece of cake?" he asked the porter. Might as well keep on the good side of the swine.

"Thank you."

The porter produced a penknife, and Chepe opened the package and cut him a piece.

Chepe stepped into the courtyard. That was a good idea, to drink it all down in one gulp. He could feel a bit higher than he had yesterday. Actually that one glass wasn't anywhere near enough to get drunk on, but it was enough to remind you of how good it felt. He sat down in the middle of the courtyard and looked at the cake. At least he wouldn't have to eat tortillas and slop tonight. That was nice of Mama. She had always loved him. She had always known he would make good, and he was doing pretty well until he met Peta. That was his downfall! Peta! Strangling was too good for her.

He'd slice her up into little slivers, beginning at her ugly toes, and moving up the line. He became aware of a circle of men forming around him.

"Well, what do you want?" he asked.

They didn't say anything, but they were all staring at the cake. Beggars! Swine! To be locked up with such a bunch!

"Don't tell me. You all feel like cake, right?"

There were nods of assent, but no one spoke.

"I am selling cake here for ten cents a slice."

Ten cents! Ten cents! they cried in indignation.

One of them offered him three cents.

"Three cents! For my mother's cake! Why, my mother bakes for the priest of our parish. He's an Italian. Five cents, the lowest."

"Okay, five cents." A man showed him five cents.

"Have you a knife?"

"Of course I don't have a knife." the man replied. "Do you think they'd let us have knives? Ask the porter."

Chepe took the cake to the porter and asked to borrow his knife.

"Five cents rental on the knife." said the porter.

Five cents! Five cents! After he'd given the swine a piece of cake!

"I'll give you another piece of cake." Chepe offered.

"Okay."

The porter produced his penknife and offered it to Chepe, who sliced the cake and offered the porter his piece.

"That's not a five-cent piece!" protested the porter.

"Listen, you set the value on the liquor, I set the value on the cake. Besides, I already gave you a piece."

The porter took his piece and Chepe took the rest back to the courtyard, where he soon had them all sold. He counted his money. Forty cents. He went back to the porter.

"Here's forty cents. Sell me another drink."

"Where's your glass?"

"Just throw the glass into the deal. Didn't I give you a free piece of cake?"

"That was a gift. That wasn't business."

"All right, all right, just give me thirty-five cents' worth."

The porter returned shortly with the glass not quite half full.

"That's not thirty-five cents' worth."

"You set the price on the cake, I set the price on the liquor."

You can't win with these swine. Chepe took the glass and downed it in a gulp, and just in time, too, because he was coming down from his previous high. He stepped back into the courtyard and looked around for the blanket, but it wasn't there.

"My blanket!" he yelled. "Where's my blanket? You thieves! Bring me that blanket or I'll strangle every one of you!"

The little old man trotted up to him bearing the blanket.

"Here it is." he said. "I was just holding it for you."

Chepe grabbed it away from him. What a miserable bunch of thieves and no-goods. At least that night was the first warm night he'd had since he entered the place.

The next day Rosa didn't come. Chepe waited for her all day long, and not until nightfall did he admit to himself that she wasn't coming. Rosa! Little Rosa! Where the hell was she? Was everyone turning against him? The only thing worse than not being able to drink was expecting that any minute you'd be able to drink and then not being able to drink. That was far worse than not being able to drink and knowing you weren't going to be able to drink.

"No booze today!" the other men on the tortilla line teased him.

How he'd love to wring all their necks, starting with the porter. He sat down on the ground with his tortillas and slop and ate them slowly. Another man, about his age, sat down next to him.

"Your wife didn't show today, huh?"

"She's not my wife, she's my sister, if it's any of your business."

"That's how it always is." the man said. "At first they come, they even bring you money, and then after a while they don't come anymore."

"She'll come! What are you saying? My sister loves me! Maybe no one loves you, and it's not hard to see why."

"They come at first, and then they don't come anymore." the man said thoughtfully. "At first they care about you, and then they don't care anymore."

"Maybe nobody cares about you, but my family cares about me!"

The man went on as if Chepe hadn't spoken.

"And then, after a while, you stop caring yourself. You know? And then all you care about is the tortillas and slop, because there's nothing left to care about."

"Wonderful! A philosopher. Listen, Mr. Philosopher, why don't you go eat your tortillas and slop over there and let me eat my tortillas and slop in peace?"

The man looked at Chepe, a long, hard look, and then went back to eating without speaking.

Rosa didn't come the next day, or the next. Chepe was beginning to get desperate. But on Saturday he was called to the main door again.

"Rosa! Rosa! Where have you been?"

"I'm sorry, Chepe, I couldn't come until today. I brought you a little money, and Mama baked you another cake."

"Listen, Rosa, thank you. But why couldn't you come?"

"I just couldn't come, Chepe. Besides, I don't have that much money. I have to eat too."

"I know you do, I know. Dear, sweet Rosa. I'm sorry. I'm no good, I know it. You know I love you, Rosa."

"I know it. You know I love you too, Chepe."

"And what about Peta? Did you talk to her again?"

"I couldn't. When she saw it was me at the door she closed the door in my face."

"The bitch! Closing the door on my sister! My door! I'll kill her! I swear, as God and all the saints are my witnesses, I will kill her with these hands!"

"Don't talk like that, Chepe! That's not a nice way to talk."

"I'm sorry, Rosa, I'm sorry. You just don't know what it's like in here, with all these bums. With all these filthy bums! And the food!"

"I know, I know. We all feel really bad, but what can we do?"

"Nothing, nothing. So help me, God! You go and tell Peta that they can't keep me in here forever. Some day they will let me out, and when they do I will kill her. You tell her that, okay? Tell her that if she doesn't get me out of here tomorrow I will kill her. If they keep me here twenty years, when I get out I will kill her. Tell her that."

"I can't tell her that! Besides, if I told her that she'd never let you out. Besides, she won't let me tell her anything."

"Rosa, please, please do something. Anything! I don't care what. Write letters to the deputy. Go back to see the lawyer. Maybe bribe the director."

"Bribe him with what?"

"I don't know. Borrow the money. Rosa, please listen, you're my only hope. You've got to get me out of here."

"I'll try, Chepe."

"And please, please come to see me every day. No matter how hard it is. When I don't see you, I die. Really, it kills me."

"I'll try, Chepe, but you know how it is."

"I know, I know, but please try."

"Okay, I'll try."

Chepe summoned the porter, who admitted the cake and the money.

"Goodbye, Rosa. I love you."

"I love you, Chepe."

"Please come every day."

"I'll try."

"Rosa, can you bring me a glass next time?"

"Okay."

"I love you."

He reached two fingers through the grill and took her fingers in his, and squeezed them. Then she was gone. Chepe turned to the porter and handed him fifty cents. He took it without speaking and returned with a little more than half a glass. Chepe gave him a dirty look, took the glass, and downed it in two gulps. He asked for the penknife and sliced the cake, offering the porter his piece. Then he went into the courtyard and made his sales.

Rosa didn't come the next day, or the next. This produced some amused comment from the denizens of the tortilla line, but Chepe ignored them. Once the man his age sat down next to him again, but didn't speak. He just looked at Chepe with a knowing look. Chepe turned away from him. When the man finished eating he stood up and looked down at Chepe and said,

"Years."

"What did you say?"

"I said, 'Years.'" the man replied, and moved away.

"Swine!" Chepe called after him.

Well, now what? He couldn't count on Rosa or his mother, that was becoming obvious. He'd have to buy his way out, but with what? There was some cottage industry in Our Lady of Compassion, some hammock weavers and a potter, but they weren't making much money. He thought about Licensiado Ruiz. The Licensiado held himself aloof from the other inmates. Chepe had never even seen him talk to another inmate. He had a runner who worked for him, and apparently he had other employees on the outside.

Maybe he needed a clerk. Chepe had studied some accounting back in high school; maybe the Licensiado would hire him.

Chepe walked to the lavatory and stepped into the pool of piss. He waded to the sink and took a look at himself in the mirror. He was dirty and unshaven, and his clothes were filthy. He hadn't bathed or changed his clothes since he'd been admitted. He removed his shirt and scrubbed it in the trickle of the faucet, and then took it out to the sun to dry. He bent over the sink and sloshed water over his face and torso, and wet his hair and tried to comb it with his fingers. He went out into the courtyard and waited for the shirt to dry. When it was almost dry he put it back on, took another swipe at his hair, and walked purposefully to the door of Licensiado Ruiz's office. He knocked and waited.

"Come in!"

He entered and saw the Licensiado seated at his desk with a sheaf of papers before him.

"Well?" the Licensiado asked him indignantly.

"Licensiado, my name is Jose Alvarez. I am a clerk and a skilled accountant. I am temporarily out of work, and am seeking employment."

The Licensiado stared at him for a few moments without saying anything. Then he turned back to his papers and said,

"What makes you think I would hire a drunk?"

A drunk! What effrontery the man had! What a swine! Chepe turned without speaking and slammed the door behind him. A drunk! The filthy drunk, calling me a drunk! Chepe kicked the ground and spat in fury. A drunk! He leaned on his arm against the post at the end of the patio and closed his eyes. They all treat you like dirt, no matter how hard you try, and then when you take an occasional drink to relieve your misery, they call you a drunk. He felt like weeping, but no tears came. He heard a sound behind him and turned around. It was the wizened old man.

"Well, what do you want?"

"You shouldn't let it get to you. This isn't such a bad place, after all."

"What do you mean? It's hell."

"Oh, it's not so bad. You get used to it, after a while. At least there's food, and no one knocking you about."

"Maybe you've gotten used to it, but I never will."

"Oh yes, you will. They all do, after a few years. Sooner. Actually, it isn't far from heaven. If there were only liquor here, it would be heaven. Sometimes there even is liquor, when you get a little money together. Then it is heaven, truly heaven."

"Maybe it's heaven for you, but it's hell for me."

"It's only hell until you get used to it; then it's not far from heaven."

Rosa came on Saturdays now. She came every Saturday afternoon, and gave Chepe fifty cents. He didn't dare ask her why she didn't come more frequently, for fear of antagonizing her. Sometimes she brought a cake, or some other little delicacy he could sell. When she brought a cake he would sell it and get drunk that Saturday afternoon. When she didn't bring a cake, he would save the fifty cents until the next Saturday, when by uniting the earnings of two weeks he could get drunk properly. Well, "properly" was scarcely the word for it, but he reasoned that a quetzal's worth of booze was worth more than two fifty cents' worth, and two weeks of deprivation made the final bash all the better. He was making a virtue of self-restraint.

Although he surely didn't consider it heaven, he was getting used to Our Lady. He was even getting used to the food. And although he still didn't like it, he began to look forward to meal times as welcome punctuation points in the boring routine of the day.

One day a new man appeared in Our Lady. When Chepe awoke that morning he spied a body lying outside in the courtyard, and out of curiosity he walked over to it and hung over the man until he awoke. Some other inmates, including the little old man (whose name, Chepe had learned, was don Ramon) also came over to examine the object. The man looked up and blinked around, and then fell back to sleep.

"Wake up!" don Ramon called, nudging the man with his foot. "Time for breakfast!"

"Leave me alone!"

"Everybody up!" don Ramon called cheerfully, lifting the man by his armpits, and indicating for Chepe to help him. Between the two of them they got the man to his feet, and began marching him to the tortilla line, albeit unsteadily.

"Who the hell are you? Where the hell am I?" the man grumbled as he staggered along.

"Our Lady of Compassion Home for Inebriates." Chepe said.

"Oh, jolly! This is very jolly! My wife! My whore of a wife! The filthy slut!" The man went on and on, disgusting even Chepe with his turns of phrase and the spittle which accompanied them, not to mention the stench of vomit and piss which hung on the man.

"Take your filthy hands off of me!" the man spat at them, twisting away from them and then falling to the ground. Chepe and don Ramon picked him up again and marched him to the line in silence, but the man carried on and on. When the food was served, he took one look at it and heaved it to the ground and stomped on it.

"What dirt! What filthy pigs! What pigs, to eat such slop!"

"Now, now." Chepe said, patting the man's shoulder. "That's no way to talk."

"Don't touch me, you pig!" the man said, turning away as if from slime.

"My wife! Dear, sweet Maria! I'll kill her! I'll kill the bitch!"

He went on. Chepe tried to ignore it. What a fool, he thought. Oh well, I suppose everyone has to go through it, but this guy just won't shut up.

"Listen, if you're going to bawl like a baby," Chepe told him, "why don't you go over to the other side of the yard?"

"Like a baby? I'll show you who's a baby!"

The man stood up and started to take a swing, but he threw himself off balance and fell to the ground. All the men laughed. The man stayed down and began to cry, and pounded the ground with his fists.

"I'll kill you, I'll kill her, I'll kill everyone!"

Later that day Chepe thought back over the incident and was amused by his reactions to the man. He still hated Peta, but somehow he didn't think about her much anymore. He had exhausted himself thinking about her. Only rarely would thoughts of Peta stimulate his murderous creativity – usually when something had happened to make him angry, and then he'd turn around and get angry at Peta. But most of the time, when the thought of Peta came up, it bored him and he dismissed it. Even when, after he'd been in Our Lady for six months, Rosa reported to him that Peta was now living with another man in his house, Chepe couldn't get the old anger flowing very well. He spent a few days trying, trying to be as jealous and hateful as he could be, but somehow the old vibrancy wasn't there. He really didn't care. He resented the aspersion upon his manhood that Peta's cuckolding him entailed; the laughter and innuendo he'd have to put up with from his friends and neighbors, but really, who cared? What the hell could he do about it anyway? And if you can't do anything, then why get all excited about it?

One day don Ramon complained of stomach pains. He slept in the same room as Chepe, on the next pallet. Chepe reported don Ramon's condition to the director, but the director said it would have to wait until the doctor came on his next scheduled round, in a week's time. The doctor was an important man, who volunteered his services to Our Lady, and he could only be summoned in a grave emergency.

The next morning, when Chepe awoke, don Ramon was dead. Chepe shook him to wake him up, but he didn't move. Chepe touched his skin; it was cold. Chepe sat down on his pallet. He couldn't think. Tears came to his eyes, but he didn't weep. At length he stood up and walked to the porter's chair and informed the porter, and the porter told him to wait until the director arrived, and then to inform the director, which Chepe did. In the meantime he returned to his room and sat on the pallet and looked at don Ramon. He hadn't really liked don Ramon, and he hadn't disliked him either. In any case, he felt very sad. He felt sad for don Ramon, and he felt sad for himself, and he felt sad for everyone. He even felt sad for Peta. She had been pretty and flirtacious. She didn't know what she was getting into when she got married, any more than he did. They were just kids. They didn't know anything. Her mother. What could Peta do? She was caught in the middle. She only could do what her mother had taught her to do.

Later, after the director arrived, Chepe helped carry don Ramon, wrapped in a blanket, out to the main door, where he was loaded into a pickup truck and carted away.

For ten days after don Ramon died Chepe felt very depressed. For the first time in a long time he strongly craved a drink. When Rosa came the next Saturday he begged her for a few quetzales, but all she had to give him was the usual fifty cents. He drank that up right away, but it didn't help much. He slept more; he slept most of the day when he could.

Then one day, about two weeks after don Ramon's death, Chepe woke up with a decisive attitude. He had to get out of there. No one was going to help him. He'd have to buy his way out. It would probably take a lot of money, to bribe the director or whoever, but he would do it.

Even his attitude about drinking began to change. It disgusted him the way the others could only talk about drinking. It was true that he was jealous of the ones whose families supplied them with enough money to regularly patronize the porter, but also he was learning to live without. He was proud of his ability to keep fifty cents in his pocket for a week and not spend it on booze. Eventually he cut his drinking down to one bout per month, and then he cut it out altogether.

He began to save the money Rosa brought him every Saturday, and the proceeds from the cake sales. He hung around the hammock weavers, and after a while he learned how to weave hammocks. When he had saved enough money, he bought some skeins of string from the porter (who had a string business too, and who bought the finished hammocks from the inmates to sell on the outside), and he began weaving hammocks. In a few months he had a sizable nest egg saved up, more than fifty quetzales. He had settled into a daze, in which nothing really penetrated except for the porter's payments for his hammocks and the daily tortillas and slop.

One day he decided to go to see Licensiado Ruiz. He pulled his courage together, went up to the man's door, and knocked.

"Come in!"

"Good morning, Licensiado. I want to talk to you about getting me out of here."

"Do you have any money?"

"Yes."

"How much?"

"More than fifty quetzales. But I can get more."

"Oh, you can. Well, it can be done, but it is very expensive."

"How much?"

"Three, four hundred quetzales. And it takes a long time to put the papers through."

"If I pay you fifty now and fifty every three months, could you get me out of here?"

"I could try. It depends. Are you hiring me?"

"Yes."

"Let me see the money."

Chepe took out his wad, which had up til now never left his person for a moment, lest it be stolen faster than you can blink an eye. He handed it to the Licensiado, who counted it, made out a receipt for it, and then placed it in a drawer.

"Here you are." he said, handing Chepe the receipt. "The next payment will be due … " consulting his calendar, "August 12th. In the meantime I will solicit the judge. You must give me some personal data, and the names of three witnesses as to your good character … "

Chepe gave him the information, and the names of Rosa and his mother as character witnesses, but it took him a long time to think of a third character witness. He finally gave the name of Mrs. Juarez, his mother's next door neighbor and best friend. Mrs. Juarez would do anything his mother asked. He got up, thanked the Licensiado and shook his hand, and left. He felt so good that afternoon that he even whistled a tune to himself as he wove his hammock.

One morning, several weeks after his visit to the Licensiado, Chepe received a message that there was a woman waiting for him at the main door. It wasn't Saturday; he wondered what the matter could be. When he got to the door, he looked out and saw Peta. He was flabbergasted. He didn't know what to think or feel, nor what to say. He just looked at her in surprise.

"Chepe." she said, looking at him in short, furtive glances.

"What do you want, Peta?" He was too surprised to be angry, even.

"I want a divorce." She looked in his eyes, then away.

"A divorce?"

"Yes, I'm in love with someone, and I want to marry him. I'll sign you out of here if you give me a divorce."

"Oh you will, will you?"

"Yes. But you must give me the divorce first. I don't trust you."

"But I'm supposed to trust you, Peta?"

"My lawyer drew up some papers. I have them with me. All you have to do is sign them, and I'll go to the director's office and sign you out."

"I don't trust you. What about the house? Who gets the house?"

"I get the house."

"Piss on you."

"Chepe, do you want out or not?"

"Peta, you're going to have to pay for the year I've spent in here."

"I've already paid for it, Chepe, many times over." she said wearily.

There was a long pause. Chepe looked at her through the grill. Her eyes were lowered. Her face was gaunt. She had a pinched look around her jaw, as if her shoes or brassiere were too tight and she was trying not to show it. She had lost weight. She wasn't pretty anymore. When he had married her, she was pretty. Well, whoever gets her now is welcome to her. She was looking at him. There was no life in her eyes; those eyes that used to smile shyly. He guessed that, if he could see himself, he would see the same thing: a hollow, dull-eyed wreck where there had once been a cocky young macho with a gleam in his eye.

"We'll split the house fifty-fifty."

"Oh yes! You live in the kitchen and we'll live in the bedroom."

"We'll sell it."

"I don't want to sell it."

"You buy my half."

"With what? No, Chepe, if you want to get out, you will give me the divorce and the house."

"I want to think about it, Peta. Come back tomorrow."

"All right."

"How have you been?" he surprised himself with that question.

"I've been all right."

"Your new man. Does he love you?"

"Ah. You know how it is."

"Do you love him?"

"Who knows? He treats me okay. He's a good lover. He brings home money. He doesn't get drunk." she said pointedly.

"Do I know him?"

"I don't think so. He's from Xela."

There was a long moment of silence. He looked at her drawn face. He felt a wave of warmth for her, but with a deep gulp he swallowed it back down.

"So I'll see you tomorrow."

"Okay."

He turned and shut the grill. He walked slowly back to his room and lay on his pallet. He felt sad. He felt like he wanted to weep, now, but no tears would come. It was funny, to finally see Peta again, and instead of being angry with her, he felt sad for her. Funny world. But he wasn't about to trust her with his freedom. He got up again and went to Licensiado Ruiz's office, but it was after two o'clock and the door was locked. He'd have to wait until morning.

Next morning he sought out the Licensiado.

"My wife has offered to sign me out of here if I will let her have a divorce and give her possession of my house. Can I get my fifty quetzales back?"

"No, that's been spent."

"Okay. Then can you handle the divorce and signing me out? I don't trust her. I think she'll get the divorce and scram."

"Who will pay me?"

"She will. After all, she's getting the house."

"All right. I'll have to speak with her."

"She'll come later today. I'll call you."

Chepe hoped Peta would come before two o'clock, and in fact she showed up shortly after noon.

"Hello, Chepe." she said, looking at him warily through the grill.

"Hello, Peta."

"Did you sleep well last night?"

"Yes. Did you?"

"No, I didn't." She paused. "Are you going to sign?"

"Yes. I'll call my lawyer."

Chepe summoned Licensiado Ruiz.

"Peta, this is my lawyer. He will examine the papers for me. You will have to pay him."

"I pay him? How much?"

"Fifty quetzales, madam." said Licensiado Ruiz.

Peta thought about it a moment, and then agreed. She handed the papers she had brought through the grill, and Licensiado Ruiz examined them. She dug into her purse and came out with a fifty quetzal note, and passed it through.

"The papers are in order." Licensiado Ruiz said. "I'll go speak to the director."

He trotted off towards the director's office. Chepe and Peta stared at one another through the grill.

"Has it been hard, Chepe?" she asked him.

"Miserable." he replied.

"Me too."

"At least you were on the outside."

"It isn't much better out here. It isn't much better anywhere."

"No, I suppose not. You look tired, Peta."

"What do you expect? You do too."

There was a long silence.

"Peta, what happened?"

"What do you mean?"

"What happened between us?"

"I don't know. I've thought about it. For a long time, that's all I thought about. I don't know. I'm sorry, Chepe."

"I'm sorry too. I wish we were young again."

"What good would that do?"

"I don't know. Maybe we would do things differently."

"No, we wouldn't. We would have done the same things all over again."

"Peta, do you love me?"

"I loved you once."

"I know that. Do you love me now?"

"I don't know. I don't know what love is anymore."

"Do you love him?"

"I don't know. I've stopped asking those kinds of questions."

There was a long silence. It got embarrassing, so they looked away from each other. Finally Licensiado Ruiz came.

"All done. Just your signature, madam, on this release … "

He passed it through the grill, with a pen. Peta signed it. Licensiado Ruiz went back to the director's office, and then returned. He handed the porter a document. The porter examined it slowly, and then said to Chepe,

"Well, you're out. Do you want to get your belongings?"

"Piss on my belongings. Just let me out of here."

The porter opened the door, and Chepe passed through. Peta was looking the other way. He walked up to her and put his arm around her. She startled and turned to him with a searching look. He felt a tear coming, so he looked down and steered her gently with his arm, and they walked together down the steps and out into the street.